The
HAWKWATCHER

The
HAWKWATCHER
Adventures among
Birds of Prey
in the Wild

D. A. Orton

Illustrated by Donald Watson
Foreword by Wilson Stephens

UNWIN

HYMAN

LONDON SYDNEY WELLINGTON

First published in Great Britain by Unwin Hyman, an imprint of
Unwin Hyman Ltd, 1989.

UNWIN HYMAN LTD
15/17 Broadwick Street, London WV1 1FP

Allen & Unwin Australia Pty Ltd
8 Napier Street, North Sydney, NSW 2060, Australia

Allen & Unwin New Zealand Ltd with the Port Nicholson Press
Compusales Building, 75 Ghuznee Street, Wellington, New Zealand

---

British Library Cataloguing in Publication Data

Orton, D. A. (Dick)
 The hawkwatcher
1. Great Britain. Birds of prey
I. Title   II. Watson, Donald, *1918–*
  598′.91′0941

ISBN 0–04–440140–X

Typeset in 11/14½ point Garamond
by Nene Phototypesetters Ltd, Northampton
and printed in Portugal by
Printer Portuguesa, Sintra

CONTENTS

ACKNOWLEDGEMENTS

I wish to record my gratitude to friends living and to friends with us no longer for companionship given while watching birds of prey, or for help with wardening their eyries, or, indeed, both. Some are named in the text, others not: there have been so many.

A special tribute is offered to Dr Fred Slater, Curator of the Llysdinam Field Centre, Newbridge-on-Wye, and to Simon and Dawn Frazer of Cwmdauddwr, Powys, for the friendship, hospitality and logistic support freely given which made ten years of voluntary work in peregrine falcon protection not only a rewarding experience, but a possibility.

Thanks are due also to Michael Radford who gave invaluable advice on improvements which could be made to the text.

Last, but by no means least, a word of appreciation is due to my wife, Margaret, who endured long weeks of desertion without a murmur of complaint, or avoided that fate only by joining the party and braving the discomforts imposed by wind and rain which upland birds of prey demand of their spectatorship almost irrespective of the time of year at which they are paid a visit.

D. A. ORTON

FOREWORD

It may be thought that the heyday of modern ornithological writing is past. James Fisher, Peter Scott, Max Nicholson, David Lack, Richard Fitter belong to the immediate post-war decades. They wrote as individuals, not organisation men. Now, in Dick Orton, another individualist restores originality to the bookshelves, and perhaps heralds a new generation. He is cast in as different a mould from that of his contemporaries as were Lord Grey of Falloden and Gilbert White of Selborne in their respective epochs. Each of them in a separate way was his own man, but neither more so than Orton is now. This I discovered when I commissioned him in 1973 to write a series of articles for *The Field*, a series which has continued to the present day well beyond my retirement from that editorial chair.

That there is nothing small about this man is as true of his purview as of Orton himself. Under cross-examination he will admit to membership or ornithological societies; yet this seems just one of several contradictions which set him apart. No man is less able to be part of a caucus, or to accept evidence unsupported by his own observation. He practises the sternest of discipline without losing the sense of wonder which, for the luckiest among us, outlasts youth. He is a challenger but not a rebel. To him ornithology is more than a pleasure or a science; it is a way of life. To his readers he will be more than a discovery or a stimulant; he is a good companion.

He lives in Worcestershire. His heart is in Wales, on those hungry mountains where falcon and raven rule the air. His eyes are open wherever else he happens to be. He is a fisherman. He was a business man. He remains indescribable and unique, just Dick Orton.

WILSON STEPHENS
Salisbury

one   IN THE BEGINNING

The night of 28/29 May had not been a cold one, as summer nights go at 1,500 feet in the hills of mid-Wales. Larks were falling silent after a brief burst of song to greet a dawn not yet perceptible to the human eye. When the sun rose to view, as it would in about an hour, they would be singing in earnest and would do so for the rest of the day.

Soon, in the alcove in the cliff-face twenty feet below us, the peregrines would stir – the tiercel on his overnight guard crag, the falcon in the scrape on the sheltered ledge and the three downy eyasses burrowing into her plumage for the comfort of her body heat as she grew restless with the approach of light.

The raid we were up there to forestall had not materialized. Perhaps we could now relax until that evening's dusk brought the next period of high risk. Was relaxation, I wondered, in the minds of our opposite numbers in the valley to the south, over the moorland hills behind us?

At 5 a.m. the previous morning the atmosphere there had been disrupted by more than the song of the skylark. A lithe, camouflage-clad young man who had driven through the night from London had at that moment leapt from concealment, raced to an accessible ledge among the rocks of the steep hillside and snatched three of the four eyasses he found there, young birds coming into feather, about a fortnight older than the ones on the ledge below me.

THE HAWKWATCHER

Cramming his loot into an airline bag, the thief had scrambled to the skyline to pass it to an accomplice, who then promptly vanished into the heather. The first villain then made a dash for his Daimler saloon, which he had concealed under the hedge of a roadside field half a mile away. After the initial shock, the response of the guard had been no less cool. By the time the fugitive had reached the Daimler a police car was parked to cut off its escape.

The thief resisted police questioning for the whole of that long hot day. Meanwhile, crowded in the airline bag and dumped in a disused railway tunnel for later collection, the eyasses grew hungry and foul with their own droppings. After dumping them, the accomplice had sneaked back to the moor to hide until the hue and cry died down and the search was called off.

After a day or two off duty I had re-entered the drama at four o'clock that afternoon just after the wireless call went out to all police cars ordering the stand-down. It was not to be. A motor cycle roared up and skidded to a halt in a cloud of dust. 'I've got the red-headed one at my garage,' said the rider. 'Came in sticky with sweat, dust to the knees of his jeans, asking to buy a bike for cash. Any sort of bike. My lad's holding him pretending to correct a fault in the bike we sold him.' The officer in the police car by which I was standing smiled and pressed the switch on his microphone.

An hour later full confessions had been extracted, charges preferred and the exhausted young peregrines recovered. As the law required, the culprits were set at liberty, whatever alternative plunder might still lie within their reach. Not only that, but the police suspected the existence of a communications network operated by a circle of bird thieves and feared the possibility of some 'grand slam' operation having been planned to attempt several of the Powys sites while the defence was overextended.

Young peregrines fetch a price on the black market high enough to attract professional criminals. One of those rumoured to be en route for Wales had at one time been the knee-capper for the most notorious of the London gangs. My companion on the cliff-top that night was an ardent young Welsh Nationalist who thoroughly enjoyed the unease bred in his English colleagues by the wicked hints he dropped of other nocturnal activities in which

IN THE BEGINNING

he might or might not have been engaged. However, firers of holiday cottages are not likely to be timorous and, with the prospect of a professional thug to be confronted, that was a comforting thought. It is astonishing how circumstances can adjust perspectives.

The light strengthened. The sun rose at last, bringing the valley far below to life. The back door of the farm at the foot of the cliffs opened and a man appeared with a large vacuum flask under one elbow and a long thumb-stick in his other hand. He had lately exchanged his smart soldiers for a flock of sheep, an elegant uniform for the joy of old clothes and the bouquet of the barracks for the sweet air of the hills. With his dogs following him he began the indirect and arduous climb which would bring him and what he carried 'for the comfort of the troops' round the rim of the short valley commanded by the cliffs and up to our guard-post.

What a bizarre situation I had landed in, in my fifties, city-born, and with twenty-five years of sober service in the world of commerce only five years behind me. It was the fifth year of my involvement in these bird protection operations. The kinfolk about me in my childhood, all of them country-bred and some still living there, had small sympathy with the interest in hawks which I conceived as soon as I saw my first picture of one. 'Nasty dirty things' my grandmother classed them, rightly detested by her brother who still wore whipcords and the others who had followed the keeper's calling earlier in life. There had been four of them.

But was the kestrel not a handsome bird, nice to look at? I asked my great-uncle one springtime afternoon, as I shared his vigil over the rearing-field, its shaded coops, penned-in broody hens and cheeping, scampering pheasant chicks. 'Yes,' he replied unexpectedly, then, after a pause for due effect, 'along the barrels of my gun.' He shot woodpeckers, too, on the time-honoured principle that 'what don't do no good might well do harm'.

Things have changed a lot in fifty years, but they had not changed that much twenty-five years ago. 'Liking small birds, as you do' said my town-bred mother-in-law, 'how can you be so interested in those spiteful big ones that kill and eat them?' On the dining-table lay the remains of the Sunday roast which she, above all else an avowed animal lover, had served to us and shared with good appetite. But her question was not absurd. I fed the small birds which visited the garden in winter and took a keen interest in them. The spectacle of a sparrowhawk soaring overhead I would have greeted with excitement, but its descent to snatch a thrush or robin with which I had grown familiar would have saddened me scarcely less than it would have outraged her.

The brevity of a small bird's life expectancy whether hawks are present or not, the service that hawks perform in culling the ailing and inadequate from a prey species, and the dire effects of severe winter weather when snow cover denies much of the natural food to a population of small birds unnaturally swollen by lack of normal predation, can all be argued in evidence for the defence, but the basic contradiction remains. How can one love the hawk and its prey sincerely? Are those of us who claim to do so vicariously indulging some otherwise suppressed sadistic urge masked by hypocrisy? The possibility cannot be ruled out completely. But the actual kills witnessed by even the fanatical watcher of hawks in the wild come too few and far between to do much in the way of satisfying a hidden cruel streak, and the moment of truth is unlikely to be enacted in the close-up one presumes the sadistic appetite would prefer.

Hawks on the wing are always supremely graceful, always an embodiment of a freedom earthbound *Homo sapiens* can envy but never share. True, their presence brings with it a tension founded on their ability to turn spectacularly lethal at a split second's notice, but to respond to that tension is not necessarily to show a sadistic streak, any more than a visit to the circus to gasp at the trapeze artists or to the lion house at Regent's Park at feeding time betrays a cruel temperament. The raptor's grace in the sky is one pleasure; the dignity of the hawk on its perch another, helped by the bird's facial structure, which enables it to stare boldly into the human countenance with both eyes, as a fellow human being gazes. Among birds they and the owls alone do this; others have to angle the head to peer strangely with one eye only, like a short-sighted sergeant-major scrutinizing the jowls of a recruit for a hint of stubble.

Then there is the plumage – in all cases sober in colour, as befits a gentleman, with such decoration as there might be in the form of streaking, speckling or barring conceived tastefully and displayed with admirable restraint. An encounter with a hawk promotes a sense of affinity tempered by respect for a capacity to perform by aid of God's gifts alone that which we can only aspire to by resort to the most complex of mechanical aids.

Such were my thoughts as my mother-in-law fixed my eye, hawklike herself, demanding her answer. She was of a generation brought up to divide creation into the good and the bad, largely in terms of positive usefulness to the human overlord. I attempted no argument but remained content to figure as a strange fellow with odd and anomalous tastes beyond the comprehension of the wholly sane.

Now, I reflected as the colonel drew slowly nearer, there has been a profound change. The pendulum has swung so far that public opinion moves towards moral doubts about the propriety of trapping a rat and extremists break into private property with a glowing sense of virtue to liberate infected laboratory animals or predatory mink bred for their fur. Fanatics! But was I so much less fanatical, spending my night awake in the open ready to do battle at first light with all comers, risking a hideous plunge to death 800 feet below or even a spell in prison if things got drastically out of hand and someone else suffered that fate?

No, I comforted myself – enthusiastic beyond the norm for a man of mature years, but not fanatical. And what I was doing was in support of the rule of law. The peregrine falcon enjoyed then (as it does now under the 1981 Wildlife and Countryside Act) special protection enforced by severer penalties than those in the case of offences involving commoner birds.

My presence on the cliff-top not only saluted that fact but represented the culmination of an interest which began with hawks on the printed page in the more generously illustrated bird books of my boyhood years, with hawks

in glass cases in museums and taxidermists' or second-hand shops (bearing witness to an odd Victorian fancy in interior decoration and furnishing), and yet more sadly in what hung fresh or decaying on my gamekeeping great-uncle's heavily-laden vermin gibbet.

The interest was at first satisfied – almost – by the smaller common hawks I encountered occasionally on the low Midland plain, where they are now seen more often. But always I had an ambition, not so easily fulfilled fifty years ago, to rove further afield in wilder places to meet the fiercer and more spectacular species I had yet to see with the flesh still beneath their feathers.

Now I had done this, and to more purpose than the mere gratification of a whim. The young peregrines I was sitting over survived the threats we guarded them against, grew apace, feathered up beautifully and flew safely to take their places in a population which had then only just begun to recover after near-extermination by the unforeseen side-effects of the new and deadly agricultural insecticides introduced in the early 1950s.

two FOCUS ON KESTRELS

Like most people in Britain who know one 'hawk' from another, the first species I learned to recognize was the kestrel. 'Hawk' goes into inverted commas in that sentence because the kestrel, as any purist will hasten to confirm, is really a falcon, in the same clan as the peregrine, but more of that later. We come to know the kestrel first because there are so many of them, because their distribution here is so widespread and because they draw the eye by the systematic hovering – 'standing still' in the sky for minutes on end above fields, wasteland and motorway embankments in a most unbirdlike way – which gives them their familiar name of windhover.

The British Isles is home to about 100,000 pairs, the population expanding and contracting in response to the severity of the winters. Its numerical strength is put into perspective when compared with the 1,000 or so pairs of peregrines here. Kestrels hover above forest glade and field from John o'Groats to Land's End, over bleak and lonely moorland hills and over sunny coastal cliffs overlooking the most crowded of bathing beaches. Wherever there is vegetation to harbour mouse, vole or beetle, the kestrel can find a living.

Kestrels are not alone in knowing the trick of hovering. All raptors are able to do it to some extent, but in Britain only the kestrel makes a virtual lifestyle of this one hunting and prospecting technique. Not only does it draw the eye to the hoverer, it ensures that the kestrel remains exposed to view for minutes or more whereas other hawks, hunting more actively, usually pass in the blink of an eye and vanish before their arrival has properly registered.

Kestrels can also be observed as they conserve energy by perching in wait on telegraph wires or the top of a pole, watching keenly for some faint movement of the rough grass of the roadside verge below as a mouse or beetle disturbs it in its passage. The traffic roaring by seems not to concern them, although stopping your car for a longer look at the bird usually does. The habit is shared in daylight hours with only the bolder members of the crow tribe, the little owl, the buzzard on some upland roads, and other birds too small to attract much attention from a passing car.

Add to these facts another. By far the majority of Britain's human population is now city-dwelling. Other hawks pass over cities occasionally and the sparrowhawk may settle where there are enough trees to offer an attractive territory to an essentially woodland bird, but only the kestrel, for whom a ledge on a rock or a hole in an isolated dead tree forms an acceptable nest site, turns ledges and decorative architectural features on large urban buildings to the same account. Small wonder that it is our best-known 'hawk'.

Time, perhaps, to examine the word 'hawk'. While in everyday parlance all daytime-flying birds of prey except eagles may be called hawks, taxonomists draw finer distinctions, comparing specimens carefully and assembling like with like into groups as far as they can in a cosmos which did not evolve exclusively to assist their schemes of classification.

The group of raptors which fly particularly fast, have long, pointed wings and a tooth and notch arrangement in the bill to assist in giving prey an efficient *coup de grâce* by severance of the spinal cord are termed 'falcons'. Another group with wings both long and broad, used for effortless soaring, an untoothed bill and a readiness to add carrion to the diet are termed 'buteos'; while another group, fierce hunters with untoothed bills and wings which when flexed in the more usual profiles taper to less conspicuous points than those of falcons, are termed 'accipiters' or 'short-winged hawks'. The sparrowhawk is the archetypal example of that group. More could be said, but need not be for the present, except that the kestrel, with toothed bill and a falcon's wing profile, mismatches them with habits more to be expected in some species of daylight-flying owl. It is one of those borderline species of the contradictory natural world which threaten the sanity of the taxonomically inclined.

The kestrel's ready adaptation to a variety of rural habitats is easily understood, but how does it maintain its toe-hold on urban territories where the rodents, although numerous, rarely expose themselves in the open during daylight? One part of the answer is that some do, though their stealthy excursions go unnoticed by us. So rodents are not entirely missing from the diet of the urban kestrel. Of no less importance is the fact that at least some of the kestrel population is able to make a change of diet from rodents to small birds, which they can catch on the ground in cities and suburban gardens as easily as mice are caught, or, at need, in the air, as the prey of other British falcons is taken.

Gamekeepers destroyed kestrels in years gone by on the assumption that they might be a serious threat to their pheasant chicks in the rearing field, as some of them certainly were. With fifty or a hundred broods of chicks scampering enticingly in and out of coops concentrated in an acre or two of rough grass, it is scarcely surprising. The nature of the terrain could not fail to attract the hawk, accustomed to finding much of its prey on exactly that sort of ground, with opportunity for easy kills increased by the inability of the cooped-up foster mothers to do anything to protect their charges beyond issuing warning signals in a language foreign to the chicks.

So keepers mounting guard over the field used to try to shoot any kestrel seen, giving the species an extra cursing for their tendency to attack at random, anywhere in the field. The sparrowhawk, the keepers said of this their other bane, was more easily destroyed because its instinct was to return repeatedly to raid the same coop until the brood had been exterminated or the raider killed in the act. To be forewarned, the keepers rightly believed, was to be forearmed.

Why, then, am I so certain that kestrels do not habitually prey on small

FOCUS ON KESTRELS

birds? There are several reasons. The kestrel, like other birds of prey, is a regurgitator of pellets formed from the tightly compacted indigestible parts of the prey it has consumed. The size, shape, colour, texture and location of the pellet enable one, with experience, to identify the bird which cast it. I have collected and investigated many, taken from roosts known to be used by kestrels and from beneath nests. One recent batch came from a local farm where the farmer complained loudly that the small birds had disappeared from about his buildings after a pair of kestrels had chosen his barn for a nest site.

Not a trace of feather remnant did I find – just the easily identifiable skulls and jaw and limb bones of woodmouse, short-tailed vole and the occasional shrew, bedded in a mat of short soft grey fur. That, plus beetle shards, would be the typical content of all kestrels pellets I have examined, except those collected from the foot of some moorland rocks, where beetle shards have often been the sole contents. Kestrels can survive on what to the human eye can seem a remarkably frugal diet. Pellet analysis has provided much of the scientific knowledge we now have regarding raptor diet and has confirmed that urban kestrels are the only ones likely to prey heavily on small birds.

Only when the rodents are hidden beneath frozen snow have I seen kestrels engaged unmistakably in bird hunting. Then the style changes and the patient hoverer takes to sprinting along hedgerows like a sparrowhawk, using cover as cleverly and snatching an unwary small bird with the same agility. Or some of them do. The dearth of kestrels which usually follows prolonged hard weather suggests that some cannot make the transition even in these conditions.

One that had made it provided more evidence for the general theory. Crossing a wintry field with laboured flight, bearing its burden with some evident difficulty, it alighted by the hedgerow on a low embankment thrown up by recent ditching operations. There it stood with chestnut wings spread for several minutes, mantling whatever it had been carrying, ready for any challenge to its possession of the kill. My vantage-point for watching developments was a good one and the telescope was mounted ready on the tripod. Soon, with a sinking sun illuminating the scene from directly behind me, I had a ×50 image of the action to help me interpret it, the kestrel's every detail sharp and clear, and enough of the kill visible despite spread grey tail and mantling wings for it to be identified as a fieldfare, one of thousands then feeding on the heavy crop of hawthorn berries which had survived longer than usual into the depths of winter.

Eventually the hawk bent to his work. 'Hungry as a hawk' is not always an apt figure of speech. Feathers should soon begin to fly on the breeze, as they would have if I were watching a peregrine with a pigeon or a merlin with a pipit. They did not. Was it a fieldfare, or had I been mistaken? I had seen only the head and a hint of wing. Could I be sure that the grey head glimpsed and now totally obscured had not been that of a young rat? They would not all be underground. One might easily have chosen just the wrong moment to emerge from the warmth of some barn or cowshed the kestrel had been perched by. And the laboured flight? Would 3½ ounces of fieldfare been such a heavy burden?

I could only wait. Whatever the kill, the kestrel had won it in far from easy conditions. The victim had lost its life to provide the meal. It would have ill become me to try to get closer and risk depriving the one of the fruits of its labour and the other of any value in death beyond some ultimate contribution to soil fertility. Fate then took a hand, in the form of a noisy tractor entering the scene two fields away. It put up several flocks of winter thrushes and disturbed the kestrel, which took off without its prey and flew back in the direction it had come from.

I opened the gate and walked quickly along the edge of the field to the solitary hedgerow sapling under which the kestrel had alighted twenty minutes earlier. There I found the expected fieldfare, with a one-inch diameter cavity excavated between its wing-roots and through which its viscera had been extracted and then consumed. Except, that is, for the crop, which had been slashed open, emptied of the rose-hips it had contained, then cast aside. The bird was otherwise untouched, every feather still in place.

FOCUS ON KESTRELS

It was not even part-plucked: the luscious meat on breast and tibia, which sparrowhawk, peregrine or merlin would almost certainly have attended to as a priority, had been ignored. The fieldfare, in short, had been dealt with as though it were a small rodent, short on muscle meat but long on nutritious offal. Here was a kestrel which did not really know what to do with a dead bird.

Another, a fully mature cock which I had the job of rehabilitating after rescue from illegal captivity, gave evidence of not knowing what to do with a live one. With a severe burn-wound on the scalp to recover from and new flight quills to grow to replace those trimmed short by his captor, presumably in some misguided experiment based on half-comprehended techniques of classical Japanese falconry, his convalescence could not be a brief one. To minimize the boredom unvaried confinement must inflict on so intelligent a bird, I employed the fruit trees about the garden to provide some variety of prospect, moving him from one to another, secured by a long leash which would permit him to sample different branches, drop to the ground and flutter back into the tree as he wished. A little judicious attention with the pruning saw and secateurs ensured that my good intentions would not be frustrated by a perpetually tangled leash.

Some of the trees bordered the lawn, enabling me to play my part in a programme of mutual observation from the comfort of a deck-chair. Doing so one fine summer afternoon, I saw the kestrel gather himself for a launch and turned to follow the direction of his keenly concentrated gaze. Grass on an unweeded path was in faint motion. Opening his truncated wings, he pounced, to be brought up just short of his target by the leash. An unworried young house sparrow emerged from the cover of the squitch-grass and continued to potter in and out of the kestrel's reach. The kestrel turned, jumped to the bottom rung of a step-ladder put there for his convenience, made his way step by step to the top, hopped into the tree, turned his back on path and sparrow and took a siesta. The movement of the grass, such as a mouse or vole would be very likely to cause, had attracted the pounce. The identity of the sparrow, once disclosed, switched off the interest.

THE HAWKWATCHER

One might argue that captivity and associated trauma had blunted the bird's instinct. But not if one had witnessed its response to a nest of naked infant mice presented somewhat to my horror by a well-meaning friend who had been moving a woodpile. Until that morning the kestrel had never consented to eat anything while under observation. For the mouselings he flew voluntarily to my fist, bolting them one after the other as though starving, for all that his crop was well laden with raw beef and rabbit's fur.

That incident helps answer one question, but asks another. How did the kestrel know mice for what they were so readily at a stage in their development at which it would never encounter them above ground? It was not likely to be by scent because a hawk's sense of smell is no keener than a man's. Could it be that kestrels sometimes expose a nest by scraping at a hole down which a narrowly missed adult mouse has just disappeared? What they are engaged in on the ground after a plunge is often something of a mystery, even to the close observer using a telescope. Sometimes far more time is taken than seems necessary for a beetle to be consumed or for the bird to assure itself that some larger target has truly escaped. When a mouse or vole is caught and eaten on site, mantling, tearing and swallowing are so evident to the watcher with binoculars as to resemble ceremonies rather than mere functions. Talons would make serviceable scraping-tools and one certainly comes across inexplicable scrapes in the turf from time to time, only to dismiss them automatically as the work of some mammal.

Kestrel, tradition informs us, is a word derived from 'Coystril', meaning 'cowardly knave', a term of abuse said to have been bestowed on the species by falconers in medieval Normandy (or earlier and elsewhere) out of contempt for the bird's uselessness in their art. Could not that unemployability, though, stem as probably from a natural human disinclination to dine off mice and beetles as from timidity in their captor? Were I a kestrel, I could, I am sure, nerve myself with less difficulty to attempt the much admired merlin's prey of lark, wheatear or pipit than well-grown rat, poisonous snake or bitch weasel, all three of which I have seen grasped in the talons of some kestrel somewhere during the past forty years.

FOCUS ON KESTRELS

Kestrels, like other birds of prey, are not obsessively territorial in the way that robins and blackbirds are, but they defend what they judge to be theirs as bravely as any of their nominal betters. I have seen hobbies in transit across kestrel territories expedited on their way; in the many aerial combats between kestrel and sparrowhawk that I have witnessed, I have yet to see a kestrel trounced, for all that sparrowhawk, both female and male, were prized in medieval falconry at their level as the prerogatives respectively of the parish priest and the 'holy water clerk', whatever that functionary might have been

If the mettle of raptors is to be judged by the aggression they display towards larger and theoretically more formidable adversaries, again I accept no slur on *Falco tinnunculus*.

The species is distributed across the temperate zones of the Old World's northern hemisphere over a vast area extending south of the Mediterranean into those parts of North Africa where, between 1940 and 1943, soldiers from Germany and the British Empire were the principal territorial contenders. Here it was that I first discovered the extent of the 'European' kestrel's range and witnessed an aerial spectacle which for me discredited for ever the 'Coystril' theory.

Above the little town of Barce in Cyrenaica a gathering of Egyptian vultures congregated regularly so high in the sky as to be invisible quite often to the naked human eye. There we returned in 1946 to help keep order while Italy's Libyan colonies were eased into history. With the war and its stringencies by then well behind us, it was my pleasure after lunch to spend half an hour seated on the steps of the sergeants' mess, a fine vantage-point from which to watch the sky for birds, especially a pair of European kestrels as they entered and left a tall cylindrical redbrick water-tower, where, on a high ledge inside, they fed a brood of well-grown nestlings.

The view to the south was of ripening barley stretching unbroken to the horizon, a curtain-raiser for what would become a commonplace in England a few decades later. Scanning it with the binoculars was the first post-prandial priority, because the kestrels often hunted its margins. Not this day, though, so I turned to check the deep-blue sky beyond the water-tower and above the gleaming white rooftops of the little town which the Italian colonists had built and over which the vultures sailed all day long.

They were not in view – but the kestrels were, playing together in the hot May sunshine as though not even a clutch of eggs, much less a family of nestlings, had yet arrived to interrupt their tranquil preoccupations.

Her mood suddenly changing, the hen abandoned her play to 'ring up' purposefully, as a peregrine might have done to climb above a flight of homing pigeons. Spreading his black-banded grey tail to contrast with her closely barred amber one, her mate followed her into the higher reaches of the sky, vanishing eventually into the blue haze beyond even the reach of my beautiful Barr & Stroud 12 × 60s. I lowered them and turned my mind to other matters, soon to be distracted by faint sounds from high above, suggesting distress. I searched the sky again and found a vulture, lower than I had ever seen one before, twisting and turning ponderously as it lost ever more height under the repeated and extraordinarily hostile assaults – authentic falcon stoops, bursting away puffs of feathers – made by the kestrel pair, fast expanding from golden stars to identifiable birds, then, at last, shortly before they had grounded and lost interest in their victim, identifiable as the kestrels with which I had grown so familiar, the subjects of my first ever systematic hawk watch.

How high had they gone? I would not put it at less than two miles into the sky. There is more – much more – to the kestrel than it commonly reveals. Had they shown that they were incapable of fear? No, as the morrow was to disclose. I had another observation post under a large tree about thirty yards from the foot of the tower and I had repaired there to see in better detail what the hawks were bringing in. In came yesterday's heroine clutching a hapless Moorish gecko in her bright yellow foot. The top of the tower was under repair, with scaffolding and ladders erected. She alighted with her prey on a middle rung of the highest ladder to check for unfriendly observers before flying into the tower through one of its several unglazed openings and betraying the site of her ledge. As she gazed around, one of the

Hovering kestrel, watched by a cock pheasant in Warwickshire (see page 18)

Kites at play in Wales (see page 46)

camp's many woodchat shrikes appeared from nowhere, perched at the very top of the ladder, bent down in her direction and uttered a string of curses in shrike language. Then it flung itself at her, struck her as hard as a three-ounce bird could and sent her tumbling to the staging below, where she sprawled whimpering for the next few minutes. His point made, emphasized by a second outburst of profanity from the top of the ladder, the victorious shrike flew off. The kestrel recovered her composure and delivered the small reptile she had clung to resolutely through all her sad humiliation.

I had witnessed for the first time the enactment of a principle I was to see exemplified again and again as the years went by. If it retreats before you, pursue it. If it attacks, retire. Never mind who's big and who's small. I had also received proof of the detestation shrikes are said to feel for hawks, a fact turned to account by the old trappers of falcons on passage over the North Sea island of Walcheren. A shrike was kept in a cage on site to alert the trapper to the approach of a quarry so that he would be prepared to spring his trap the moment his victim fell on the tethered pigeon.

Cyrenaica is not the only place in which I have seen kestrels display remarkable intrepidity or an equally surprising lack of it. Golden eagles in Scotland commonly suffer persecution by peregrines and even the little merlin. A few years ago I rented a cottage in Morvern on the edge of moorland where kestrels had taken over that role. There were plenty of both and I cannot recall ever watching an eagle soar for more than a few minutes without a kestrel going up to challenge and pester it. I was not alone in noting this. The laird, too, had watched them and shared my surprise.

Kestrels on a shooting estate in Warwickshire where I do much of my wintertime bird watching follow the plough as the black-headed gulls do elsewhere. The attraction is mice and voles disoriented by the earthquake which has just struck their homes. Kills are often carried for consumption to the edge of the field, probably to escape the noise of the tractor. If so, the kestrel does well to select a quiet spot where there is not an old cock pheasant prowling in wait under the hedge. The pheasant charges and the hawk takes to its wings, unburdened by anything which could impede retreat. One might expect the possessor of a hooked bill and talons to come off best in such encounters, but my money says that 4 pounds of cock pheasant has the edge automatically over 8 ounces of kestrel. Those who relish the flesh of the pheasant should not count on their dinner's diet having been exclusively vegetarian.

Should one reconsider the derivation of the name 'kestrel': If not 'coystril', what? The modern French name the bird 'crécerelle'. Stand within earshot of a nest when a parent brings in a mouse. Listen to the gabble of infant kestrelese. Onomatopoeia is, I am sure, the key to the mystery.

A bird so widely observed as the kestrel has few secrets so far undisclosed, but I stumbled on one of them during a fine autumn afternoon in Warwickshire. The local vole population had reached a cyclical peak and the behaviour of the birds of prey had adjusted to that fact. One particular cock kestrel, recognizable by the exceptionally rich hue of his dark-chestnut mantle, had found a concentration of prey in long grass at the field's edge, well situated for observation. He was hovering above it when I began my watch. The usual progressive drop from a hundred feet or more to ten or less led to a well judged final plunge rewarded by a capture. The fat grey vole was carried to a low branch growing almost horizontally from a big oak in the immediate background. The kestrel scrambled sideways along it until he reached the trunk, dragging the prey still clenched in his foot.

Then, after poking the vole into some recess out of sight from where I sat, he flew from the tree to resume hovering. Two hours later, after the seventh vole had been so dealt with, he left the scene and I walked to the tree for a closer investigation. I found a deep, dark fissure in the bark of the trunk just visible above where the big branch jutted out and quite deep enough, by the look of it, to store voles by the dozen. With my tree-climbing days some years behind me, it had to be left at that, but I harboured no doubts as to what the hawk had been doing. Why he was doing it is another question.

When prey is abundant and there are young to be fed, peregrine falcons are well known for their way of making hay while the sun shines and making caches of the result. On this day we were between breeding seasons; nor had

FOCUS ON KESTRELS

I ever seen a written reference to this habit in kestrels. It may be a coincidence that a short spell of unseasonably severe frost and snow followed soon after, but I wonder. I wondered also whether what I had seen was something any kestrel might do and many, in fact, did, despite the absence of reports, or a misguided aberration unlikely ever to be witnessed again.

That was not the sole instance of unexpected behaviour on the part of that same cock kestrel. Through the winter of the following year he and his mate had as a regular associate another cock, not yet fully mature. The juvenile kestrel of either sex wears a plumage very like that of a typical adult female, and the young males progress by stages from a barred to a speckled mantle and the unbarred tail of male adulthood, concluding the transition after two or three years with a tail bearing only the broad black subterminal band, and the terminal white tip of each feather.

This hanger-on, accepted by his elders with surprising equanimity, combined a speckled mantle with ten or more intermediate black bars on the tail, suggesting that just one more moult would carry him through into the uniform of full maturity.

Then came early spring and the revival of the reproductive instinct. The young male was not immune and attempted one afternoon to mount the hen within a few yards of her mate while all three birds were resting in the same tree after a prolonged spell of hovering, strung out in a line along the foot of the low but steep hill bounding one side of the field. The hen offering no welcome or co-operation, he abandoned the attempt and withdrew to his perch. The adult cock then trod her and his rival in immediate succession, both accepting the service without evident emotion. My experience of an authoritarian and enforcedly celibate male community had already led me to speculate that not all male homosexual connection was founded in simple lust. A dominant male's urge to assert personal authority in an unforgettable way might also have played its part at times.

The fine cock kestrel who recalled these reflections lived to inspire no more. Before the year was out I found his squashed remains spread-eagled on a lane nearby. Broken, bedraggled and dusty though the remains were, enough of that splendid dark-red mantle was left intact for there to be no doubt as to which of the estate's kestrels would no longer be there to answer the roll-call.

Aeronautical engineers (according to whose classical theories a bumble-bee cannot fly) make brave attempts to explain the technology of bird flight. When dealing with gliders such as the gannet and the albatross, or, for that matter, the kestrel when it stiffens its extended wings to become a simple little aeroplane, they are on reasonably secure ground. When the kestrel turns into a light breeze, drops its spread tail and holds station aloft at a precisely chosen altitude on fast-fanning pinions, aerodynamic certainties tremble like the feathers themselves.

According to them, a bird's ability to remain airborne owes nothing directly to the down-beat of the wing (for all that one may see a slow beater like the crow or raven bounce up an inch or more in rhythmic response to each one); it is all a matter of lift, created and maintained when air flows faster over the longer convex upper surface of an aerofoil than over the concave under surface. Hence the camber from leading to trailing edge of both avian and aeroplane wings. This creates a suction effect which keeps the flying machine flying. All no doubt true as far as it goes, but to produce the flow in still air the whole aerofoil must move forward. The object can head into fast-flowing air and remain airborne without further effort if the relationship between its weight, shape and the wind speed is sufficiently favourable. In a high wind, even a fat woodpigeon can demonstrate this fact for a few seconds, especially if there is a kestrel or buzzard up there wind-hanging to set an example. Woodpigeons are odd creatures.

I draw a deliberate distinction between hovering and wind-hanging precisely because there is so much difference between a mere leaning on the wind, adjusting geometry to offset unwanted excess of lift as it gusts, and generating lift in nominally still air for as long as necessary by a mysterious and evidently sophisticated series of fast wing articulations which has never, so far as I have been able to discover, been explained aerodynamically. One day, I suppose, it will be. If the theory does not require an abandonment of the doctrine that direct downward pressure of wing on air does not contribute to lift I shall be greatly surprised.

Is hovering a uniquely effective technique? For all that kestrels devote so much time and energy to it, I have doubts. Harriers and owls hunt the same prey in open territory by quartering the ground slowly at low altitude. I shall never forget the culmination of a December afternoon spent watching the same Warwickshire field, once a gamekeeper's rearing field, where I witnessed the vole caching and homosexual assault. A different pair of kestrels had been hovering over it all afternoon, without success. As dusk fell a barn owl arrived and hunted by quartering for fifteen minutes, during which time I saw him (or her – only barn owls can tell the difference) catch and eat three vole-size rodents. Three rodents – three impressive gulps. Any hawk would have been far likelier to pick at and fiddle with each one for as long as the incredibly effective owl had taken to catch and eat all three.

So the kestrel has evolved to hang motionless, if necessary in virtually still air. Can it also fly fast, as becomes its official status as a falcon? On the rare occasions a kestrel really exerts itself in this way, I believe it can. Once, watching one perform a fast circuit round familiar countryside, I was struck by a happy impulse to track it accurately, counting the passing seconds. Tracing the timed flight afterwards on a 1:25,000 OS map – along its route behind that stand of elms, beyond that church steeple, directly over that railway bridge, and so on – I calculated the speed as a mean 60 m.p.h., give or take 10 per cent.

I never saw a kestrel go so fast for such a distance – more than a mile – before, and have never seen one do so since, so I offer no further evidence regarding kestrel speed. After timing peregrines by the same method, however, and watching the remarkable distances covered in a few seconds by hobbies during their occasional high-flying displays, I do not seriously doubt the prowess I attributed to the energetic kestrel I timed at the foot of Bredon Hill. I therefore suspect most authorities of underestimating the speed at which raptors can fly, principally because the birds rarely attempt their maximum speeds.

I also suspect the same authorities of underestimating the ability of raptors to resolve objects at immense distances. Comparisons based purely on anatomical examination have equated the raptorial eye naked, at best, with the human assisted by ×8 binoculars. I do not know an experienced fellow observer in the field who would not think that a serious underestimate, a point to which I shall revert when discussing the peregrine in detail.

Returning specifically to the kestrel, one gave me a valuable demonstration one afternoon in conditions which could not have been bettered in a laboratory. From a perch in one distinctive tree at the foot of the low hill already mentioned, it stooped suddenly to the turf at the foot of another, equally distinctive, some distance away. Returning to its perch, it ate from its talons an insect just detectable by telescope from where I sat, a field's length away. I saw the dark wing-cases flutter down. When the kestrel had gone I walked over to the foot of the hill, paced the distance from perch to kill and inspected the ground. The distance was 60 yards; the turf coarse beneath the second tree. The hawk had gone straight as a bullet from perch to kill, suggesting a prey detected, not one merely hoped for. Could you sit up a tree with ×8 binoculars and detect a beetle sixty yards away climbing a grass stalk or making several tremble as it crawled through them? You could? Congratulations.

If one can find the patience to sit quietly in the same place – and the right place – for several hours at a stretch, waiting for something of interest to happen, it usually does. That is how I spent 30 August 1987, perched on a coastal cliff west of Lynton, North Devon. The something of interest which eventually happened involved a kestrel.

Two new friends I had made that afternoon sat on my left; to my right a gully bit deeply into the line of the cliff-top. They had yet to see and recognize their first sparrowhawk; I had just told them how this gully often generated a powerful thermal used by sparrowhawks to regain altitude after chasing some small quarry unsuccessfully down the cliff-face. 'And there's one now,' I concluded, as the full-spread wings and tail of a sepia-mantled hawk circling up from below caught my eye. With all binoculars trained on it, the bird rose to eye level, banked, made for one of the small boulders projecting from the muddle of scree and turf at the head of the gully and perched on it breast-on. Several things were not quite right. The end of the soaring bird's tail had seemed rather too rounded for a sparrowhawk's; there had been a suggestion of barring, distinct if slightly reminiscent of a photographic negative at the same time, just perceptible as it circled below us displaying its upper surfaces. Nor was it typical of a sparrowhawk to choose so exposed a perch.

It was the work of mere seconds to bring the tripod-mounted telescope into play. The ×45 image clarified every detail, including the lustrous dark eye and streaked breast of an undeniable hen kestrel. Turning her back, she spread a tail dark as a sparrowhawk's but with ten fine intermediate bars displayed, not a sparrowhawk's five much broader ones.

My companions had not seen their first sparrowhawk after all. Just another kestrel, but the first melanistic mutant of that species I had encountered in a lifetime of hawk watching. Taking off, the bird resumed her journey along the cliffs, pausing for spells of hovering as she went, as though to dispel any possible doubt as to her identity remaining in the mind of any watcher.

That was my last visit to the cliffs that holiday, so the dark kestrel and I did not renew our acquaintance. She had served a useful purpose, though, issuing a reminder to all three of us that birds cannot be identified with certainty on the basis of a single salient feature observed, or by the fulfilment of an expectation encouraged by precedent.

Does anything else remain to be said of the kestrel, its status in 1989 Britain and its prospects thereafter? The winter of 1987/8 having proved so exceptionally mild in England and Wales, the outlook as these words are written is promising. The 1988 nesting season was productive and survival during the following months high. There are currently few unoccupied territories.

As the most adaptable of all our raptors, the kestrel has a long-term prospect of weathering all foreseeable environmental change as it has adjusted to change in the past – for example, motorway construction, as any driver with a corner to his or her eye must be aware. Whatever changes in the pattern of agricultural subsidy may impend, one fact seems certain: cultivation will not be intensified further in the near future. As mice and voles are fundamentally seed-eaters, cultivation as such is not bad news for kestrels, provided some rough vegetation survives on the margins to harbour rodents where a hawk can see and reach them.

An increase in the provision of that, if I read the pros and cons of agricultural debate aright, seems to be the one outcome of impending change which can be predicted safely. The industry's chemicals, as ever, will need a close eye kept on them. Because mammals eliminate organochlorine residues better than small birds do, the kestrels were not prominent among the victims of that scourge. If they are to escape the next (and there will be a next, somewhere at some date in the inescapable passage of time) we shall need to be more vigilant than we were in 1950. With that experience behind us, there will be no excuse for us if we are not.

three # HOW SPARROWHAWKS
BEHAVE

Twenty years ago the sighting of a sparrowhawk anywhere in England east of a line running north–south down the middle of the country was an event to warrant a telephone call to the editor of the local newspaper. Twenty years earlier still the bird was as common as the kestrel and almost as widely distributed, although much less obviously so. Where the kestrel conspicuously exemplified the virtue of persistence, the sly sparrowhawk personified stealth as it so cleverly exploited speed and cover that neither the intended prey nor the casual human observer was likely to see more of its approach, passage and departure than a hint of a shadow in silent transit. One oblivious member of the feathered congregation would never, indeed, live to see anything else ever again. Or so the textbooks insisted, surrounding the sparrowhawk with an aura of mystery which, for me, it has never entirely lost.

The twenty-year absence of sparrowhawks from the eastern half of England was caused by the side-effects of a great advance in the effectiveness of agricultural insecticides, stemming from a laboratory experiment as far back as 1874 – the combining of substances to produce the compound given the code-name DDT, thought at the time to have no commercial value. Put very simply, this branch of chemical engineering was founded in the art of combining a powerful toxin such as chlorine with mineral oil derivatives to form compounds so highly stable that a few showers of rain could no longer turn the farmer's outlay on crop protection into so much money running literally down the drains.

DDT was first used indoors, against domestic pests such as bedbugs and body lice. Employed out of doors with due care, its effects were not drastic. Dieldrin, Aldrin and Heptachlor, which followed it into use in 1948 as sheep dip and seed dressings, posed a threat of a different order, producing side-effects which had, by the mid-1950s, proved disastrous. Birds began to die like flies – small ones which had eaten their share of the treated seed, larger ones which killed and ate them after their contamination. Birds, it was discovered, could not eliminate small dosages in the course of digestion – as rodents and other small mammals proved able to do – but responded to the poisoning by extracting the toxins for storage in their bone marrow and livers, where the capacity to kill or injure is for the time being inactivated.

Not a good prospect for the small birds; a fatal one for the hawks and falcons which, in killing and eating them, received repeated doses in concentrated form from the contaminated organs consumed. Immediate death was one risk; destruction of the capacity to reproduce effectively another. An interim stage was reached throughout arable Britain at which adult hawks might still be about, but those which succeeded in laying eggs either broke them because the shells were too thin to stand the weight of the incubating parent (eggshell thinning was at the heart of most of the trouble) or failed to hatch them because the embryos were too damaged chemically to live and grow properly inside the shell.

In pastoral Britain there was less trouble, except for the effect on peregrines (whose collapse was never thoroughly accounted for) and species which ate sheep carrion or lined nests with wool shed by sheep which had been dipped in the splendid new pesticide. Hence that division of England and Wales by a line running north–south, roughly through Derby. Scotland was not entirely unaffected, but in that country the pattern of arable farming, stock rearing, forest and moorland wilderness is too complex for simple definition by straight lines drawn on maps. Also, with so much wild and uncontaminated land to harbour unaffected raptor populations, there was a big reserve to be drawn on when casualties occurred on the less traditionally farmed mains and crofts.

East of the line through Derby, 1955 England was predominantly arable: west of it, increasingly pastoral, culminating in the hills of Wales and Cumbria, where virtually all the farming was then animal husbandry. That truism still holds, but its significance has been muted by improvement east of the line, first by voluntary agreement among farmers to restrict the use of the organochlorine poisons to seasons and circumstances in which the threat to birds would be at a minimum, and later on by the introduction of legislation by way of reinforcement.

That tale of woe had a marked effect on my connection with birds of prey. Not living far enough west of that rough-drawn line to benefit from the fact that my home was situated to the west of it, the years in which I would otherwise have added experience of bird-eating sparrowhawks to an expanding knowledge of mouse-eating kestrels were the very years of the sparrowhawk's disappearance from cultivated land.

When my fortieth birthday arrived in 1964 I was able to speak with some confidence on the habits of the former bird, but my sightings of the latter – fleeting glimpses included – could still be counted on the fingers of both hands. Living specimens, that is. The bodies of three pesticide casualties had passed through my hands and, as the great-nephew of a Warwickshire gamekeeper still walking his rounds, I had seen more than enough dead sparrowhawks swinging over his garden on an ingenious swivelling mount erected to frighten away small birds tempted by his seeds or fruit, or nailed to his vermin gibbets about the estate. There they kept grisly company with kestrels, jays, crows, magpies, owls, stoats, weasels, grey squirrels, hedgehogs and rats, drying, withering and decomposing as sun, wind and rain performed their immemorial offices in disposing of the uninterred dead.

There was a broader sense in which my life really did begin at forty. A change in private circumstances brought in its train greater mobility and new contacts, which included a gentleman who did me a great favour in terms of hawk-watching possibilities which he had not intended and neither of us foresaw at the time.

The intention (also fulfilled) was to improve my prospects of catching salmon. The beat on the lower Wye to which he gave me access is one of those on the river where it runs hard by the Forest of Dean through a steep-sided valley scarcely less generously timbered than the forest itself. The area, of course, is well to the west of the critical line. Salmon were showing on the day of my first visit, so they received my concentrated attention. Likewise on the following day and the day after that. But by the fourth day of the long weekend for which the beat was mine the run had gone through to overexcite the anglers further up river and I felt able to take time off from fishing to take proper notice of the glorious countryside about me. Buzzards I had been aware of from the first morning, but with buzzards I was sufficiently familiar for there to be no more than a faint sense of satisfaction at their presence. Buzzards haunt the sky as conspicuously as kestrels. I had often fished beneath their indifferent scrutiny in streams on either side of the Welsh Border. Kestrels were hunting, too, hovering above the high skyline the far bank reared up 350 feet to form.

Restoring my tissues with fresh-made tea at 4 p.m. after a long stint of casting at unoccupied water, I became suddenly aware of another and nearer kestrel, hanging motionlessly on the wind at tree-top height, right over the river a few yards downstream from where I was seated. A *kestrel*? Not on your life. This bird had broad, spread-fingered wings, a distinctly smaller head, a square-ended tail and underparts barred everywhere – closely on breast, flanks and inner wings as seen from below; less closely but more boldly on primaries, secondaries and the main quills of the spread tail.

At long last a living sparrowhawk had presented itself at close quarters and remained for detailed inspection. But not for long, though. No sooner, was it positively identified than the hawk banked, turned across the freshly blowing breeze with quick nervous flicks of wings by then neatly half-furled for a dive towards the tall trees lining the foot of the far bank, through whose interwoven canopy she threaded her way expertly to vanish swiftly up river.

HOW SPARROWHAWKS BEHAVE

No salmon that day, but the fine hen sparrowhawk had crowned it memorably enough.

Why, though, had I mistaken her initially for just another kestrel? How could the 'short rounded wings' of the textbooks be mistaken for 'long pointed' ones? Easily, because a hen sparrowhawk's wings are but marginally shorter than a kestrel's. The principal difference lies not in the length from root to tip but in the measure of breadth, from leading to trailing edge.

Skins I have since taken for preservation from hawks killed on the roads, by poisonous pesticide or flying accident show that the kestrel's wing from carpal joint to tip measures on average 9½ inches, that of the hen sparrowhawk 9 inches. Contrasting with this small difference, the secondary quills (which give the wing its breadth) average 5 inches in the hawk, only 4 inches in the pseudo-falcon. Put another way, 5 per cent in length, 25 per cent in breadth. Nuff said?

That was not the only way in which the old books misled, a fact of which the sparrowhawks in the lower Wye Valley soon acquainted me in a rewarding connection which lasted through four years of frequent visits and remains part of my bird-watching programme to the present day. A year after the first visit I was offered a rod on the beat at a nominal rent which enabled me, if I wished, to spend every Saturday in the delightful seclusion of that valley, fishing when conditions hinted at a chance of success, studying sparrowhawks when they did not.

The first lesson was in arithmetic. Sparrowhawks, male and female, rose to soar above the crest of the hill in such fast succession on a fine day that it soon became obvious that it was not a question of a single pair claiming the hill as territory. Thermals bubbling up from among the bracken, gorse and sun-warmed rocks of the steep slope drew hawks from the depth of the surrounding forest as catnip draws cats.

Some came to raid across the bracken or 'steal' through the scattered hawthorns which studded the hillside to 'surprise some flock of unwary finches' (to quote a familiar old text), but most of the arrivals came to soar up to heights so great that the binoculars might sometimes lose them and, with luck, recover them as they fell back into view like falling stones, to drop with long yellow legs finally at full stretch into some tall tree in one of the plantations further along the hill.

Why, if not as some form of territorial display, were such flights undertaken? If that was the reason, why did challenge and conflict not follow more often? Sometimes it did, showing that these high-altitude flights might be founded in that motivation, but not often enough to imply that declaration of territorial possession was their only purpose. Failing that explanation, did the hawks go up to broaden the vista and spot gatherings of potential prey over a vastly expanded area? I think not, because the prospecting flights seen to culminate in a stoop after prey never seemed to take the hawk more than 500 feet above the skyline.

Long deliberation brought me to the conclusion that the answer to another question, if one existed, might solve this mystery too. Why do men and women with comfortable homes and a pub conveniently round the corner drive fifty miles or more to a distant pub to drink in a crowded bar merely that much further from home? The urge accounting for both these classes of expedition is hard to explain in strictly rational terms in both of the contexts, but *Accipiter nisus* can justify its vertical wanderlust by the fact that the sky at 5,000 feet is seldom as crowded as the bar of a country pub on a Saturday night.

Put more simply, the urge to explore is universal, except for limpets and such.

How, though, can I be so explicit in the matter of altitudes – 500, 5,000 feet, and so on? The visual image of a departing bird, horizontally, vertically or at some angle between the two extremes, halves with every doubling of the distance. That of a bird seen first at a distance of 100 yards halves at 200, halves again at 400, and has to reach a distance 800 yards away before it has halved yet again. That is why the image of a bird flying directly away or climbing steeply into the sky at first shrinks rapidly, then more and more slowly, until it seems that it will never vanish completely, however long one watches. When the departure is in a roughly horizontal line the sighting usually ends when the small image blends into the typically rural background, while a departure into the sky usually ends the long, arm-cramping track with the binoculars by a melting into the high haze.

The binoculars, according to their ratings (×8, ×10, ×12, and so on), give an image equivalent to that of the human eye using them at a distance the binoculars reduce to an eighth, a tenth, a twelfth, or whatever, of what it would be. Having taken these facts on board, one needs only to own a large-scale contour map of the district, learn its features on the ground and calculate. The theory applies to the judgement of height and speed of all soaring species of bird; one gets better at applying it reliably with experience and growing familiarity with the maps. None of us, though, ever reaches a point where a heartfelt thank-you would not be said to the giver of an anti-aircraft gunner's range and height finder found in the stocking one of these Christmas mornings.

Whatever the motivation for going there, the sky at 5,000 feet is a fine place for a sparrowhawk to demonstrate that the woods, fields and bracken, heather or gorse-clad slopes below its advertised presence are, as far as its own species is concerned, personal property. Although the sparrowhawk is not territorial to the degree the truculent little robin is territorial, there is not a month in the year in which I have not seen one of these hawks perform such a flight somewhere. Usually, the bird has been a hen, leading to an assumption that the larger female (about twice the weight of her mate) is the true tenant of the territory, the male merely a useful appendage. Yet, although it is the female which in my experience takes the lead in proclaiming territory, any conflict which results, invariably between females, may be spectacular but does not expose the combatants to serious risk of injury.

With cock sparrowhawks it is different. That was another lesson the hawks taught me in the lower Wye Valley, driven home by others inhabiting a great wooded combe behind the Exmoor coast in North Devon. Dismounting from the car right by the river one fine June morning (a parking concession which concentrated fishing tackle, food, drink, shelter and optical instru-

ments most conveniently), I first employed my binoculars. A handsomely mature cock sparrowhawk dropped obligingly from above to alight on a boulder at the edge of the shallows, either to drink or bathe, probably the latter, since healthy hawks drink little, if at all.

He was given no chance to do either. Before he had done more than take a glance into the water flowing gently by, a ruddy-breasted, slate-backed facsimile fell like an arrowhead from the big horse-chestnut beneath which the victim stood, struck him between the shoulders, bound to him with wings flailing, dragged him into the water and set about treading him under. Fortuitously or by calculation I cannot say with certainty, but the assault was methodical enough to satisfy the majority of the human spectators that the aggressor had properly appreciated his opportunity.

I do not readily intervene in the affairs of wild creatures I am watching, but I fell from grace and made an exception that time. A quick clap of the hands was enough to break the spell. The hawks broke apart; he with the upper foot departed; the vanquished required a few seconds to shake himself dry and perform an emergency preen. The feathers of hawk and falcon are more than insulation or the means of transport: they are the equipment of their profession.

Next time I saw cocks fight I was in no position to interfere. The Devon valley from whose rim I watched lies about 1,200 yards behind coastal cliffs and runs roughly east–west for a mile. It is deep, splendidly wooded with a variety of fine deciduous trees, and at that time harboured not fewer than six displaying pairs of the hawks. A high-soaring sparrowhawk may or may not be engaged in a display over territory; one which ascends to perform a strange flight of undulating climbs and short stoops with untypically slow and weirdly syncopated wing-beat is doing that for sure. Thus, in favourable conditions, may one correctly estimate the number of nesting pairs likely to be found in a wood and the extent of the territories they are defending.

One I had found beyond the range of the human eye with the help of the binoculars. While marvelling at the altitude it had climbed to, I was astonished further by a second falling violently upon it from higher still. They grappled immediately and fell together a mile or more, threshing and twisting like fighting tom-cats to crash into the rough pasture on the opposite valley-shoulder a quarter of a mile away. Incredibly, they were not even damaged by their fall, though the bird with the skill or luck to have hit the ground with the other providing a cushion stood triumphantly on the loser for something like half a minute. There was no attempt to deliver a *coup de grâce* or make a meal of the conquest, though. Instead, one hawk stepped quietly off the other and permitted a departure which was made without further defiance. Adrenalin, though, still flowed in the victor's veins, a fact of which he gave evidence by taking off after a short rest to beat up a nearby line of hawthorns and rowans standing along a stone dyke from which a dozen fat woodpigeons were expelled in hasty panic.

Sparrowhawks here provided not only a dramatic fight between cocks for my entertainment, but plentiful evidence of an inclination to emerge from cover to hunt for small birds on the slopes of the open cliff-top downland and among the nooks and crannies of the actual cliff-face. One must accept the dogma that the sparrowhawk is fundamentally a woodland species, for one does not find them far away from it. Let their woodland fastness be within handy reach of open country, however, and they will not ignore it, whether or not it offers hedgerows to skulk along.

Many reaches of coastal cliffs in Wales and the West Country and much of the moorland above them are patrolled by sparrowhawks these days, offering a far better chance to look at one than the heart of any forest. Indeed, one sees sparrowhawks properly only when they have left the thickets in which they loaf between expeditions. One such observation, on a small bare hill in Radnorshire, provided one of my few experiences of a sparrowhawk which failed to inspire terror among the vulnerable.

The hill bears the typically Welsh name of Little Mountain. It rises 300 feet above a valley bottom on the 700-foot contour to form a hog-back half a mile long, crowned with an earthwork. Stunted hawthorns grow there in profusion; crows, jackdaws, magpies and a few ravens haunt the hill for whatever pickings it offers. Watching from a lane on the opposite shoulder of the valley as they reduced the remains of a sheep to gleaming bone one cold February day, I noticed a young hen sparrowhawk flying in to try her luck among the hawthorns. So did the corvids, all of them except the dignified ravens rising in a cloud to torment and frustrate her as she tried to flush prey from the bushes by methodical patrolling. The size of the corvid horde drawn to the scene by the precious February carrion was too much for her. Outclimb them, twist and turn however sharply, check however cleverly to induce overshoots as she might, it was impossible to give attention to her business while simultaneously evading the spiteful bills aimed to stab and tweak.

She persevered bravely, but in the end had to acknowledge defeat and accept grounding. Once she was down in the shelter of a hawthorn, the corvids lost interest in her and all returned to the dead sheep to resume gorging.

Now came the remarkable incident: the failure to intimidate the vulnerable. From the cover of the nearest gorse bush a quarter-grown leveret came lolloping confidently to edge up to the standing (and astonished) hawk, then attempt to cuddle up to her as though she were its long-lost mother. The expression on that merciless face as she stared down at this strange sparrowhawk nestling, every feather on her neat little head erect, had to be seen to be believed.

She took a pace to the side: the leveret cuddled up again. Another pace: the leveret again closed the distance. This was too much. Leaping into the air with wings beating sharply, she quickly gained height. Then she stooped almost vertically at her innocent new tormentor, but seemed careful not to strike it. She flew away, presumably in search of some less Alice-in-Wonderland habitat and the leveret beat a hasty retreat back into the gorse bush. It had learned something which might be useful to it if it ever crossed paths with a goshawk. Why does everyone not see sights like this? I believe the answer to be simple – impatience, and 'bird watching' in large, mobile parties. I had been sitting with legs turning to ice for five uneventful and almost motionless hours, attended by only one companion, equally im-mobile, when the little comedy was played out. Hawks accept the presence of people who have made themselves part of the landscape. For that it is not necessary to deny an eyelid a flicker, but a growing conviction after half an hour that something more interesting *must* be happening over the hill or down the valley is fatal to the prospects.

Perhaps all hawkwatchers should serve an apprenticeship as anglers. Everybody knows that sport for one where nothing ever happens!

So, for sparrowhawks, familiarity may breed either contempt or at least a suggestion of the possibility of coexistence with the human neighbour. Can there ever be more? A great hawk-watching friend of mine who farms in Shropshire believes there may be. At one time not so long ago his daily routine included a drive down the same narrow lane at the same time with a van loaded with eggs from his poultry unit. He began to notice a sparrow-hawk flying with him, ready to pursue small birds his passage disturbed from the hedgerows. Next, he formed the suspicion that she waited on a gatepost for the van's arrival, clearly aware of the help it could provide. He never entirely satisfied himself of a coldly rational chain of cause and effect, but still wonders whether he might be the only man in England entitled to describe himself truthfully as the employee of a sparrowhawk?

Whatever the leveret's surrogate mother thought of crows, hawkwatchers often owe them a thank-you for services rendered. When *Corvus corone* is on the prowl in search of mischief, few hawks loafing in cover, however dense, escape that beady eye. Why there should be such bitter animosity I do not know, but one can count on the corbie to flush the watcher's quarry and put the common target through its paces.

Although by comparison clumsy in manoeuvre, the carrion crow and its near kin are fine all-weather aircraft, making up in persistence for what they lack in finesse. Sparrowhawk, kestrel and buzzard all suffer these attentions – all of which encounters can be turned to the observer's account as the victims produce every twist and turn in the repertoire, show every variation in the geometry with which the watcher needs to become familiar, and show them from every angle of view. Observations are helpfully prolonged; the crow, so densely black and so commonplace, is measuring-stick, colour datum and the one surviving optical certainty at distances where hawks dwindle down to metallic twinkles in the black speck's orbit as a sunray touches the fiery red of a kestrel's mantle or the broken silver of a hen spar's breast.

What then are the true colours of the hen sparrowhawk? The ground colour of her breast ranges from white to pale buff; the bars which decorate it may be bold or faint, sepia, paler brown than sepia, grey or nearly black. Any hint of rufus fades with age. Beneath the tail she is unblemished white, a badge prominent in display. The old textbooks endowed the adult with a generally sepia upper plumage, mantling only her adult mate in grey and those of her sisters which lived into advanced old age.

Nowadays, after much handling of trapped specimens during sparrow-hawk research in the south of Scotland, adult hens, too, are described as having grey mantles. Am I, like an earlier generation of ornithologists, colour-blind? Are the scientists? Or is there some likelier explanation of the anomaly? I believe so. All agree that young birds of either sex are brown-mantled. Watching populations systematically has persuaded me that males adopt the plumage of maturity not later than the third calendar year of their lives, females remaining brown for significantly longer. Relate that theory to the rate of destruction among sparrowhawks by keepers when the old authorities were writing and their illustrators painting and an explanation takes shape.

Life expectancy in the pheasant- and partridge-rearing lowlands was such as to award few grey mantles to hens: those which evaded the shot that long would be the likeliest to go on doing so, never to become artist's models or the subjects of post-mortem reports. So: a strong bias in the records towards brown-backed hens. Yet a reservation remains. I have scarcely ever identified a hen sparrowhawk at close quarters whose upper plumage I could describe as 'grey'. They have all been brown – a warmer shade in the case of birds judged to be young or youngish, a drab sepia in that of the older ones, but no more 'grey' than the bark of an oak-tree is grey.

I sometimes wonder whether the same plumage might register one colour impression in the hand and another when viewed in flight half a field away. Iridescence is the common denominator of the plumage of birds, causing its responses to changes in the direction or intensity of the light falling on it to be quite dramatic in some circumstances.

One sees rather more hens than cocks, reflecting the smaller number of long-term survivors among the latter and, I suspect, their weaker inclination to emerge from cover and take to the sky. When one does so in the right place at the right time, though, the experience can be visually memorable. The most handsome I ever saw outside a glass case broke from a stand of tall Douglas firs on Radnor Forest one bright January afternoon after an overnight fall of snow followed by hard frost.

The track I walked wound round the shoulder of a valley, the plantation on my left, a steep fall to pasture and a stream lined with tall broadleaves down to my right. The hawk came like a bullet from between the trees on my left, narrowly missed my ear in his passing, gathering yet more speed as he fell to the valley bottom where fieldfares, redwings and chaffinches searched for food where the wind had blown snow away to expose patches of open ground. They sensed his approach and rose in a scattering crowd making for the protection of the streamside trees, but not quite soon enough. Using the momentum of his stoop, the spar shot up among them like a rocket, half-looped, and reached to clutch a cock chaffinch successfully. It, too, reached the tree-tops, but by then unaware of the journey.

That hawk had a mantle with more blue in the grey than some of the merlins I have watched and a breast so ruddy that it seemed to be blotched with blood. Nor could the encounter have been at better advantage. Nothing so enhances the brilliance of bird colour as sunlight reflected by new-lying snow.

The witnessed kill, too, added its dimension to the incident. Many sparrowhawks are seen while hell for leather after prey. A kill already gripped in a passing hawk's foot is no great rarity, but a moment of truth truly witnessed is another matter. The fingers of one hand record my tally. The odds, when all is said and done, are on the prey escaping unless subnormal, juvenile or taken utterly by surprise. The sparrowhawk's speed, phenomenal powers of acceleration, tactical sense and cunning have evolved so that it can survive, not prove triumphant in every encounter.

Even a quarry so feeble as the blue tit is not irretrievably doomed. Standing on the road bridge at Llangedwyn late one winter's afternoon, bidding the River Tanat adieu at the end of a day spent happily with soaring hawk and rising grayling to keep me company, my eye was suddenly caught and riveted. A hen sparrowhawk had emerged from a tunnel formed by the bankside alders downstream, twisting and turning in hot pursuit of something at first invisible in the failing light. As they sped towards the bridge I saw that the quarry was a blue tit on the verge of exhaustion but by the blessing of its small turning circle just able to go on escaping the clutch of the talons.

When so close that I could make out the glassy orange of the hawk's ferocious eye without help from the binoculars, the tiny blue tit vanished inexplicably from sight – mine, and, as it turned out, the sparrowhawk's too.

HOW SPARROWHAWKS BEHAVE

She braked, circled two or three times below me at reduced speed, glared up angrily (it seemed) at the spectators on the bridge, then flew off. A careful binocular search of the ground below where the disappearing trick had been performed recovered the blue tit, spread-eagled still as death in the winter-dingy sheep-cropped turf tussocks. It, too, departed safely soon afterwards, saved by sagacity or syncope and the fact that the hunter's eye responds above all to movement. Ask any opossum.

The isolation of the crepuscular blue tit was not in its favour but did not prove fatal. Might the hawk have fared better with a choice of targets? It might have, but not necessarily. Much can be no better than too little. On a well wooded shooting estate near my Worcestershire home there is a steep bank rising 200 feet from the plain to extend half a mile, most of it overgrown with hawthorn. This bank draws winter-migrant thrushes like a magnet and sparrowhawks to prey on them again these days – or to make the attempt. It draws me, too, on a fine winter afternoon and although I have recorded eight unsuccessful attacks in a single afternoon, made by relays of hen sparrowhawks, old and young, I have yet to witness a kill there. There are always too many targets for the attacker to concentrate lethally on one amid the distraction of the bird-storm, too many to blunder into the line of attack and obscure the intended victim from the hawk's view as soon as one is selected.

Seen in the hawk's perspective, I judge both extremes to be undesirable. A single target not seized at the first snatch is all too energetically aware of the trouble it is in; flocks spell protection by confusion – one of the reasons for their existence. If ever I am reincarnated as a sparrowhawk I shall pray to Horus for finches sent in parties of half a dozen. Enough for each to trust to the other chap being the unlucky one; not enough to muddle the issue.

Some sparrowhawks cope better with profusion than others do, which may reflect the making of perfection by practice. In the grounds of a local stately home in reduced circumstances there is a massive willow on a small island in the middle of a twenty-acre ornamental lake. Generations of sparrowhawks have roosted there over the years and now do so again. The dense reedbeds bordering one side of the lake provide a summertime roost for starlings by the thousand, which fly in party by party towards sunset, but if there is a sparrowhawk in residence they do not immediately settle but wheel and whirl about the sky in contingents, until one stands beneath at one's peril. Gradually the flock assembles until a critical moment arrives. Then the sparrowhawk leaves the willow for what the anglers who used to fish for roach there called his or her supper shopping expedition, when first I was part of the spectatorship.

The starlings, too, know the ropes and by instinct or split-second response to the flock leader's telepathic orders sweep up into a curtain of birds, change front, transform from curtain to counterpane, dive en masse, climb en masse, but always so as to present the hawk with a swarm of targets. At last a false move leaves one starling cut off and isolated. Its fate is sealed. The hawk returns to the willow with the kill, the starlings drop immediately into the reeds and settle down for the night, as though aware that a toll has been paid. Sometimes one sees the actual clutch; more often hawk and prey seem only to brush together momentarily before the hawk drops back to the island to perch and bend to its nice warm supper.

The big broad wings of the sparrowhawk grip an impressive square footage of air, generating a remarkable momentum. Such 'oars', though, cannot be plied without strain. Watch a sparrowhawk in the attack and a salient impression will be typically of momentum unprofitably sacrificed as energetic flight is interrupted by inexplicable glides towards the target. These, I am sure, are to allow oxygen refreshment to overtake blood toxification, to avert cramp and crash. There was, indeed, a time when I doubted the sparrowhawk's capacity for sustained fast flight as a falcon employs it in a long-distance overhaul.

As ever, though, as soon as a theory is formulated, the time arrives to question it. The cloud came over this one as I watched a high merlin territory in Shropshire. The valley was small but deep, the merlins' shoulder well bushed. All day, a blackbird had carolled from a thorn on the opposite skyline. Shortly before 6 p.m. he attracted the notice of a cock sparrowhawk,

Peregrine and male hen harrier in Radnorshire (see pages 101–116)

Two young hobbies in an oak tree, the adults in flight (see page 146)

HOW SPARROWHAWKS BEHAVE

which shot down past us from the ridge behind to open the drama. Employing – as usual – the momentum of the stoop to swing up to the prey from below, the hawk made one error. As we viewed him, Blackie was in the right-hand side of the bush. The spar unaccountably decided to flick round the left-hand side and take him as he departed. That he certainly did, squawking fortissimo and climbing with just that trifle of edge his well-dished wings – designed for such a task – conferred on him.

Never ceasing his clamour, he gradually opened the gap as he tore off down the valley. Blackie, I surmised, was not entirely new to this game. Four hundred yards they sped, Blackie aiming for a patch of dense cover in a little re-entrant, spar flailing away with never a break, closing the gap, losing the advantage, closing it again. But not fast enough, it seemed, with Blackie almost home and dry. Then a treacherous puff of crosswind blew the victim just sufficiently off course for the pursuer to take the inside of the bend, cut off retreat, shoot out a long yellow leg and strike a glancing blow. A few dark feathers danced on the breeze and Blackie was spurred into finding a second wind. Great stuff, this adrenalin. It brought him back up the valley, regaining height and maintaining his astonishing lead. Still the hawk beat hard, taking no break from the action, and when the two birds passed us for the second time both were tiring visibly. As they disappeared beneath a big overhang jutting immediately below us, the horrified cackle Blackie had kept up throughout the pursuit reached a peak which I assumed to be his final message to an unfeeling world. Not so. On galumphing down the slope to where a view of the outcome could be obtained, I found the blackbird deep inside another – and thicker – hawthorn, still uttering vigorous protest, with the sparrowhawk spread among the bilberries at the foot of it, gasping for breath.

He had both broken a rule by which his kind commonly lives and was demonstrating the price his particular physiology charges for that indiscretion. On this occasion, though, not the full price. After a minute or two spent gulping air avidly, he recovered, collected himself, sprang into the air and flew away confidently enough, favouring us with a baleful yellow glare as he passed us for the fourth and last time that afternoon.

Let my tale of sparrowhawks conclude with the strangest experience of their affairs I have yet to recount. I stumbled upon it in Galloway, while driving along the shore of Wigtown Bay one June afternoon. A grey hawk was seen in flight over the rock-pools and shingle, with small birds in pursuit as small birds will occasionally risk mobbing their fearsome enemy. A swift dismount improved the view, the bird turned, flew directly overhead with broad sparrowhawk wings to perch most untypically on the nearest telegraph pole.

The stance was upright, the eye orange, the legs long, the bill fittingly hooked and the breast properly barred. Or was it? No. The belly and flanks were, but throat and breast were immaculately grey, as a cuckoo's would have been. The bird repeated its flight, a cuckoo fluttered from a gorse patch nearby and quietly left the scene.

The hawk returned to the pole, the mobbing wagtails vanished into the gorse. All appearances at the top of the telegraph pole were checked and confirmed. Not a normal sparrowhawk, but what? Africa's pale chanting goshawk was the only accipiter known to me with a plain-grey upper breast. An escape from a bird garden, perhaps? Not impossible at that time. Donald Watson, the distinguished ornithologist and bird painter, lived not distant. Speeding there, I laid my mystification before him.

'Have you not read Ash's paper?' he politely enquired, then did me the further courtesy of searching his library shelves and putting it in front of me. The bird had been the cuckoo's mate. Ash had shared my experience of the fantastic impersonation in every particular but the stretching of legs to adopt a vertical stance. Presumably, the bill is 'shortened' when the feathers of the throat are fluffed out to mask part of it, and the wing usually carried in a point is given breadth and spread fingers when one primary quill is folded over another.

At last – at long last – I knew how the old writers had brought themselves to report and reiterate the story of cuckoos destroyed by gamekeepers in mistake for sparrowhawks. Kestrels, by all means, especially if the unlucky cuckoo had been a youngster or a red-phase adult; even a merlin, if the light were poor, but how do you confuse the broad wings and powerful, incisive flight of the spar with the flutterings of the feeble cuckoo which did not even parody its profile? Now I knew – and why the cuckoo did it, I thought. What better way of drawing attention from the hen cuckoo while she deposited the egg? There could scarcely be any, as I had seen for myself.

Why was it not seen more often? Had gamekeepers blasted the habit out of the unfortunate cuckoo, as I suspect the motor car to be in the course of selecting for survival any hedgehogs which do not happen to roll up into balls when frightened? Natural selection takes an eternity to arrange its marvels when left to nature. It might be different when *we* put a foot on the accelerator.

The sparrowhawk in England is no longer a scarce and threatened bird. Few shots are now aimed deliberately at them, so few are aimed at cuckoos. Perhaps the one bird will respond in the long run by coming to seem less of a 'skulker along hedgerows' as the progeny of free-soaring parents survive to perpetuate their inheritance. Perhaps the lesser bird will perform its weird mimicry in such safety that it, too, will reimplant as a common instinct something else which the gun may nearly have eradicated from the package.

Stranger things have happened.

four   THE KITE IN WALES

When I first heard of the red kite (as it was then sensibly named) the impression left on my ten-year-old mind was of a rarity standing at only one remove from the dodo and the sabre-toothed tiger. 'Only two or three pairs surviving, found in remote hill country on the Carmarthen–Cardiganshire border' – no mention in those proudly insular days of secure and substantial populations in Continental Europe, found from Sweden to Spain, in Asia Minor, on Mediterranean and on Atlantic islands.

Nor, in fact, was the Welsh population quite so desperately reduced as it was then asserted. Then as now, it existed in the form of separate nuclei which might not have totalled more than a dozen pairs, but the oft-quoted 'two or three' related not to the entire population but to that sector of it centred on the upper Towy valley, in the heart of what was then the 'Great Welsh Desert'.

Most of that once congenial 'desert' of rolling sheep-grazed hills has since been sacrificed to the abominable Sitka spruce, so that one is fortunate nowadays to find a gap in the trees through which anything but the odd crow and the ubiquitous coal tits flitting about the plantation coastlines can be glimpsed.

During the initial stages of the tree planting, though, it was different. That was when I began to visit Wales regularly in search of kites and I have no doubt that the replacement of sheep by seedling conifers contributed at first to the bird's recovery there, now advanced to the point at which a good year may encourage forty pairs to attempt to breed, with almost as many again roving the skies between Dovey and Usk as they progress through the several years which separate fledging and the attainment of full sexual maturity.

Sheep in the hills of mid-Wales were traditionally ranched rather than farmed, with heavy losses in hard weather accepted as inescapable. The resulting supply of plentiful sheep carrion from November to March was without doubt a major factor in keeping a kite population ticking over in Wales – as it also made the Cambrian Mountains a fine habitat for buzzard and raven, too, in far larger numbers – but sheep cannot feed these birds throughout twelve months of the year.

Remove the competition from grazing sheep, and voles – exploitable by raptors when there is no sheep carrion to be found – prosper. Add the first few crops of conifer seed as the trees begin to grow to the seed of ungrazed grasses not yet extinguished by the conifer canopy, and vole populations explode. One did not need to trap and count voles to discover this. The sky above the new-planted hills was in those days permanently alive with kestrels and buzzards. Half a dozen and more could be counted in one 360° sweep of the binoculars wherever one halted the car on the hill tracks between the A483 and the A485. My short-eared owl record on the mountain road between Llanwrtyd Wells and Tregaron was ten seen in an evening's drive which did not include a single halt to scan for them.

As a presence among these commoner species, the kite was no longer a rarity. Find the right place to stop, and a careful search of the sky above the horizons might easily disclose several on patrol at the same time. Now it is not so easy. Kites are present in even better numbers, but the open spaces which so attracted and concentrated them have dwindled drastically and the hill road from which one is trying to watch is almost bound to be lined by conifers now grown to a view-excluding height. There has never been a more callously brutal assault made on the beauty of the British landscape than that perpetrated by the foresters of the twentieth century, driven by their sole serious consideration – a maximized financial return on an investment whose economic justification accountants are still at loggerheads over.

Obsessed as I still was by notions of their imminent extinction, it is small wonder that the kite should have been the first bird to draw me into the wilderness when I made the big decision to organize myself to watch hawks purposefully, not just to enjoy them when they happened along as I was doing something else out of doors. As so often happens, the road I had applied my foot to was not a direct one. A son then in his mid-teens had taken a fancy to make birds the new subject of his water-colour painting. Displaying an admirable initiative, he had made a contact at Birmingham's combined Art Gallery and Natural History Museum in pursuit of interesting artists' models. The friendly curator had provided him with both a kite on a pedestal and a map reference for a hillside between Rhayader and Devil's Bridge where he knew a living specimen was likely to be found. I, enjoying at the time a marked improvement in personal circumstances which included a nice new motor car, responded in the obvious way.

Our first expedition culminated in a seat torn from a pair of new trousers as my son lost his footing on the steep hillside while a bird with a body like a bullet sprinted along the skyline. In the mid-1960s it was not everyone who could claim a peregrine falcon in the audience as he exposed his nether end to the autumnal breeze through the tattered remnant of a square foot of worsted fabric. That hillside remained the principal focus of interest throughout the following winter, but not until a summery day in the March which ended it drew us further west were our efforts rewarded.

North of Tregaron there is a small village whose road sign reads Pontrhydfendigaid. Approaching it from the north, one notices a rounded hill to the left of the road. As it came into view a fortissimo croak from the back-seat passenger rent the air. 'Forked tails. Forked *tails*.' He had a leg out of the car before I could stop the wheels turning; I followed a second behind him. There they were – two undeniable kites at play a hundred feet above the field. Creamy heads and napes; sharply arched wings; mottled mantles and long forked tails so assertively red that I still protest at the deletion of the adjective from the modern textbook.

'Kite' forsooth! There are numerous species of kite about the world, with the splendid possessor of the handsome red tail neither the commonest nor the most widely distributed. If taxonomy felt obliged to dub one of them 'The kite' the black kite was the logical candidate. *Milvus milvus migrans* and its scarcely differing local races are distributed solidly from central France to the isles of Japan, from Jutland to the Australian outback. 'Our' kite does not occur east of the Caspian or south of Cancer.

The pair soaring above the Cardiganshire pasture that fine March day did not remain in view for long. After turning towards each other for a brief moment of talon-grappling amorous display, they broke apart, dropped below the horizon and were gone. That, as I was to discover in the years to come, was fairly typical of the time allowed by kites for the viewer to enjoy a sight of them. Where the much commoner and far less spectacular buzzard may hunt over the same hundred yards of skyline for hours on end, the majestic red kite appears briefly and passes on. This habit of ranging widely probably reflects a preference for easily won carrion and that such is to be seen by sharp eyes on the first inspection of the ground it is lying on. Vole, rabbit and much other living prey reward persistence by being likely at any time to emerge suddenly from cover which has been under scrutiny for half the day. Of this fact the buzzard is obviously aware.

Not that the red kite confines itself to carrion. An eminent British Trust for Ornithology scientist I meet in Wales now and again while bird watching told me once of the remains of 23 juvenile magpies he had just identified at a single kite plucking post. As magpies roof their nests, some element of pursuit and energetic capture was implied. Nests are robbed, though, as witnessed by a sequence in a film the Royal Society for the Protection of Birds made, in which a kite is shown as it successfully evades a cloud of black-headed gulls over one of their colonies high in the hills to take a chick. Indeed, a habit of snatching the progeny of domestic fowl is often cited as a prime reason for the nineteenth-century extermination of the kite from England.

That is probably true, because the invention of the breech-loading shot-gun and an expansion in the popularity of poultry keeping were contemporaneous developments. In Scotland, where the notorious Glen Garry vermin book shows the kite to have been extremely common as late as the 1830s, there is no doubt that the suddenly fashionable sport of grouse shooting was responsible. The red grouse is naturally scarce in West Wales: Victorian Royalty set up no trend-setting establishment in the Principality. These facts taken together could throw a little more light on the as yet unanswered question of why it was here that the species hung on during the decades in which it was dying out everywhere else in these islands.

The topography of the Cambrians is one of small but deep valleys bounded by a complexity of spurs and re-entrants, with such roads as there are constructed to follow the contours of the higher – and drier – ground. Before the conifer plantations matured, one was often rewarded there by the pleasingly unusual view of a hawk or daylight-flying owl hunting or travelling at eye-level, or even below it. During the big explosion of vole populations there, I saw several kites pass by at eye-level, eating a vole out of the foot as they flew, without detectable prejudice to the controlled elegance of their stately flight.

A friend who lived on the edge of the kite country had a closer and rather more surprising encounter one midwinter's day while paying a social call on a peregrine site we had wardened together and would again. Among the reasons for the visit was concern for a ram and his group of attendant wethers with which we had formed a firm friendship based on a supply of stale bread. Coming quickly to recognize our cars, they would greet our arrival by racing down the hillside, bleating, to stand in a circle round us until tribute had been offered.

Bread was taken that day, but the sheep were not the first to benefit. No sooner was it scattered on the roadside grass verge where we parked and its scatterer back in his car to shelter from the fierce blast of the December wind than a kite, unnoticed during the scattering, fell from the sky to eat the bread as eagerly and knowingly as a crow might have done. One assumes desperation, as I did on another winter's day when I saw a kite invite disaster by scavenging mummified remnants of bone, skin and feather from old peregrine kills littering the rocks of an eyrie some miles to the west. Happily for the dicer with death, the peregrines were not at home or within easy reach of it.

Although the distinction I drew between the different styles of kite and buzzard in their methods of covering ground as they search for food is a valid one, it is a generalization, not a dogma. When a kite demonstrates this fact by concentrating buzzard-fashion on a limited section of hillside, investigation may prove profitably instructive.

A regular companion during the heyday of my kite-seeking years was a senior colleague from the American company for which I then worked. Manchester-born, Bill had crossed the Atlantic while still a young man but had never lost his passion for the birds of his native land. It was one, like my own, which had been conceived but not fully indulged during boyhood. Now, as he paid his frequent visits of inspection to the British subsidiary, the ball was at last at his feet and the goal open. We made the most of the opportunity together. Wandering in search of birds is always enjoyable, but best of all when done in congenial company.

Following a morning of such wanderings and scannings, from vantage-point to vantage-point along deserted tracks, we pulled up at mid-afternoon beside a small stream racing limpidly over clean gravel and filled the kettle. A big grassy bluff reared some 200 feet above the stream's little valley, over which a buzzard soon hung head to wind. It was joined by two more while we watched – then by two kites. They gave the impression of bird-shaped artefacts hung on strings, lowered, wound back up, let fall again. So they continued throughout the boiling of the water, the making and drinking of the tea. What was implied? When duly refreshed, we decided to face the steep climb and find out what anchored the big hawks so magnetically to whatever lay beyond the ridge.

THE HAWKWATCHER

The climb was at least as stiff as it looked from below, causing the fatter man (in his forties) to puff and blow harder than his trim and energetic companion, for all that the latter had a sixtieth birthday to look back on. Eventually, we got to the top but what we found there was nothing of note – certainly not what we had half expected, the remains of a sheep we had suspected the birds of squabbling over out of our trackside view. There was just a waterlogged depression on the hill-top plateau, a neat rectangle measuring about fifteen yards by ten, excavated, presumably, by peat cutters of another century.

No living thing was visible, but every large puddle we had examined in the rutted track beneath the bluff had been wriggling with well developed tadpoles. The Welsh uplands, when left bare, support a population of frogs and toads to astonish anyone brought up to expect them on only the lowest-lying and marshiest ground. I had never seen a kite or buzzard carrying a kill positively identifiable as one of these amphibians, but I had little doubt of what had kept the five hawks over that hill-crest with such persistence while Englishman and adopted American sat below celebrating the special relationship with tea and their shared enthusiasm.

That friend and I had many adventures with birds as we travelled Wales, Scotland and North Devon together, tracking down the dreams which had escaped us in our boyhoods. Often I read in his face the signal of some private ambition realized or was told of it in triumphantly plain language. Never with more emphasis, though, than when a friendly field officer of the Nature Conservancy Council braked his Land-Rover to a halt by where we sat at the side of a mountain road, dismounted and put into Bill's hand a big pale egg, faintly speckled in brown, which he had recovered from a failed kites' nest for laboratory analysis. 'Gee!' breathed my friend, duly stricken with awe. 'If anyone had told me fifty years ago that I should live to have one of these *in my hand*!'

Fifty years was just about what it had taken for a whole package of protection measures to raise the red kite population in Wales from a dozen pairs or fewer to forty pairs or more. After the chemically induced contribution to the wipe-out of Welsh peregrine falcons on the same scale had been halted, the species took little more than a decade to make a complete recovery – rising to a hundred pairs and more – despite only half-hearted protection measures and persistent interference from egg and chick thieves.

One has to ask whether there is something wrong – genetically wrong, perhaps – with the Welsh population of red kites. It could well be so, with the gene pool once reduced to the contribution of twenty birds or fewer, cut off by several hundred kiteless miles from any source of reinforcement. Then why, for heaven's sake, one might ask, were steps not taken to reinforce it artificially from the abundant Continental population?

A remarkable Herefordshire character, the renowned 'Barmy' Gilbert, authority on Wye salmon fishing and nearly an England test cricketer, took those steps unofficially in the 1930s, introducing young kites from Gibraltar which he arranged to have reared to maturity in the chicken run of a well-known Radnorshire gamekeeper before releasing them to the wild.

With what outcome no one knows for certain, but there are those convinced to this day that the result was disastrous, as birds of a supposedly stronger Iberian strain fought with and killed off the male remnant of the old Welsh stock. That is mere conjecture, but there was – and is – a scientifically sounder argument against interference on this scale.

Most of the Continental red kites are migratory; among the idiosyncrasies of the Welsh relict is an absence of either that instinct or the need to respond to it. We cannot be sure which, but introduce the gene which, for all we know to the contrary, houses the migratory instinct and the scarce Welsh kites may vanish in winter to poison themselves with the by-products of the agricultural chemicals banned here in the interests of bird protection and for which the manufacturers found an open market beyond the Mediterranean as soon as this one was closed.

Kites, God knows, suffer sufficient casualties from poisoning in Wales without receiving encouragement to search further afield for this fate. Sheep pasture is spoilt by the excavations of moles, of which there are millions in the uplands. Lambs are sometimes taken by foxes, or fatally damaged by crows, which pick out their eyes and nip off their tongues as soon as they are born if the ewe is not up to defending them. After a hard winter, many of the ewes are not. The conifer plantations now bordering many of the sheep pastures are notorious for the foxes they harbour, nor are they devoid of crows, once the trees have reached a height of fifteen feet or so. Strychnine is used lawfully, underground, to destroy moles; unlawfully, above ground, to kill foxes and crows. These are killed by intent; buzzard, raven and kite more often by casual side-effect. Strychnine proverbially kills the fox, the raven or buzzard which feeds off the body of the dead fox and the hungry sheep-dog which consumes the dead raven or buzzard – or kite! In the old county of Radnorshire, I was told authoritatively in 1976 that enough strychnine was sold to farmers to kill the entire human population of Western Europe, if administered economically.

Losses of kites to poisoning in mid-Wales are lamentable, but this does not offer a satisfactory explanation in itself for the sluggishness of the population recovery. Welsh kites desert their eggs at the least provocation, leave them unincubated for longer than is wise, abandon their young or fail to work hard enough to keep them adequately fed. Because of this, attempts have been made to mend the situation by the transfer of eggs from the nests of kites fertile but known to be incompetent parents to those of other kites or even of neighbouring buzzards with a good record in rearing chicks. The same food serves both species and, while an understandable caginess in official circles restricts publication of the results in detail, one may reasonably guess that successes have been achieved.

Because of an extreme official sensitivity to the affairs of the kite in Wales, I give the bird as wide a berth as I can during the nesting season, stifling any interest I might otherwise take in the location of the breeding pairs. Were there no such official concern and no legal protection for the species, I should still steer well clear of kites in the nesting season. One cannot expect to gain a view of a woodland nester at the nest without getting too close to it for its peace of mind and, as I have already mentioned, kites in Wales have a reputation for deserting all too readily.

One year, though, the guard post I used high on a hill to warden a family of peregrines gave a good view over the crowns of an oak wood and right into the nest of the local kite pair in one of the wood's finest old trees. Naturally, I took the odd look at it through the binoculars. It is not the seeing which breaks the law: it is the disturbing in order to see. Looking down from a distance of 400 yards does not cause a disturbance.

I was witness to several interesting incidents, but none to rival that of the carrion crow which alighted on the nest beside the incubating hen kite to insert itself under one of her wings and lever her up off the eggs he intended to break and suck. The kite erected the feathers of her nape in protest and bent upon the intruder a look of shocked disdain. No employment of her hooked bill, though, to punish such insolent intrepidity, and had not her mate arrived in the nick of time and, more to the point, the peregrine tiercel in company with him to discover what was so intriguingly in progress in the tree-tops, I think that would have been just another kites' nest going into the archive as 'failed: theft of eggs suspected'.

There cannot be many people nowadays who wish to see a kite in Wales but have failed to realize that ambition. If any of them read this book, they will do so without finding detailed guidance. This alone I feel free to tell them. Draw on the map of mid-Wales a rectangle with its angles seated on Builth Wells, Llandovery, Lampeter and the little village of Eisteddfa Gurig in the north-west corner. Not strictly a rectangle; more a tetragon, but never mind that. Explore those of its roads and tracks open to the public, halting where a parking-place is found outside the forests in command of broad vistas, and be patient. Keep the glasses scanning the sky above the horizons, focusing on every large bird seen. Above all, do not leave the road and enter woodland on foot.

Kite nests are wardened; intrusion by the unauthorized carries heavy penalties and magistrates in Wales value the kites. Penalties aside, there are villains enough in search off eggs to steal for wealthy collectors without otherwise harmless imbeciles blundering about the kite hills irresponsibly, distracting wardens from the arduous work they are trying to do.

If the thirst to see the red kite in springtime is insatiable, satisfy it elsewhere. On Minorca; on the hills of the Eifel or the Hunsrück, between Mosel and Rhine; in the valley of the Saar, where I have counted five from a fast-driven car in 100 kilometres of motorway. There one is favoured by an extra dimension of interest. The next kite sighted might be a black one, *Milvus milvus migrans*, which you will see in Britain, if at all, only during very infrequent incursions.

five FARTHER AFIELD

A steep hog-backed hill in the lower Wye valley had taught me how emphatically a topographical feature may concentrate hawks for the watching. Wandering the byways of the Cambrians had underlined the lesson, although here it was changing land use rather than a critical pattern of contours which had produced the effect. The Wye valley hill had demonstrated the value of repeated observation; the Cambrians had provided scope and incentive to learn by self-teaching how the finer detail on Ordnance Survey maps, the sun's changing position in the sky as the hands moved round the watch face and meticulous journey planning could be concerted profitably in one's efforts to get the best out of watching hawks.

Reduced to essentials, nothing helps more than sunlight illuminating the vista from behind the watcher's back; nothing hinders worse than bright sunlight shining directly into a watcher's eyes. So, use the maps intelligently to find observation points from which wide vistas are commanded. Use the maps, cosmological fact and the wrist-watch so that one is at each one when the sun in its fast passage across the sky most favours the situation there. Remember that a vista to the north never confronts the watcher with a blinding sun burning the cells of the retinas and veiling cliff-faces to the front in impenetrable black shadow. Cliffs are extremely important, if only because they usually offer high and secluded vantage-points from which the ever-watchful hawk can replicate the strategy of the man or woman watching it – maximize the vista!

Peregrine and merlin had always been secondary objectives in my searches made in the Cambrians for kites. My son's new trousers had been mutilated under the imperious and all-seeing eye, but no other peregrine had obliged, nor any merlin. The plight of the former had by 1970 become common talk in the newspapers; there seemed at the time small reason to hope for improvement. If I was ever to see another peregrine or watch either species as instructively as I had observed sparrowhawks, something positive would have to be done about it.

But where to do it? That was the key question. One had seen or heard reference to famous peregrine eyries said to have been occupied continuously through the centuries, but that was before the population collapse. How many of these territories were occupied now? Few, it was obvious, and neither time nor resources permitted random search. Hitherto an entirely private bird watcher, I had joined organizations for their literature, in hopes that advertisements for holiday accommodation might be specific regarding the local attractions. Two were: one in terms of peregrines; the other, of merlins in the vicinity. Both led me to the birds and to friendships with the advertisers which have survived to the present day.

Both, incidentally, plunged the advertiser into hot water with some protection body seized with the notion that people who contribute towards their work should remain contented by tom-tits in the binoculars and falcons on the TV screen. Obviously, there is a dilemma, but it does not help to grow paranoid over it. Having passed in and out of the paranoid phase several times, I can speak with some authority on the topic.

My introduction to *Falco peregrinus* having been by way of Henry Williamson, the North Devon coast seemed a singularly proper place to begin my adventure. The skies over the 'estuary of the two rivers' was where he set much of his story; the guest-house at which I finally drew up in dense fog late one April night stood within twelve miles of the Taw's tidewater and much nearer than that to a peregrine's cliffs. Cliff-paths were walked, wooded valleys a little inland watched over assiduously in the mistaken belief that peregrines *must* come to them to hunt woodpigeons. The bird watching in general was splendid, dotting the odd i and crossing more than one t in the matter of sparrowhawk behaviour (as mentioned earlier), but brought no peregrine to the binoculars in six long and earnest days.

The evening of the final day was calm and inviting. Dinner digested, I headed for the most productive of the wooded valleys and cliffs beyond it, so far unexplored. A way was found over close-shorn pasture trodden by none but thick-woolled Devon sheep. Suddenly, I was on the land's edge, with a breath-taking vista open to view. High, secluded and rugged cliffs swept in a gentle curve six miles to the west and two miles to the east, the view bounded in that direction by a rising gradient which marked the highest point on that cleave of the coast.

Away to the far west, beyond a calm but sparkling sea, Lundy pushed a prominent dark headland into view. On either hand, gullies bit deeply into the coastline. Massive rock-falls in ancient centuries had piled up secondary cliffs, ground slanting edges jagged and razor-sharp to the eye, but fit perching for gulls, as gulls were then demonstating. Might this be the haunt and sanctum of the peregrines, too? Did one of these deep gullies hide a ledge where previous and healthier generations of falcons had reared their eyasses decade after decade? The sun had set; no answer would be forthcoming that evening.

Morning at last arrived. Certain in my bones what that answer would be, a deferred departure was proposed and, Madame consenting, Fate was offered an eleventh-hour opportunity to unveil her smile. My wife, who had her reasons for wishing to get home without undue delay, is nothing if not willing to meet a chap half-way. We arrived on the newly discovered watchpoint at 10 a.m. She, an enthusiast for coastal scenery, found reasons going beyond the mere watching of birds to register her approval. Noon, though, was the hour of departure firmly agreed.

The morning was such as one hopes to enjoy in heaven. The sun shone brightly, but a breeze tempered the heat. Fleecy clouds rode high in a soft blue sky, mirrored in the crinkled blue beneath. Gulls and cormorants came and went; a buzzard passed along the cliff-edge fly-way, carrying something I could not identify. A cuckoo flew by, a whinchat sang from a bracken frond. A kestrel came to hover above the sloping cliff-top turf, moved away, melted into the haze half a mile to the east.

The wrist-watch ticked on. All too soon the hands stood at 11.45. A brownish bird was approaching from the right, travelling the cliff-edge fly-way so many other birds had favoured. Not a buzzard – too elegant a profile, too swift a wing-beat. Another kestrel? Up with the glasses I had not quite returned to their case as we began to gather ourselves for departure. Into their window flew a perfect young falcon peregrine, broad of shoulder, wings tapering neatly to feather-perfect tips, mantle touched with blue, tail still flushed fox-tawny and closed down for transit to the reversed wedge by which the peregrine completes the streaming of its drag-free line.

The first I ever saw had materialized as though by magic among the escorting gulls some distance off the cliffs of Crete to exchange scrutinies across the starboard rail of a troopship's boat-deck. The second had been spotted as it watched my Inverness-bound train go by from a track-side fence post near Newtonmore. The third, as reported, had briefly joined the audience in Wales when my younger son ventilated the seat of his new trousers on a steep hillside from which the hoped-for kite had been missing.

This North Devon peregrine, though, was the first ever seen in fulfilment of a deliberate intention. Accomplishment in the fiftieth minute of an eleventh hour added its own piquant contribution to the atmosphere of the occasion. An urge to celebrate the consummation with a clumsy hornpipe danced on the perilous turf of the sloping cliff-top was restrained with difficulty. As well, perhaps.

Home we went, as agreed, but were soon back. And many times afterwards, right through to the present day. The evident age of that first North Devon peregrine, a bird of the previous season's hatching, encouraged hopes of fertility and a new lease on life for those cliffs as a nursery for the most splendid member of Britain's wild bird community. Those hopes were destined to be realized, but not immediately.

Before that happened, there were events to be recorded at the opposite end of these islands. Some years before, a friend dwelling in Easter Ross had cited the great lochs of the Inverpolly Estate – Oscaig, Lurgainn and Bad a' Ghaill – as a paradise in which no angler should fail to cast his fly for sea trout ere his account was closed. This wisdom having been passed on to certain friends at home, plans for a fortnight's sampling had been formulated. For them, sea trout were enough; for me, possibilities assumed to be strong for golden eagle, peregrine and merlin (with merlin as yet undiscovered in Wales or England) added further allure to the prospects.

There are, of course, substantial populations of all these birds in the Scottish Highlands, but there is an awesome amount of Highland Scotland for them to vanish into. The mountains are bleak, which fact inhibits density of occupation, relatively trackless, which limits opportunity for the short-term visitor, and present on so vast a scale that there is a sharp lesson to be learned by those who cut their teeth on the cosier splendours of wilderness Wales, Devonia, or the English Lake District.

I learned it on the road to Lochinver, at an observation post pressed into service on impulse, without reference to the one-inch map. From that lay-by on the high altitude road the vista was one of blanket bog, heather moor and scrub, undulating away to a fine cliff-face in the distance, backed by the great mountains of Suilven and Canisp. All I needed seemed to be on offer.

The folding chairs were opened and erected, the vacuum flask put handy, the binoculars uncased and suspended. Peregrines on the cliff? Eagles over the mountains beyond? Hope ran high. The binoculars picked up two objects in motion on a little ridge beyond the blanket bog. Rabbits? A vixen and her cub? Not unless Ross-shire foxes were equipped with antlers. Peregrines over that cliff would have registered as grains of dust on the lenses; over the peaks beyond, eagles not even as that. Nothing smaller than a Boeing 707 would have been identifiable.

Eventually, I found pockets of watchable wildlife in the Highlands, but their chief characteristic for me remains the perfection of the habitat as it strikes the human eye, coupled with the smallness of the likelihood of anything of interest except deer being encountered in it by the unguided traveller. That is an opinion formed or confirmed in the Trossachs (most pointedly), in the Monadhliaths, at Inverpolly, in Morvern (to a lesser extent) and in the wilderness of Ben Eighe. For a chaffinch enthusiast it would be another matter. Wherever one parks a car by a Highland roadside, two things will happen. A chaffinch will stroll up to beg for crumbs (as a robin would in England and may in Scotland) and a wren will fly to the nearest safe perch from which to scold you back home. For those for whom black-headed gulls make the pulses race, there may be that pleasure in store, too, as the chaffinches are displaced by one or two of these.

There was talk in the hotel of a peregrine here, a peregrine there, a pair on yet a third site, covering between them a hundred square miles and more of wild terrain. Eventually, we found the third pair, and in memorable circumstances. Using the one-inch map to bring optical expectations within the realm of reason, we had settled on a little dead-end road which runs above the head of Loch Broom for about a mile on the south-east side of the glen. The view from our observation post was over Inverlael to the east, over Rhidorroch to the north, with endless wilderness stretching beyond.

The loch itself was well populated with the more interesting species of duck, with herons, gulls, cormorants and a pair of black-throated divers exploring the band of shallows at the very head. Buzzards mewed in the sky behind us, a pair of sparrowhawks ascended to challenge and spar with a third above the conifer plantation on the hill opposite. Two eagles appeared in due course, the occasional beating of their vast wings like the 'shaking of blankets', as my wife aptly described the motion.

After we had watched for about two hours, a party of woodpigeons sped from the tops of the conifers lining the crest of the hill opposite, the falcon which had presumably flushed them climbing in pursuit. She did not attack them, though, but continued to climb until she was so high that even in the glasses she resembled nothing so much as a twinkling black star in the pale grey September sky, then a black shooting star as she found a current of high wind to her liking.

It was my first experience of how high and immensely fast a peregrine at times chooses to fly for no detectable reason except the sheer pleasure of it. At last we had found action as intense as it often was in Wales and Devon. I remember regretting only that it was all taking place a thousand yards away and more.

We returned the next day, again watching birds for which the immediate horizon on the opposite side of the loch appeared to form some strange boundary. Appearing from the east or north to soar briefly above it, they all retreated after only a short performance. In hawk watching it is easier to exchange the better for the worse than the good for the excellent, but I was inspired at 2.30 that afternoon to take a memorable decision. Overcoming inertia with some difficulty, I opened the map and sought for and found a route which should take us to the back of those hills and wherever it was that the eagles had come from every time we had seen them. It led to a deep gorge with a river flowing out of a loch a mile in length on the way, and another leading into the loch after it had emerged from a more dramatic gorge bounded by steep and rugged cliffs on the northern side. The road was shown by the map to deteriorate as it continued, but should be drivable far enough for the enticing gorge bounded by the tall cliffs to be brought within 400 yards of the binoculars without abandoning the convenience of the four-wheeled umbrella.

In the event, the road ran initially through a dismal quarry which promised only disappointment, but after it had passed through a jagged gap between blasted rocks an elbow-bend turning down a gradient disclosed all we could have hoped for. About five miles of rough road wound across moorland bounded on the north side by low, smooth-textured cliffs, skirted the loch, and arrived at lodge gates bearing a forbidding notice. This being one of those instances where the terminology is more draconian than the intent, a head stalker, approached with all the deference due to his status, graciously gave permission for the journey to be continued to the great crags now in clear view, for the car to be parked and birds watched for until dusk, if we wished.

Eagles and peregrines? Not the latter, he thought, although there had been an eyrie on the main crag in years gone by. Eagles, though, he often saw and believed we might too. We jolted on, found a patch of dry enough grass by the track just short of the high crags, pulled off and halted, turning the car first so that the tail-gate could be lifted for us to sit beneath it while facing the mouth of the gorge, sheltered from the rain which the sky implied to be imminent. Chairs out, glasses at the ready.

Half an hour passed. Unheralded as almost all raptorial arrivals are, there was suddenly something remarkably like a light aeroplane approaching along the edge of the cliffs 700 feet above, gliding, rocking slightly, a wingtip nearly brushing the rocks. Reaching our end of the feature, it turned, adjusted geometry and became an eagle. Turning again, it passed from view over the skyline. Five minutes later it reappeared, much higher and in stately company with a consort.

Rotating the milled wheel for a sharper focus I found a third bird, a smaller one, even higher in the sky directly above the eagles, hanging on the wind they were edging into. As I found the peregrine, so it tipped over, beat its wings quickly a dozen times, drew them in and fell like a stone on its target. I had seen my first stoop, a classical one into the bargain. The eagle shifted clumsily, the peregrine (a tiercel, I had by now decided) shot up to its original pitch, using only the momentum of its descent to do so, then came down again, even faster, this time beating its wings all the vertical way.

And so it went on – twelve minutes, by my watch, of uninterrupted drama. Previous peregrine sightings had been measured by the second.

The eagles drifted from view beyond the cliffs, the tiercel alighted on the rim of the nearest to stare down at us inquisitively, his head canted on one side, remarkably like that of a friendly parrot at the zoo hoping for a nut. Unexpectedly, the dense cloud which had threatened rain all day, although high, began to clear for the sun to break through. Eagles now lit to a warm bronze reappeared high in the sky again from behind the cliffs; a peregrine

Donald Watson
1989

now of blue steel and milky silver rose to do battle afresh. What can I say of round two – except that it was a repeat of round one, but staged in glorious technicolor, as the old film ads used to put it.

When the first eagle sailed into view, the hands of my wrist-watch registered the time at 4.30. When the tiercel broke away from the eagles for the last time, they said 5.35. One of the friends who had come for the fishing had an amusing way of pricing his pleasures. After a day of hard work with the rod and poor sport he would growl about pleasure at '£5 a minute'. I, naturally, had responded by doing sums enabling me to pull his leg with claims of peregrine watching pleasure priced at more £s than that per second. Now, I had to return to the hotel with a happy confession that the bottom had dropped completely out of the market.

Nor was that the end of the glory. The peregrine did not return to bully the eagles, but the latter treated us to another two days of more-or-less continuous entertainment. On the morning of the second visit the show opened as they flew comparatively low over our heads, coming from the other side of the glen, turned towards each other, grasped talons and came spinning down with an audible whoosh of wings, whirling about each other as a horse-chestnut leaf comes helicoptering to the ground when the frost of an autumn night gives way to the power of the climbing sun.

Breaking apart twenty feet above the heather, the great birds resumed their prospecting for blue hare and red grouse as placidly as if they had never performed an aerobatic feat in their entire lives. The conspicuous white areas on the tails of both birds proclaimed that those lives had not at that time been long ones, a fact which may have gone some way towards accounting for such spectacularly lively behaviour. One of them returned later in the day, after an hour's rain had cleared to bright sunshine, to circle over a corrie bitten from the scree at the foot of the cliff which marked the spur's end, yelping like a fox terrier pup and showing with hackles agleam why that species of eagle is dubbed 'golden'.

The last day but one of the holiday arrived. Eagle sightings had become almost a commonplace; a peregrine experience which has never ceased to be memorable was in the diary. Only the merlin remained to be added. I had travelled to the steep banks of the Kirkaig in search of a reported pair. After a report of an angler having seen one kill a pipit down on the shore of Loch Oscaig, I never drove by it in a gear higher than second. The day had been earmarked for another visit to the eagles' glen. The road from the hotel led in that direction by a small inlet from the sea bordered on one side by extensive sand-dunes.

On impulse, I halted the car and suggested a walk through the sand and marram grass. Several times, I had come out here before breakfast, always in hope, but so far hope had been a deceiver. We found a comfortable seat on a sandbank well tunnelled by rabbits, giving views over both beach and the moor's edge. Wheatear, meadow pipit, redshank, purple sandpiper, curlew and whimbrel enlivened the next hour, but nothing of greater interest. At 12.30 I rose to stretch cramped limbs and opened my mouth to propose departure. But other words came out. 'There she is!' A neat little falcon had rocketed up from the moor's edge, her lines not all that unlike a kestrel's, but more vigour in every movement. A redshank followed her aggressively, dicing it seemed, with death. The merlin accelerated her wingbeat, increased her angle of climb to one near vertical. Having thus gained room for manoeuvre, she turned above her pursuer, tucked wingtips to tail, and fell. The redshank did not remain to argue. Having seen it off, the merlin flew energetically to a derelict fence post 180 yards away from us (afterwards paced) and posed for inspection.

For ten minutes she remained, then flew away fast, a yard above the ground, to vanish behind another rabbit-bored sandbank, twin to the one we were sitting on. She did not reappear from behind it. Walking over a few minutes later, I found a deep-cut little watercourse so narrow that she could not have made an unobserved escape along it with wings fully extended. We returned to the car to resume our journey. Before we had covered a hundred yards the merlin was racing us, to turn and flash across the bonnet, flush her bright blue mate from the roadside heather and sweep up with him to perch together on the telegraph wires. I stopped and dived from the car for a better look. The birds took off, tore to a ridge which formed the skyline a hundred yards away, vanished over it. Running to and up it, I soon had miles of splendid heather moor in view. But no merlins. As time was eventually to teach me, I could not have been given a more typical introduction to the species. 'Émerillon' – the sprightly one, as the French name the bird. Our own connotation with Arthur's wizard mentor is no less apt. They appear like rabbits from a conjuror's top hat, to vanish from view by what seems some exercise of an even more potent magical art.

Twelve days had been filled to overflowing without a team of flies once being thrown at a sea trout. Those who did had but little to show for their endeavours. Perhaps my strictures on the empty Highland wilderness should be modified. Given natural distributions, peregrines are spaced farther apart than in Wales, North Devon or north-western England, but the real difference is in terms of raven and buzzard. In most of Scotland, they are rarely present to link the sightings of the more exciting sky species in anything like the densities met in western uplands south of the border. It is that lack, above all others, which makes so many regions in the Highlands seem virtually devoid of exciting birds.

six ON GUARD IN GALLOWAY

Galloway I was once able to regard as the outstanding exception to my rule that falcons are spread thin in Scotland. I made that discovery hard on the heels of making the rule. About six months later, in fact, when the urge to expand my experience of birds in the wilderness took me there for my third visit, though the first made for a strictly ornithological purpose.

The first visit, made for another reason, had been in 1960, when few people went there, choosing instead to bypass that geologically strange appendage of moor and mountain jutting south beyond the soft hills of fertile Dumfriesshire as they sped north from Carlisle towards more distant highlands and islands of greater historical glamour.

James Robertson Justice, the celebrated actor, dwelt there and flew his falcons over Galloway moors. John Buchan knew those moors well, setting his novel *Huntingtower* in the north of the province and some of the action of *The Thirty-Nine Steps* on a moorland railway line which now serves as a nature trail that one can walk on the way to a viewpoint from which peregrine rocks can be seen in the distance.

That first visit followed the return of the golden eagle after a fifty-year absence following extermination in the interests, real or supposed, of sheep farming. The intensive conifer afforestation had not yet cast its sterilizing mantle over the land; nor had its impact grown insupportable ten years later, when I made my third visit. When I made my last, in 1986, the conifer blanket denied it any useful purpose or pleasure worth the journey. Conifers grow fast. I inspected seven eyrie-rocks during the third week in June, when eyasses should have been standing conspicuously on ledges, or developing their breast muscles by frequent flights from rock to rock in the vicinity of the eyrie. I saw no eyas, not so much as a single feather plucked from a kill, and only one adult, observed as it left the site, to remain absent for the next three hours, the period I spent on watch. In six of the seven cases what ten years earlier had been extensive moorland commanded by the eyrie-rocks, with only conifer seedlings or saplings breaking through the heather, was in 1986 sterile forest floor hidden from the falcons by the closed canopy of trees grown to fifteen or twenty feet in height, forming a blanket which stretched as far as the eye could see. Cause and effect are not proven, but where in Galloway inland peregrines would now hunt profitably enough to rear good broods I cannot imagine.

Happily, some of the beastly trees themselves are now beginning to die, presumably from the acidified moisture they themselves have sucked down from a hostile sky.

Conifers in 1970 had pronounced sentence of death on almost all of Galloway's once lovely moorland, but the sentence had yet to be carried into execution. Wide views of moor and sky there still were, above the endless ranks of seedling and sapling. Ornithologically, Galloway in those days had a centre of gravity – Murray's Monument. Beneath it runs the Palnure Burn. Between monument and burn stretched moorland on which one could sit at ease looking over more extensive bird-haunted heather all the way to the slopes and crests of Cairn Edward and Cairnsmore of Fleet, above which eagle and peregrine might be found soaring at any hour between the rising and the setting of the spring and summer sun.

The first day we spent there was a gloriously fine Easter Saturday. Binoculars remained riveted to the crests of those mountains from 2.30 p.m. until dusk. An eagle came and went, but no peregrine. Disappointing. We went further afield, to Carsphairn, to Carrick. We saw birds, but still no peregrine. The hotel where we stayed was situated in the little town of New

ON GUARD IN GALLOWAY

Galloway, and trips to almost anywhere we were likely to visit took us past Murray's Monument. Passing it on the return journey on the last full day of the visit, our eyes were drawn to the crest of a massive rock by the road. Over it a tiercel displayed, while people stood photographing wild goats as they played on its lower crags, obliviously engrossed in their art despite the raucous din of the tiercel's excited screaming up in the sky. We got out of the car to discover his mate, perched on an abandoned ravens' nest, making her own contribution to the melody.

The irony of it! We had spent five hours within 300 yards of that rock, but seated facing away from it, our glasses trained obsessively on the other side of the valley. First light next morning found a parked car glazed by ice, its occupant huddled into all his warmest clothes, and white feathers streaming down from the rock as the falcon fed from a kill her mate had delivered before the sun had risen.

Then they copulated ecstatically. Falcon peregrines are not only larger than tiercels, by as much as a third in some cases, but when there is an appreciable difference in colour intensity it is the female which is conventionally the darker bird, in respect of both the upper plumage, with its stronger hints of brown in the grey, and the lower, which is creamier and more boldly marked than the tiercel's. The mantle of this falcon, whose sex could no longer be a matter of debate, had as blue a sheen as I was ever to see reflected from the plumage of the smartest tiercels between Land's End and John o'Groats, and a breast white as milk under its fine black speckling and barring. My experience of peregrines was beginning to come on apace.

I spent the rest of the day there. The final high-spots were a hen sparrowhawk which soared so high she melted from ×12 glasses into a sky of sharp clarity and a tiercel which crossed the valley at about 5,000 feet, carrying a kill so large that it gave the impression of a double peregrine, one beating its wings and one gliding just below it. Some large wader, no doubt, had paid the 'debt of nature'. That was the first peregrine I had seen carrying a kill. The visual impact of that double image, so high in the otherwise vacant bowl of a grey April sky, remains etched on my memory sharper than most of

the painters' art to which I have been expected to render respectful salutation. Hope for moments of such emotion is what keeps the dedicated hawkwatcher out in the uplands year after year, regardless of all discomfort, for as long as the eyes will focus and the arms lift a pair of binoculars towards the sky.

Peregrines had now taken me over. Six weeks after the Galloway sightings I was back on the North Devon coast, and again in September, to coincide that time with a stable high pressure system over the Bristol Channel which kept the peregrines soaring as freely as buzzards in a sky devoid of cloud for five consecutive days. Which satisfied me most? The spectacle of the peregrine in flight viewed from below, as it usually is inland, or from above, from high coastal cliffs, the blue-grey bird held with difficulty in the window of the binoculars as it speeds indistinctly over waves which almost reciprocate the steely hues of its own dorsal plumage? I could not make up my mind then; nor can I now.

An outward-bound osprey passed through that week, and, to remind me that birds from outside the raptor family can provide drama, a Dalmatian pelican strayed Devonwards from its home in the Adriatic. Soaring over Lynmouth with the ever-present buzzards, it resembled a four-engined bomber of Second World War vintage protected by an escort of twin-engined fighters. Intriguing, to see buzzards dwarfed; even more so to reflect on the fact that this was an afternoon on which bird watching had been foregone in favour of more conventional holiday pursuits – postcard buying, cream-tea eating, and so on. Even a hawkwatcher betrays the occasional streak of humanity.

The reserve maintained at Slimbridge on the marshlands of the Severn Estuary by Sir Peter Scott's Wildfowl Trust attracts large numbers of wintering wigeon and even larger flocks of various wader species. In most years one or two peregrines join the party for obvious reasons, and so my watching did not have to end as the days grew shorter. An hour's motoring takes me from door to hide. It was there and then that I first learned something of the peregrine's epicurean predilections when prey is varied and plentiful. The resident during the first winter I watched there was a large, stout and handsome adult falcon. When she hunted one was left in no doubt of her firm intention to catch a wigeon, a redshank, an oystercatcher, or whatever else fancy might dictate.

A thousand birds of assorted species would be flushed skywards in successive clouds to expose her hapless target, to whose tail her single-minded purpose would then leash her until her talons closed on flesh or the price of the candle rose to exceed the value of the game. Never did I see her change targets. A failure was followed by an immediate return to one of her operational bases, a fence-post, a stag-headed tree or one of the massive tree-stumps which some memorable spate had beached in years gone by out on the Dumbles. There she would sit, giving careful reconsideration to the matter of her supper while the disturbed ducks and waders calmed down and resumed their own feeding.

Such preselection of prey was the first reason the peregrine gave me for suspecting that hawks are capable of conceptual thinking in the human sense. To go looking for a victim of predetermined species strongly implies a capacity to make an image of that bird in the mind and to match reality against it. What, after all, is the prime requirement for the development of mental capacity? Leisure – something of which bird-hunting hawks, which usually earn their day's livelihood by less than half an hour's energetic labour, are not stinted.

The following spring took me again to North Devon; the summer, back to Wester Ross, and a cottage actually *in* the glen of the eagles. Yet no eagles that year, nor a peregrine. Devon, too, had not been memorable. Such is hawk watching – indeed, all bird watching. Success can be built on, but not without reverses.

That autumn of 1972 saw my 25-year career in the world of minor business come to an abrupt but not unwelcome end, to be succeeded by a life of greater freedom financed by journalistic and other odd-jobbery in which conveying my thoughts on birds to the readers of *The Field* played a prominent part.

ON GUARD IN GALLOWAY

The first season of liberty took me back to both Devon and Galloway. Devon presented me with my first sighting of an Exmoor merlin – a fine, brilliantly blue-backed cock giving a raven a rough time over the head of a small shallow combe – but nothing of note on the peregrines I had found on the cliffs except that there was no evidence, in June, of any successful attempt to breed that year. Galloway, too, gave me my first sighting of one of its merlins, another colourful male, put up from a roadside boulder by the approaching car as we explored a narrow, unfenced moorland road.

During that visit, I learned something of much value respecting peregrines. It was the strange resemblance borne by the profile of a newly flying eyas to that of the woodpigeon. For this there are two causes: one, a tendency to fly with the neck extended; the other, flying with the tail permanently spread from fear of stalling. The head of the flying adult is usually carried retracted and dipped to keep the ground and air below under scrutiny; the tail is confidently tapered to almost a point in most circumstances, to minimize drag. These differences are accompanied by a third, readily apparent to the experienced observer. Whereas the flight of the adult impresses first and foremost by the apparent ease with which it is performed, the juvenile – not unnaturally – flies initially with conspicuous effort.

I blush at confessing that these characteristics, undiscovered at the time, caused me one morning to spend two hours by a recently successful moorland site with a family of eyasses passing swiftly to and fro above me one, two, and three at a time in their journeys about the extensive glen as I waited impatiently 'for the peregrines to show up'. Until they became excited by something and began to scream in flight, the penny remained jammed firmly in the slot.

That morning, though, promised much not foreseen at the time which would come to fruition in the same place the following year. It would bring about my metamorphosis from the caterpillar which, with luck, might see a peregrine to the moth which could usually find peregrines on demand, guide other watchers into seeing them and account quite confidently for a great deal of their minute-by-minute behaviour while they were under observation. A new way of life was growing on a foundation of well structured routine.

One evening the following April I stuck a judicious pin into a map of the English Lake District and the next morning drove two hundred miles to the destination indicated in rational hope that it might prove to be the home of England's one and only pair of golden eagles. It was. The eagle allowed me time to raise the tail-gate of the car and fish the vacuum flask from the muddle (but not to unscrew the cup) before it came sailing above the car-park to investigate me.

Beating over from the great cliff which closed the head of the valley, a peregrine arrived a minute later to share the scrutiny from a pitch head to wind a hundred feet above the eagle's circuits and to satisfy me that Fate's smiles upon my new style of life in the previous year had been more than the empty gesture of an absent mind.

The prompt eagle was a triumph of a sort, but that Easter was dominated by the peregrines. Because she was on point of lay (as it afterwards transpired), the falcon's behaviour was subdued, but the tiercel was magnificently in the full grip of spectacular oestrus. I had watched others before him and many more since, but never another tiercel with a gift for aerobatics to equal his. More than that – he alone of his kind has sent me writhing anxiously out of line as viscera stressed beyond continence in the g of what aviators term the 'zoom' and falconers (inelegantly) the 'throw up' discharge their burden earthwards like whitewash flung from a bucket. There are hazards, more apparent than real, perhaps, in serving as an aiming-mark for a tiercel coming down vertically from a pitch a mile above the heather one is lying in. But one remembers these small courtesies with affection. They certainly focused my thought for the first time on the incredible mechanical efficiency of the peregrine's structure. Visualize the membrane confining the giblets of a domestic chicken and the ease with which a blunt human thumb can be thrust through it. Arrest that membrane and its contents suddenly in a dive at a speed of 200 m.p.h. or more and reverse the momentum in a fiftieth of a second. How, then, were the tiercel's mutings not accompanied by the intestines which had discharged them? Why did the wings not dislocate? Or the bones bracing their leading edges not snap with a bang audible a thousand feet below?

There is something very special about a peregrine's construction. If the ability to dive at 250 m.p.h. is remarkable, the capacity to survive that exercise is phenomenal. But can it really reach that speed? If the stooping peregrine and the aerial bomb represent respectively nature's and mankind's best endeavours to design objects perfected for controllable free fall (as their shapes when falling certainly suggest) the known mathematics of the one must apply sufficiently to the other for the result of calculations based on carefully checked weights and dimensions of peregrines to be relevant. Two formulae are involved: one to determine the maximum speed to which the 'bomb' is capable of accelerating before it accelerates no more; the other, to determine the distance it must fall in order to reach that speed. Both of these formulae are given in the note at the foot of this page.

When applied to a 2½-pound 19-inch falcon they indicate that she must fall vertically for 12,000 feet to reach her maximum and that in a 5,000-foot fall she would attain 239 m.p.h., a speed within 11 m.p.h. of that maximum. A 15½-inch tiercel weighting 1 lb 6 oz would have to fall 13,500 feet to attain his maximum of 243 m.p.h., reaching 233 m.p.h. at 5,000 feet.

Formula for calculating maximum attainable speed in fall

$$\sqrt{\frac{2 \times \text{mass} \times 32.2}{\text{air density} \times \text{cross-sectional area} \times \text{drag coefficient}}}$$

(speed given in result in feet/second)

Formula for determining velocities after particular distances fallen

$$2 \times \text{distance fallen} \times \text{constant (C)} = \log_e \left(\frac{g}{g - C\,\text{Velocity}^2} \right)$$

where $C = \dfrac{\text{air density} \times \text{drag coefficient} \times \text{cross-sectional area}}{2 \times \text{mass}}$

THE HAWKWATCHER

There is a tendency nowadays to scale down theories of the speeds attainable by peregrines in both level flight and the stoop. I have turned briefly to mathematics (not one of my subjects) to show another side to the possibilities, one more in accord with the tales told fifty years ago by RAF fighter pilots of having been overtaken by a stooping peregrine while diving aircraft at speeds of more than 200 m.p.h. during aerobatics performed over the Scottish Highlands.

Peregrines do not commonly stoop that fast or as far as 5,000 feet when hunting – there is no general need – but display under the pressure of oestrus in springtime can be another matter, as that splendid Cumbrian tiercel spent much of a glorious afternoon demonstrating.

I had now seen a peregrine assaulting eagles, had seen peregrines copulating, a peregrine reach a speed something like the maximum the species is capable of attaining. I had seen pursuit. I had seen a peregrine – more than once – with prey in its talons. A far cry from a brief sighting from a North Devon cliff-top, but I had yet to see in clear view a peregrine making a kill. That too lay just around the corner. It happened seven weeks later, across the Solway, while I was engaged upon my first spell of duty wardening a family of these handsome birds in as perfect a setting as one could possibly wish for.

The word had gone around among those specimens of *Homo sapiens* who occupy the other end of nature's spectrum that there were again enough peregrines on the cliffs to be worth the risk and trouble of removing some of them for black-market sale in defiance of the law. The M6 had put Galloway within reach of both the villains' urban rookeries and their markets, so eyes were on its more accessible eyries.

Some of these are so near the road that tourists stream by unawares. Others are on cliffs so remote that only the energetic are ever likely to see them close to. Because even the typical passing holidaymaker, speeding by en route for the beaches, may notice a man hanging from a rope on a roadside rock-face, the remoter sites were judged to be the ones at the greater risk.

ON GUARD IN GALLOWAY

One of these, reached by a ten-mile drive through a series of locked five-barred gates followed by a two-mile struggle on foot through heather, rock and ruined moorland then already trenched for conifers, was occupied by a falcon generally agreed to be Galloway's finest. She was, by about three inches in her wingspan and – I would guess – four ounces in her weight, the largest peregrine I have ever seen.

Her character matched her size. When invited to warden her threatened brood, I was cautioned that a guard-post 600 yards from the cliff would be the nearest approach to her ledge that she would willingly tolerate. Her raucous protests, in fact, began at 1,000 yards and rent the air until the ominous apparitions on legs had shrunk to become mere humps projecting from the heather of a bank 600 yards from the cliffs, not quite motionless, but static enough to calm apprehensions.

That, as I was to discover again and again, is typical. Whatever the temperament of the individual peregrine suffering the disturbance, people walking are resented far more keenly than people sitting down. To approach is to spark off one rumpus; to rise and retire, another, despite the fact that the intruders by that very act are moving away and, one would suppose, thereby beginning to reduce the threat the bird suspects them of representing. To try to puzzle out what motivates a bird, it helps to start with a view of the world as seen through that bird's eyes. The peregrine knows, if it 'knows' anything, that the threat it offers to any other bird while it sits motionless on its crag is only potential. Potential becomes actual only when it launches itself into action. Nor should movement initially *away* from the target be construed by that target as a siren blowing the all-clear. It is likelier to be a manoeuvre to get the sun or the wind at the angle which will best favour the attack.

To credit the peregrine with enough brain to weigh the options open to an enemy and attempt – in however limited and misconceived a fashion – an appropriate reaction is to make a large assumption. Not to make it, though, is either to dismiss the bird as too stupid to know the difference between something coming and something going, or to leave an interesting question.

In the beginning, this falcon could not bear any kind of rumpus, whether the movement was just a stretch of the legs or a stealthy descent from the bank to answer a call of nature. By lunch time on the second day, though, she had relaxed sufficiently in her guardian's presence to glide over quietly and inspect from above with keenly turning head as she circled any action in the heather – from fetching an extra pullover from the waterproof bag (guarding peregrines is not for sissies of either sex) to relieving the bladder with a modestly turned back. Not easy, when the inquisitive eye is airborne in a small turning-circle and, in power, human × at least 20! Nor, perhaps, strictly necessary; but such is the personality of the peregrine that one's inclination is soon to treat them as people. Sometimes, the tiercel accompanied his mate on these voyages of discovery, but more often not. Curiosity was ever a female attribute.

Six hundred yards south-west of our guardpost the forbidding crags and cliffs of the mountain wall which enclosed the glen on that side stretched two miles to the head of it and rose 1,000 feet above the high moorland to frown at the feature's south-east extremity upon the placid waters of a loch fed by a foaming burn which came racing down the glen. About 300 feet above the junction of still and running water, time had eroded a sheltered alcove in the rocks, protected against intruders on foot by fifty feet of sheer cliff below it and from the weather by an overhang of harder rock above.

A grassy shelf in the alcove had been chosen by the peregrines for their eyrie, now occupied by three fat and vigorous chicks clad in the off-white down of their third week of life lived outside the egg. In the morning, when the sun shone upon them from an angle over the left shoulders of the watchers, their antics could be observed quite distinctly through binoculars. When past its daily zenith, all detail was progressively lost in deep, dark shadow in which even the adults in flight took on the appearance of images on a photographic negative. Towards its setting, the sun would dip below the crests up the glen, improving but not perfecting visibility. The brighter the weather, the bigger both contrasts, and visibility problems when the sun was high. As peregrines prefer cliffs facing north-east for their nurseries, the situation was not an uncommon one.

ON GUARD IN GALLOWAY

If a raid occurred, what should we be able to do about it? One thing was certain: we were in no position to prevent it physically. If the fact that we were there on watch did not deter the raiders, there would be a race against time. The nearest ungated public road was seven miles away, beyond the hills we were watching. Our line of communication with a telephone was shorter, but obstructed by several gates. The success or failure of a raid would turn on how fast the raiders could get down from the top, back up after taking the chicks, and over at least seven rough miles of moorland to their parked car, set against how quickly one of us could cover two equally rough miles on foot, drive several more with halts to unlock and open gates, then, finally, the time the alerted police would need, exploiting their mobility and radios, to string out a cordon to cut off the thieves' line of retreat. After that, it would be a matter of getting the recovered chicks back to the ledge before darkness fell. Quite a tall order.

Pending such excitements, the job was one of observing and recording progress. There was plenty for me to discover as I watched peregrine chicks on the ledge for the first time. The first two watches were carried out on days of blustery winds, during which the tiercel surprised me by demonstrating that a peregrine can glide tail-first under perfect control, provided the wind is strong enough, and even gain altitude quickly while doing so. His mate surprised me more by leaving the down clad chicks unbrooded in the rugged conditions for several hours at a time and feeding them at intervals of three or four. I learned that she fed fresh kills to her charges as carefully as she might have been expected to had they been newly hatched, but might (or might not) leave the remnants on the ledge for the chicks to pull about and squabble over while she and her mate mounted guard on the crags above. One such remnant, having come near to going over the edge during a tug of war, was retrieved cleverly by the largest and most advanced of the brood, at considerable risk of accompanying it to the loch shore below had it mismanaged the exercise. Were young peregrines at real risk of falling from a ledge? Time might (and eventually did) tell. So the hours passed entertainingly by.

THE HAWKWATCHER

Then came the first Saturday of the watch and with it racing pigeons passing through the glen, in ones, twos, and larger flights. A singleton provided the first kill, a pale-plumaged bird chased by the tiercel until both birds had vanished from view in the distant sky, and brought in a few minutes later by the falcon, which had followed in the track of her mate. A second kill was made away from the site early in the afternoon, this victim only thrush-sized. At 4.45 p.m. another pale homer entered the glen, this time from beyond its mouth, flying low over the loch. To my astonishment, it alighted by the burn where it ran in, directly under the eyrie, and drank.

The falcon took off from a high crag, but did not attack. Instead, she worked her way up-valley close to the cliffs, the tempo of her wingbeat very fast but her actual progress slow and deliberate. Reminded of a motor car driven carefully in a low gear, I began to consider the possibilities of some parallel motivation. Not for long, though. As she entered an area of deep shadow now masking the rocks up-valley from the eyrie, two pigeons broke suddenly from a high cranny to attempt escape downwind.

The dawdling falcon exploded into the assault faster than the eye could follow. The pigeons tried to evade her and regain shelter among the rocks, but two bursts of small white feathers hanging in the air like the smoke from exploded anti-aircraft shells signalled two glancing blows which sent the victim staggering. Closing for a third strike, the falcon seemed merely to halt suddenly in flight, then turned – once again at her leisure – to emerge from the darker shadow with a pigeon dangling casually from one foot. What happened to its companion I did not succeed in following.

The falcon carried the less fortunate bird first to a high crag for a quick *coup de grâce*, then the body to a patch of rank grass at the same level to be cached against future need. That done, she circled up and left the scene, presumably in search of more pigeons. With whatever concentration one watches for peregrines approaching or leaving a site some hundreds of yards distant, some of the arrivals and departures are missed. Suddenly a bird is found unexpectedly in the sky, or equally unexpectedly on a crag, as it turns a snow-white breast towards binoculars trained blindly on the perfect camouflage of a steely-grey mantle backed by rock of very much the same colour. So the afternoon wore on, as I found, lost and rediscovered the adults, in the sky or on their crags, and caught glimpses of the chicks as they awoke to fidget on the ledge, or exercised their long narrow wings, conspicuously white except for the tips, now blackening with emerging primary feathers. Time for departure approached, but there was a final spectacle in store.

Both adults had left the cliffs to soar above the glen at a height of a mile or more, just recognizable as peregrines through the binoculars. Tipping over on his beam, the tiercel closed his wings and fell, accelerating to a speed at which he changed from an expanding silver star into a grey streak passing behind another pigeon duo then attempting their escape from that deadly glen. Rocketing up with the momentum of the stoop and perfect calculation, he bound at the apex of his full loop to the breast of the leading pigeon just as his larger mate crashed into the other from behind, in the third blizzard of pigeon feathers witnessed that day.

Dramatic though the spectacle had been, I left the site willingly, somewhat surfeited by so lavish a ration of violence. Pigeons too, are birds, innocent and extremely likeable as they croon and flirt in their lofts or potter amiably among the pedestrians in the city squares.

The drama was finished for that day, but not for the fortnight. Four days later, a ten-hour vigil was drawing to its close in fading light. The falcon, having sat for a noisy hour nagging at her not conspicuously energetic consort (few tiercels are), left the site in disgust to hunt supper for the chicks herself. The tiercel kept watch from the highest of the crags, with breast so bright as the setting sun gilded it that one might have thought it devoid of a single speckle or bar.

Half an hour passed. After a few excited rasps, the tiercel took off to climb with an unusual display of urgency. Reaching his chosen pitch quickly, he rolled, shrugged in his wings and stooped. A pigeon sighted? Yes – a woodpigeon in his mate's talons, en route for the ledge. The stoop was aimed and timed so perfectly that by merely flicking over through 180 degrees as he passed like a bullet beneath the falcon's vulnerable belly he gashed the pigeon from end to end, leaving a vapour trail of snowy feathers in the sky behind the protesting falcon and a pigeon with blood-bright, viscera dangling a foot below its opened body.

Returning, to his high crag, the tiercel burdened the evening air with a ten-minute obligato of disappointed wails. The falcon landed some distance from him to feed with appetite from the prize she had so nearly lost, surrendering what was left of it twenty minutes later to the hungry youngsters on the ledge in the armchair alcove.

Much has been written about the fear which some suppose falcons inspire in their smaller spouses. Some falcons may. Others certainly do not. That episode did not suggest a tiercel overawed. Perhaps he needed to be a particularly bold fellow to risk a mating with such a big and splendid falcon, to whose size he conformed in the classic proportion.

In all, accompanied by some other member of my family, I had watched that site for 41½ hours, spread through five days spaced over a fortnight. The three chicks immaculately down-clad on the day of the first duty, were eyasses golden-breasted with feather on the day of the last.

All survived to fly safely without any attempt being made on their liberty to do so. With such parents, the genes they added to a British population then beginning to recover well from its disasters were a valuable contribution.

It was not my fate ever to see them on the wing – so far as I know – but September had a bonus awaiting me four hundred miles to the south. The North Devon pair, too, fledged three eyasses that year, after rearing them on a ledge in a gorge to be viewed by none who set store by a neck in one piece. The wind on that journey down the M5 to Devon was a force not easily to be forgotten. On arrival, we braved it far enough to sit for a while on a big rock in a small and sheltered cove whose western shoulder broke the force of both wind and wave. Connected as it was to that shoulder receiving the wild buffets of the stormy sea, it shuddered and throbbed under us in time with each blow the cliffs round the corner took from each crashing wave. Could even peregrines remain safely aloft in such weather? Their absence from the sky visible from the cove suggested that they might not be making the attempt.

The wind next morning, still fierce, had dropped to about half its previous strength. A day spent on the exposed cliff-top would not be comfortable, but the risk of being blown to join first the gulls and then the congers was no longer unacceptable. We arrived on the cliffs to be chilled in minutes, despite several layers of wool under the wind-cheaters, but our hearts were warmed as quickly by the ascent of five peregrines in a line staggered in two dimensions to do battle with what was left of the gale. I had now learned something else. Families might remain a cohesive unit for at least three months after the eyasses were on the wing.

During the next six days, the peregrines demonstrated both the strength and elasticity of the bonds linking that family, as its members scattered east and west along the cliffs, individually or in a variety of combinations, but never so as to leave the vicinity of the eyrie gully entirely unattended for longer than an hour or two. Such loyalties earn their reward. They have evolved, I am sure, from the necessity for young peregrines to be taught their craft. Some basic skills and the urge to acquire others may be implanted by instinct, but the skills are developed and refined by parental example and the juvenile impulse to imitate.

To what degree the adult is conscious of the process in which it is involved one can only conjecture, but in that week I saw the tiercel race out over the sea to catch a pigeon which he brought in alive to be released right in his daughter's path for her to recapture unassisted. More evidence is offered by the wild chases induced by the parent carrying prey brought in dead and dropping the booty in flight to whichever eyas persisted with the greatest determination or won the race to catch up with the tantalizing fugitive. The fact that prey is presented to young so long after fledging proves only a need for support, but the manner of the delivery implies far more than that.

On Saturdays and Sundays flights of pigeons passed frequently along that coast, separated at times by intervals of only five or ten minutes. Some were ferals (flocks formed by deserters from races earlier in the year which had found the stress of their swift journeys from the South of France, Spain or Portugal too much for them), others were birds still bound by their discipline, heading dutifully for home when seen. One could usually tell the one from the other. Apart from a growing familiarity with the composition of a flock of ferals – so many blue chequers, so many red, so many Antwerps, sweeps, and so on – their behaviour when threatened was distinctive. Where the birds on the race-track would accelerate or disperse from a broken flight to seek their individual salvations wherever they might be thought to lie, the wilier ferals would condense the formation, speed for the cliffs and circle tightly as near to them as they possibly could. The peregrine might try a cautious half-speed stoop, but I never saw one accept the insolent invitation to overshoot and break its neck in a collision with the all-too-proximate rock. Some, no doubt, do – especially inexperienced eyasses.

The eyasses in this brood demonstrated their inexperience in another way. Several pigeons cut out from flights by a parent and shepherded towards the youngsters where they circled over the sea, screaming with excitement, were seized confidently enough but soon released accidentally in good enough condition to make good their escape. One may assume that the pigeons, too, derive some benefit from this kind of training. Any doubts a young homing pigeon might have harboured as to the reality of the menace presented by those sturdy anchor-shaped forms in the sky above could scarcely be more convincingly dispelled.

The eyasses, two male and one female, were a lively group. The brothers specialized in the torment of kestrels as they hovered (or tried to) above the cliff-top turf and scrub; their sister, in assaulting herring gulls in immature plumage as they passed along the cliff-edge flyway. Perhaps their colour, size and shape caused her to view them as a vulgar parody of her own more elegant form and colour scheme, calling for protest and chastisement.

One of the brothers cost me a hot cup of coffee one lunchtime by choosing the psychological moment to pester a kestrel into dropping a mouse hard-won by half an hour's assiduous hovering, stoop after it, catch it half-way to the waves, sample its flavour while still on the wing, then drop it in disgust to its burial at sea. Next day, he or his brother, leading the trio in a noisy and frantic hunt over the sea, summarily concluded an injudicious endeavour by a swallow to make its departure for Africa a solo flight.

That was a memorable spectacle, but the violent dispersal of a formation of fifteen high-flying cormorants in an attack which involved the entire peregrine family was one to be recalled without the regret one feels for the death of so likeable a bird as a swallow. Emphatically, the brothers preferred the exclusive companionship of each other in their frequent skygames (more training), leaving their handsome sister in no doubt of her redundancy. When not engaged in bullying young herring gulls, she alleviated boredom by studying the antics of the peregrine watchers from a near perch chosen obviously for that purpose. While we remained static she remained there; when we moved, if only to don or doff a garment, she would come to circle low over us or off the cliff-edge as near as she could to where we were sitting.

One morning we decided on divided activities, and that day the cliffs were left for me to enjoy in solitude. The route to them was circuitous, winding at one stage round a steep hillside closer as the crow flies to where we habitually sat while watching the birds than was the field-gate where I always parked the car. On that hillside stood several dead oaks. On that morning, I spotted the eyas falcon perched in the top of one of them as I approached. Falling immediately from her vantage-point in a stoop, her dive into the valley on my left took her low across the road a few yards in front of the braked car. Her head as she shot past was turned to gaze full in my face behind the windscreen. And that, I told myself, was the last I should see of *her* for a while.

Parking the car and collecting my accoutrements, I crossed the close-cropped turf of the familiar sheep pasture, climbed the usual gate and joined the path which leads along the top of the cliffs. Two hundred yards beyond the gate I had climbed, the stone wall bounding the path on one side was decorated at that time with a line of derelict fence-posts. The young falcon was perched on the first of them, looking in my direction. Taking off, she flew low over the grass towards me for a few yards, then turned towards the sea to fly along the cliff-edge flyway until drawn level, then she turned inland again, to escort her friend, circling slowly low over his head, hers turned and angled to keep him under close scrutiny, all the way to the usual observation post. Having seen him settled safely in, she made off down the coast to attend to other business.

A chain of coincidences may explain the sequence of events that day, or have made an important contribution to them. Nevertheless, I have since then been less sceptical than hitherto of claims made by falconers that the sentiments a peregrine falcon often displays towards her master do not differ greatly from those shown by his spaniels.

My wife and her friend had shared most of the week's excitements on the cliff, but when told the story they mourned for what they had missed that morning. Had I not been alone at the time, though, there might not have been anything to miss. If a current of feeling can pass reciprocally between a man in the right frame of mind and a wild hawk, as I believe it can – just occasionally – isolation at the time may well be one of the prerequisites.

seven   NOT THE BOLDEST
OF HUNTERS

'Variable' is the adjective the French apply to the noun 'buse' in their name for the buzzard we define as 'common'. Aptly, for common buzzards differ not only in colour through a range running from blackish sepia to off-white, but vary in temperament no less profoundly. Most are as easy to handle in captivity as Rhode Island Red pullets, but one handed to a friend of mine for rehabilitation after a collision with a motor car was so savage that after a few days he reached the conclusion that he could cope with it no longer. A gun was used with much reluctance to resolve the dilemma. Leashed as it had to be, he could not place food within its reach without approaching it, much less inspect the progress of the treatment of its injuries. Every approach was greeted with an attack at his head and, undramatic though a buzzard's talons might seem when compared with a falcon's weaponry, they could still do nasty damage to human features when driven by 2 pounds of furious bird.

Admittedly, that buzzard's first intimate contact with our species had not been made in promising circumstances, but neither had that of another I heard of which accepted attention as though with gratitude. That bird had lost half a wing, severed neatly at the carpal joint by some moron with a .22 rifle, and was thus reduced to foraging on the ground for beetles and such until weak enough to be rescued for veterinary assistance. A gun in the right hands is one thing; in the wrong ones, very much another.

THE HAWKWATCHER

These references to captivity do not imply that buzzards may be taken into it at will. Their lives and liberties, too, enjoy the protection of the law. Since the 1981 Wildlife and Countryside Act came into force, even injured buzzards in need of help can receive it from only those people who have been licensed to give it.

However abnormally dark or pale the plumage of some common buzzards might be, the distribution of darker and lighter elements in the individual's plumage and the pattern of markings is more nearly uniform. Dorsal plumage is dark. Tibial and belly feathers are relatively pale, bearing barring, fine or coarse, which, after a fade-out (sometimes) on the lower breast, strengthens to unite into a 'shield' of solidly dark feathers shaped rather like the plastron worn by a lancer in full ceremonial dress in the days before the horse gave way to the armoured car and smart primary colours to ubiquitous khaki. The spread tail, short by raptorial standards, bears about a dozen fine bars, of which nine are plainly visible. The terminal bar may be a little broader than the rest, but only a little – certainly nothing like as bold as the bar terminating the tail (which otherwise has little in the way of marking) of the rough-legged buzzard, a Continental species which overspills into eastern Britain in winter, usually in very small numbers. Sometimes a few stray farther west, so one always looks carefully at the tail markings of any buzzard seen in winter, even in Wales or Devon. Where is the best place to hide a leaf? In a tree.

The skin of the legs of the common buzzard is yellow, like that of nearly all adult raptors, the leg feathered with 'trousers' reaching the tibiotarsal joint (the bird's back-to-front 'knee'), whereas the leg of the rough-legged species is feathered – appropriately – down to the bottom of the tarsus, where the toes emerge. One needs a very good view of a rough-legged buzzard, though, to see that detail. The iris of a buzzard's eye is dark tawny, a colour between the hot orange of the mature sparrowhawk's and the rich vandyke brown of the falcon's. The bill is not massive. Wings at full stretch span from four feet to a few inches more, with females, as usual, exceeding the size of the males.

NOT THE BOLDEST OF HUNTERS

Full-stretch is how the wings of a buzzard are usually viewed, for no other raptor in Britain spends a greater proportion of its time on the wing. Nor, where present at all, are buzzards likely to be thinly distributed. Twenty-eight soaring together is my personal record, a collection counted on a fine October day as the birds accumulated for some reason never fathomed over a one-acre plantation of young spruces standing among fields just to the west of Llandrindod Wells in Radnorshire. The spectacle of threes, fours, fives and sixes circling in the sky together is a commonplace.

Exactly where and when in buzzard country does one come across these airborne parties? Only a knowledge of the terrain and a familiarity with it in all wind and weather conditions can answer that question. Soaring buzzards ride thermals some of which are as much as a quarter of a mile in diameter. These bubbles of warm air climb skywards as the temperature of the land beneath rises in response to the interplay of sun, wind and cloud. Thermals may follow one another into the sky from the same patch of warmed land, to drift on the wind when they reach a critical altitude. Eventually, they cool and disperse, sometimes releasing moisture to form clouds as they do so. If one could predict thermal behaviour, one could predict that of buzzards, too.

All soaring birds exploit these currents, but none in Britain with an instinct more perfected than that of the buzzard, which uses them with the facility of a seasoned traveller surfacing by escalator from a station on the London Underground, and with much the same benefit in terms of personal energy conserved.

A buzzard soaring in typical fashion describes perfect circles within but near the circumference of the thermal. It does so because movement is necessary to generate a flow of air over its aerofoil surfaces and to keep it buoyant. Even so, the bird can lose height within the bubble, imperceptibly to the human observer, perhaps, because the loss is often compensated by the speed at which the bubble rises through the colder air surrounding it.

A circling buzzard's path across the sky indicates the track of the thermals drifting on the wind before they dissipate. When the bird is seen to begin beating its wings, it means that the thermal he was occupying is weakening and that he will soon leave it in search of a stronger one.

It is for the purpose of riding thermals that the buzzard (and not the buzzard alone) is believed to have evolved its spread-fingered wing profile. If it were not for the subtle influence exercised by the tips of these emarginated primary feathers on the air, the slower flow over the slower moving wing nearer to the centre of the turning circle would cause wing-tip stall. Loss of equilibrium would follow and a fall from the thermal with a loss of yet more height as the bird dives urgently to recover both control and flying-speed.

Why buzzards soar so continuously and so high – unless for pleasure – I have never discovered. Conventional answers, based on a theory of per-petual prospecting for carrion, do not satisfy me. True, buzzards take advantage of carrion, especially in winter, but one sees them hunting for living prey for too much of their time aloft for so simplistic an explanation to be acceptable. Except, perhaps, in an indirect way, because habitual soaring cannot fail to increase the prospect of observing profitable developments below. But if that benefit is a by-product of soaring for the pleasure of the exercise, does the simple cause and effect relationship stand up? I think not. For it to do so to my satisfaction, it would have to be shown that the bird ascends with carrion firmly in mind. These polemics are not merely academic. One sees raptors confined in wildlife parks and such. If one protests, one is invariably informed that the enforced inactivity is not tedious to the bird because 'it only flies because it is hungry'. Having been fed, idleness is perfectly congenial to it. I am sure that is false, and especially so in the case of the buzzard.

The role of carrion in the buzzard's natural diet, though, goes a long way towards explaining the remarkable local instability of populations in mid-Wales, and possibly elsewhere. As with kites, so with buzzards: careless – or lawless – use of poisons lies at the heart of the matter, with buzzard losses numerically heavier because there are far more of them to be poisoned. Once the carcass has been opened by jaws or a stronger bill, poisoned baits laid for foxes or crows attract buzzards too. Then the poisoned possessors of the jaws or stronger bills themselves become bait for buzzards, multiplying the casualties.

Add to these losses others caused intentionally by farmers who cannot believe that a hooked bill and talons poised above a lambing field do not threaten the lambs below, and one begins to understand why buzzards seen regularly over a hill in one season are so often missing in the next. Some lambs are stillborn; others die soon after birth from maternal rejection or incompetence. Yet others die from the shock of injuries inflicted by crows or magpies while they are helpless and before the birth-exhausted ewe rallies sufficiently to provide protection. Experienced buzzards haunt the skies above lambing fields in the early spring in anticipation of placentas. Is it surprising that a dead lamb, too, may attract attention, or the farmer find the hawk in what he may immediately assume to be flagrante delicto? Life is too hard in the hills for the niceties of the law to be weighed as carefully as they might be in less demanding environments.

So limits are set to the expansion of buzzard populations in the hills by local 'thresholds of intolerance', which, when reached, may be followed by disproportionately drastic crashes. Fortunately for those of us who like our skies decorated by hawks, there will be others on other hills not too far away which, although expanding their numbers sufficiently to provide reinforcements for the replacement of casualties elsewhere, have not yet reached the level where poison is laid or the guns loaded.

Thus, despite these local instabilities, one rarely has cause to fear general decline over areas as large – for example – as Devon or the modern Welsh mega-county of Powys. In a more local sense, too, recoveries tend not to be long delayed. A bird able to exploit animal protein from sources as diverse as the maiden dew earthworm and violet ground beetle at one end of the scale and moles, rabbits and carrion lamb at the other is a bird hard to keep down.

If the buzzard could receive in fact the protection of the law it enjoys in theory, the passage of ten years free from persecution would see the species nesting again in every county in Britain, as they are believed to have done three hundred years ago.

When first I met the buzzard on the printed page, that print cited the rabbit as the bird's principal prey. Soon after I met the buzzard live in the feather, myxomatosis reared its ugly head above the horizon. The year before it struck, I was presented by a friend with the fishing on four miles of a Shropshire border stream draining hills above which the buzzards soared all day. Duck fancying had been for generations the preoccupation of the family which owned and occupied a minor stately home in whose parkland the stream had its source. Despite elaborate fox-proof fencing to pen them in, exotic duck – Carolinas, Mandarin and so on – escaped to nest and rear their families down on 'my' water.

In the spring and early summer of that first year, indeed, these duck and their scampering broods of ducklings were the chief obstacle placed by Fate between my fishing rod and the trout I attempted to entice. Then came the dread disease, a buzzard population reduced locally by at least three-quarters, and far, far, fewer broods of ducklings. I never witnessed an attack, but noted that the surviving buzzards had begun to follow the course of the stream in their prospecting flights and occasionally to hang hovering above it. Two and two traditionally equals four.

These observations have since had me toying with thoughts of how artificially induced myxomatosis might have applied an accelerator to a process of natural selection, as I had come to suspect the gamekeeper's gun to have done in modifying sparrowhawk behaviour, as proposed in Chapter 3.

Assume the possibility of prey-selection tendencies being subject to genetic influence and the buzzards' preoccupation with the rabbit as true as the old books asserted. Any buzzards not wholly subject to the rule would be the likeliest survivors of the rabbit famine, transmitting their independence of bunny flesh to their descendants. Their descendants would then become the archetypes of a new and revised strain of buzzards, destined to dominate the species of the future.

THE HAWKWATCHER

To test the hypothesis, one needed to find post-plague buzzards demon-strating indifference to rabbit once rabbit had again become the most readily available form of prey. Such buzzards I eventually found, sixteen years later, on the Polly Estate in Wester Ross. Rabbits infested the dunes where I saw my first certain merlin; buzzards were numerous. So abundant were rabbits above ground at first light that the buzzards, soon aloft, could have taken them two at a time, one in each foot, as they passed over the warrens. Yet all those I saw as I waited hopefully for a merlin to show up passed without distraction on their journey to a heathery hillside half a mile away, where they wind-hung or hovered in clear expectation of voles. For the fattier body tissue of these little animals, a generally well informed friend insists. But, if so, why the reported predilection for lean rabbit in all those years gone by? The voles are not recent arrivals here, nor the special beneficiaries of changed systems of agriculture and husbandry. Just to clinch the argument, the rabbits in the dunes seemed to fear the big shadow passing overhead no more than those of the gulls or lapwings to which they were equally indifferent.

The temperamental variability of *Buteo buteo* is reflected by regional variations in choice of prey, which extends beyond the fur-bearing animals. Among the fur-bearers, incidentally, the mole – for whose lawful poisoning below ground much of the strychnine which kills buzzards in Wales is nominally purchased – makes an extremely large contribution. A friend who photographed a nest under licence saw eight brought to it in a single day; I have watched many buzzards perched on the posts of fences bounding mole-infested fields as they waited for the earth to betray surfacing prey by beginning to heave. If the buzzard reacts quickly and clutches decisively, the mole, sensitive only to earthborne vibration, is without defence. The buzzard is a well-documented species, with plentiful references to moles in the Continental literature.

Exmoor buzzards are noted for taking adders; New Forest dwellers for taking birds of many species, including carrion crow and tawny owl – information we owe to Colin Tubbs, who wrote the definitive study of their behaviour in that habitat. All the stranger a small adventure of mine on the Radnor Moors while watching the crest of Glascwm Hill one afternoon in early August in hopes of seeing a hunting merlin.

Buzzards – survivors of a fourteen-bird casualty list resulting from a poisoning incident – crossed the sky at frequent intervals, sometimes turning to patrol the skyline over which we expected the merlin to appear. Finally, one of these buzzards made a shallow stoop which flushed a party of three red grouse. Buzz flopped down in their wake, and we spoke a small threnody for grouse number four.

The struggle was fierce and prolonged: the prey (never seen to move above the heather) escaped the buzzard's clutches several times, to be recaptured as a maimed mouse is recovered by a playful cat, and was eventually dispatched. With the kill mantled by wings spread wide, the buzzard bent to plume and feed. A quarter of an hour passed busily up on the crest. What should we see when the buzzard flew again? Doubtless a crop bulging with contents Fortnum and Mason might have been proud to supply; possibly the remains of the grouse in carriage to a nest somewhere for consumption by a brood of buzzard chicks hatched late in the season. When the sated hawk did at last take to the air the talons were empty and the crop scarcely detectable, let alone bulging out from the normal curve of the breast as it would if recently filled to capacity. We had been presented with a mystery.

Within a few yards of where the action had taken place, there stood on that otherwise bare skyline a small solitary hawthorn bush which would serve as a marker. This was fortunate, because there can be profound differences between the aspect of a hill-crest as viewed along two hundred yards of steep hypotenuse and as it appears when one has climbed to it. So, with a code of signals worked out with my accompanying better half (now left below to direct me), I started to climb. Helped by her signals (a performance good enough to earn her a job among the tic-tac men on the racecourse at Epsom), I zero'd in to the critical spot without difficulty. There, exactly where the buzzard had been dancing, floundering and feeding in the sparse ling and bilberry scrub, fresh-plucked meadow pipit feathers lay heaped in a neat pile. Search as I might, nothing else of animal origin came to light. Erasing the word '*Lagopus*' from a metaphorical headstone, I inscribed '*Anthus*' in its place and returned to the foot of the hill to report my findings.

How could one account for so strange an incident? Much might be accounted for by the variability of the buzzard, but this seemed to be going altogether too far. Possibilities were reviewed, among them the fact that buzzards may lay as early as mid-April, hatch their eggs in a month and fledge the product six weeks later. In August it was not too early for the spectacle to have been one of juvenile ineptitude by a youngster which had been on the wing for less than a month and not, as originally surmised, that of a parent hunting to feed a brood hatched in the season.

When all's said and done, dusk in any well wooded buzzard country is likely to offer the view of one brushing the canopy as it steals towards a roost to try for a snatch at one of the woodpigeons as it settles down for the night. The wariness of the woodpigeon being rightly proverbial, captures are infrequent, but the regularity of the attempts argues a success rate sufficient to justify the expenditure of effort and an instinct for dealing with feathered prey which should be equal to the prompt dispatch of a pipit.

Had we, then, been watching an extremely young buzzard as it took early steps in the development of its professional skills? To age a buzzard confidently, one needs to hear it call or see the tail clearly from below. The call of the juvenile echoes the cat-like 'mew' of the adult, but in shrill and broken-toned parody; the feathers of its tail, like those of so many other young raptors, are tipped with white or cream much more conspicuously than those of their parents. This buzzard had neither called nor spread its tail for a clear view of the terminal bar, so the question of its age remains an open one.

Watching birds seriously presents one with many mysteries, but far fewer solutions.

Basing his report on experience of buzzards in the New Forest, Colin Tubbs told of young carrion crows taken by them from the nest. Could that, I wondered when first I read the words, have something to do with the bitter and conspicuous dislike of buzzards shown by all carrion crows whenever the raptors are encountered and at whatever season? Still wondering, I have yet to find a likelier explanation. Crows pester all hawks at times – even the lethal peregrine, occasionally – but none with quite such determined persistence as the buzzard. Some victims vacate the disputed area of sky without offering resistance; others are more truculent, rolling over in flight and shooting out feet spread to fend off assault. The number of these engagements I have watched must run well into four figures, but only once have I seen a buzzard suffering harassment turn the tables.

It happened over my hog-backed hill in the lower Wye valley where I learned so much of sparrowhawk behaviour. Conflict witnessed there between hawk and corvid had until then followed the common pattern. On this memorable afternoon, though, a crow chose the wrong buzzard, the wrong place, or the wrong occasion. When noticed, the buzzard was patrolling inoffensively along the crest, the crow accelerating to catch up. On closing to stabbing or tweaking distance, it gave one croak of anger or triumph, which proved to be an error of judgement. Buzz was round in a flash, the roles reversed and the atmosphere utterly transformed. The difference in demeanour between a bird bullying a bird and a bird hunting a bird is unmistakable. Corbie fled for its life, confirming my diagnosis with anguished croaks and squeaks more fitting to a terrified barnyard fowl than to a seasoned bandit. Buzzards not being swift on the wing, it escaped.

There has to be some reason for such untypical behaviour. It may be that the buzzard was a specimen somewhere near one extremity of the variability bracket in terms of spirit, or a bird of only average valour challenged near the heart of its territory and drawing courage from that fact, as we are all likely to do in similar situations. Somewhere among the trees which clung to the rocks and soil of that steep gradient was one which harboured a buzzard's nest. The would-be crow-killer might well have been its incumbent.

Another useful insight given to me by the buzzards of that hill concerned the weight a buzzard could lift. Such a wing area obviously adapts the species well to the task, but expressing possibilities in figures is another matter. However, if the size of the carrier is a known fact, one may make a reliable estimate of the size of the burden it is carrying. Especially, as on this occasion, when the porter is the familiar buzzard and the burden the equally familiar rabbit, grasped obligingly by the head, and so hanging to display its full length.

Having, as a fellow predator upon the species, handled and weighed a fair number of rabbits, I had no hesitation in estimating this one's weight as somewhere near the textbook maximum of 4½ pounds. The buzzard, weighing at most 2½ pounds, carried its prey from tree to tree without difficulty as it searched the hillside for the one which its fancy would select that morning as a luncheon table.

The buzzard in 1988 Britain is confined as a regular breeding species to the western and northern uplands (with unoccupied gaps here and there) and a tongue of terrain in southern England reaching east through the woodland of Dorset, Wiltshire, Hampshire, Berkshire and West Sussex, thinning out in density as one progresses east.

Buzzards breeding freely in Shropshire and Herefordshire exert a coloniz-ing pressure eastwards which meets a barrage of gunshot on the borders of the well keepered pheasant-rearing counties of the English Midlands. Keepers there have grown tolerant of the smaller hawks, but those of a size to carry off an adult pheasant or partridge fare less well. Some buzzards, though, make the penetration and survive the consequences. Hence one of my local ornitho-logical mysteries, for every harvest time for at least twenty years has been signalled by the arrival of buzzards on the shooting estate in west Warwick-shire where much of my winter bird watching is done. Usually, several of these immigrants remain to haunt the extensive woodland and the skies above it until spring. Once, the keeper then employed on a neighbouring shoot set himself the task of destroying the season's influx and accomplished it, but otherwise I have no reason to doubt the toleration professed locally.

Yet the theoretical abundance of the food supply – voles galore, and rabbits by the hundred laid low by myxomatosis – and thousands of mature oaks and ashes in traditional forest from which to select a nursery have not persuaded a pair, so far as we have been able to discover, to mate, remain and build a nest. The buzzard's pile of sticks is one of the most conspicuous to be assembled in any British tree; a pair of buzzards bearing prey to it from all quarters of the estate in turn for seven or eight weeks would scarcely go unnoticed, nor would the shrill cries of the young buzzards, to be heard for several weeks thereafter in the general vicinity of the nest.

Either I have been sadly obtuse or extremely credulous, or something required for the propagation of buzzards is lacking these days in that part of the county. Unless, of course, colonization is a by-product of some strangely directed form of winter migration which does not take root as readily as one might suppose. Whatever the explanation, I have no tears to shed. Having to travel for some of one's pleasures adds a dimension to them. The buzzards soaring over the Wye thirty-five years ago when I made my first visits to that lovely river, fishing rod in hand, added to the pleasures of the day as they could not have done had they been as familiar an experience as the kestrels sailing among them were.

Not long after that first visit to the middle Wye, I found a minor road running along the northern flank of Mynydd Eppynt where a buzzard might be found crowning every third or fourth telegraph pole for nearly two miles. I should be surprised by a failure to find them there today, or indeed on any day till the end of the century. Ornithological prophecy thereafter would be folly. Such is the population density in the counties of the buzzard's occupancy as often to inspire the words 'only another buzzard' as the binoculars are lowered in mild disappointment.

Perhaps we should not be so blasé. If the day ever dawns in Wales or Devonia when that bulky figure with the long, broad, tip-tilted wings set spread-fingered in a shallow dihedral ceases to grace the sunny sky, bird watchers of that era will have cause to appreciate – and bewail – their loss. There is no doubt that our successors will do at least the latter.

My saddest encounter with a buzzard was at the roadside just outside

THE HAWKWATCHER

Mortimer's Cross in Herefordshire. A car passing through earlier in the morning had struck it fatally – just as its short and not especially sharp talons had closed on a full-grown buck rat. Buzzard and prey lay in the gutter, locked together in death. A dead rat is always good news: the slaughter of any creature which assists us in our never-ending war against them, invariably bad.

eight   THE 'FUNNY LITTLE TIERCEL'

A crow laboured along the skyline, a hawk in pursuit. The rate at which the gap was closing implied peregrine; the extent of the size disparity between fugitive and pursuer suggested kestrel. The sun broke through a veil of grey cloud for a few convenient moments, turning the second bird into a twinkle of blue-grey and silver. 'What a funny little tiercel,' said my son Stephen, and a bird destined to play a large part in my life for the next nine years had received an undeservedly dismissive baptism.

Funny or not, he was certainly small. Compared with the tiercels I had watched in Galloway, Cumbria and North Devon, he looked positively frail. So this was the peregrine whose progeny I had committed myself to spend much time in helping safely into a hostile world. I hoped my time would not be wasted. Had I foreseen how much discomfort I had volunteered for, that hope would have been a fervent one indeed. Watching a peregrine falcon site through the sunny hours of a fine spring afternoon is as pleasant a way of spending them as any I know, but peering up at it through snow or sleet blown horizontally on a gale-force wind at 5 a.m. is a different matter. In those conditions, one has to struggle to remain conscious, let alone alert. Without a stern effort to dominate them, priorities narrow towards prayer for a change in the weather so that the egg you plan to fry in the back of the car three hours later will not congeal into a tasteless sallow obscenity before it can be carried round to the driving seat for sheltered consumption.

THE HAWKWATCHER

As the little tiercel raced along the Radnorshire skyline in the wake of the fleeing crow on that fine March morning, though, knowledge of hardships in store – and of much else – lay hidden in the future. An officer of the Nature Conservancy Council had asked for the job to be done. By the time I had begun it, responsibility for peregrine welfare in Wales had been handed over to a newly opened office of the Royal Society for the Protection of Birds. I asked for a brief. It was to protect against intrusion, casual or criminal, one of the two sites in mid-Wales known to be occupied by a fertile pair that year; to be as nearly invisible as possible while doing the job; and to know in some detail what transpired on the ledge, but not to be caught anywhere near it – 'or we shall have to prosecute you'. I had not been licensed to make close inspections, nor did I wish to be, nor did Authority wish to issue a licence. Might there be help with the job? Possibly, later on.

That briefing, too, lay in the future on 23 March, as I stared up at the landmark I had been given by which to identify the ledge the birds were expected to choose. Showing no interest in the ledge or anything else near the landmark, the speeding tiercel concluded his pursuit of the crow by vanishing over the steep shoulder which reared up from the road and beneath which we stood. That road, I knew, led round a sharp spur which separated two long reservoirs. Bare rock was conspicuously visible on both flanks of the high feature from which the spur projected, but the geology of the west-facing shoulder around the corner included a fine complex of sheer cliffs rising 350 feet above the road, itself about 1,000 feet above sea level at that point. The line taken by the tiercel as he disappeared led that way. We followed by road to discover whether he might concur in the view we took of the possibilities those cliffs must offer.

The cliffs topped a steep heathery bank with a handy lay-by bordering the road at its foot. There we parked, to dismount and await events. They were not long in materializing. Harsh croaks of peregrine protest rent the air. Caused by us? It seemed unlikely. If these peregrines disliked people that much, why choose a public road to dwell by? A buzzard floated out from behind the skyline, the 'funny little tiercel' in hot pursuit, stooping, pulling away, stooping again. A falcon followed him from behind the skyline to join in the fun, signalled by the resonantly hoarse din rising in a crescendo. From an enormous cleft running from top to bottom of the cliffs a second falcon emerged like a rocket to turn a demonstration into a battle. Lack of ounces, one might now conjecture, neither inhibited the tiercel's libido nor diminished his sex appeal.

Nor did they imply mental inadequacy. Leaving the ladies to fight it out in the sky, he dropped quietly to the skyline to find a perch from which he could command the cleft, into which we were by now staring keenly from a vantage-point along the road where the view into it was better. Having seen off the flirtatious intruder, the incumbent falcon returned, flying straight to the top of what had until then been mistaken for a vast clump of dead or moribund ivy growing from the rock. Now, we saw it for what it really was, an old nest ravens had been building up for decades, until it was a stick pile ten feet or more in height. It was not merely the tiercel's taste in domestic architecture we had discovered; it was his private address.

Motivated, perhaps, by an urge to restore self-respect, the tiercel greeted his mate's return to duty by crossing the lake to inspect a soaring hen sparrowhawk. Presence recorded and examination completed, he troubled her no more. Not behaviour I would have predicted – he was an odd fellow indeed.

At 3.30 p.m. the falcon left the ravens' nest, the tiercel immediately taking over what was obviously incubation – at least a fortnight before the date on which I had expected to assume duty.

The falcon muted copiously and preened on a skyline crag for thirty minutes before leaving the site – behaviour on her part I should come to know as typical. The expedition, conceived only as a preliminary reconnaissance to be made well in advance of any need for action, drew to its close, but not before a roving kite and a handsome male hen harrier on patrol over the moor beyond the lake had embellished the day by crossing in the searching window of an idly aimed binocular.

Lessons had been learned: that the timetable had to be adjusted; that tiercels are not necessarily hefty fellows breasted like Norfolk turkeys; that flirtatious conduct was not a phenomenon confined to one of the Galloway sites I knew, one with a record of unexplained failures; and that not all peregrines in Wales waited until the second week in April to begin laying their eggs. I had discovered also that the topography of this Welsh site would enable me to watch peregrines lawfully at a distance less than a sixth of those imposed elsewhere, if at the hazard of a permanently cricked neck. We left for home that evening with light and hopeful hearts.

Commitments made before the discovery that my intended charges were 'early birds' indeed kept me from them until 5 April. Anxious for reassurance that there was still something to be guarded, I climbed that day round the cliffs and up to the moor behind them to risk a look over into the nest in the big cleft, if a view should prove possible. I found that the ravens, as usual, had chosen and built judiciously. Astride a rock pinnacle which promised swift death as the penalty for vertigo, I looked down at my Dinky Toy car on the grass beside the ribbon of road, and from about twenty feet into the lustrous dark eyes of an unafraid blue-mantled tiercel who did not look the least bit 'funny' or 'little' at that distance – just splendidly handsome and unforgettably dignified. He sat tight for the three seconds my head remained in view, making no sound. The letter of the law had been broken, but now I knew that I truly had something to guard. I hope Nelson's conscience gave him no greater trouble when he opened fire on the Danish fleet in Copenhagen.

Following one of the higher contours, I found a sheltered guard-post about two hundred yards south of the cleft. By the time I came down from it that evening, more lessons had been learned. One, that Radnorshire in April can offer at 1,400 feet blinding snow showers on one compass bearing while the landscape shimmers in heat haze on another. Two, that a man enjoying that vista might with luck intercept eyrie robbers, but would be ill placed to react if they sneaked in under the cover of moorland ridges from an unexpected direction and offered resistance. A minimum of ten minutes would be needed to get back to the car and five more to reach a telephone. Obviously, two men formed a desirable minimum – one down by the road, as close as possible to a telephone, in visual signalling contact with another up high, where he had the best view of all approaches to the site. However, on 8, 9 and 10 April I would be single-handed.

The next discovery – that one did not need to visit the northern uplands to find midwinter in spring – helped me make up my mind where I should guard from. Apart from other considerations, a descent by a man locked double with lumbago would take rather more than ten minutes. The decision to operate from the roadside at the foot of the bank brought other benefits. A lawful watchpoint on top disclosed little of what went on in the cleft; one below gave a view of reliefs and other incidents I ought to record, for both the official record and my private interest.

In the latter respect I did my best, but the peregrine's talent for clandestine arrival and departure (practised assiduously at that stage in the cycle) coupled with drifts of low cloud and curtains of falling snow denied me all the records I wished and planned to make. Later on, as experience grew, weather improved and the peregrines lost their early-season caution, I did better. Time's influence on the attitude of the birds is consistent and interesting. We may detect small difference in the vulnerability to predation of eggs, small chicks and well-grown chicks en route to eyas-hood, but the peregrine sees the matter differently. With *Homo sapiens* on the prowl bearing stake, sledgehammer, horsehide gloves, climbing rope and crampons, the instinct grows obsolete, but it was relevant enough when the peregrine evolved it. In those terms, man is a newcomer to the scene. Fox, polecat, raven and eagle are not.

Reliefs continued through my first three-day stint. The tiercel brought in kills, all of them small passerines. By starting – and losing – a fight with a cock sparrowhawk over the lake on 9 April, he suffered yet further damage to the figure he cut as viewed by his guardian. As he declared personal identity by blueness of mantle, snowy upper breast and primary quills which closed to lend his angled wings neatly sharpened points, so the mantle of his bulkier mate reflected a lilac sheen in clear sunlight and her breast a creamy tinge darkened further by the boldness of the black barring she bore. As she sailed in or out overhead her wing-tips suggested a nicely symmetrical clip with well wielded secateurs at the very ends. Almost all falcons are dingier than their mates, with wings which come in typical carriage to distinctly blunter points, but the extreme form in which this pair demonstrated such standard variations in plumage helped much in distinguishing between authentic reliefs and mere visits to the incubating bird for whatever other reason, as well as unsignalled intrusions by other peregrines. The crags of an eyrie rock may at any time attract a passing peregrine from elsewhere to pause in the absence of a sentry and take the weight off its wings for a while somewhere out of view of the bird recumbent on the ledge. As observing and correctly interpreting comings and goings at and about the ledge may be for a human guardian the sole practicable indication of how matters progress up there during the first eight weeks of the season, the identification of peregrines as individuals is a matter of more than academic or sentimental interest. On this occasion, a quick look into the ravens' nest was physically possible, but ledges chosen so obligingly are few indeed.

The artist's impression of falcon and tiercel published in a textbook can be no more than a depiction of Mr and Mrs Average for the species. Reality watched through binoculars or telescope at a distance of a hundred yards or less is more subtle. No two peregrines are identical any more than any two tabby cats are identical. Profiles in flight differ, facial markings differ. So do plumage tints and patterning, with all due allowance made for the strength of the light and the angle from which it falls. The variations are not profound, but taken together they are usually enough to inform an observant eye. The art of individual recognition is not acquired in a few hours, but after fourteen long days spent on this site in all weathers between 8 April and the month's end I had begun to get the hang of it.

Galloway had given me insights into the pattern of events at an eyrie after the chicks have hatched. Now I was well placed to augment that information. I discovered that the task of incubation was shared quite fairly between this pair, but that its division from day to day was erratic and unpredictable, bearing no obvious relationship to the progress of the embryos until the very end. Responses to an offer of relief were no more predictable than the timing of it. Sometimes the change-over was immediate, as though urgently awaited; sometimes it was leisurely; occasionally it was refused outright. It was not unusual for the falcon to be called off to accept a kill presented by the tiercel before he took her place on the warm eggs.

There were times when I wondered whether the relative comfort of the sheltered eyrie might be a prime factor in the behaviour of its occupants in that bleak valley. If so, one is tempted to trace the subtle hand of natural selection at work. The object of incubation is to keep eggs warm; the more frequent the reliefs, it is reasonable to assume, the greater the risk of heat loss. Chilling, if prolonged sufficiently, causes embryos to die in the shell. If not that severe, I suspect that it may still delay development, adding to the time the vulnerable eggs lie there at risk of attracting predation if left unguarded, as when the parents are disturbed or, as occasionally happens, they are confused as to each other's immediate intentions.

For either bird, a stint on the eggs might last an hour, two, three or four. On two occasions I have observed five-hour stints but the average is usually nearer two hours than four. The relieved bird might leave the site immediately or remain to preen. If presented with a kill as part of the ceremony, the falcon would enjoy her meal somewhere on the eyrie rocks before preening or leaving. Occasionally she would not leave the site at all, going back to the eggs as soon as her preen was complete. As incubation proceeded and the weather, on the whole, became less harsh, falcon and tiercel alike might emerge for a preen and a respite lasting up to twenty minutes once or twice during a stint. That worried me at the time, but the eventual success of both hatch and fledge were to prove their instinct sounder in the matter than my rational misgivings.

Copulation after incubation began was not astonishing, but its continuation until after the hatch was. At that level of evolutionary development, one began with an assumption of a clinically functional character for that exercise, but experience soon suggested that even for creatures whose intercourse is external it may serve to reinforce the pair bond. As it has long

THE HAWKWATCHER

been known that peregrines do not lay repeat clutches unless robbed of the first within about a week of completion, one has difficulty in accounting other than in pair-bond terms for treadings seen daily in the course of the relief ceremonies at an eyrie containing eggs a fortnight or three weeks old.

By the end of my April visits I had begun to learn the rudiments of the peregrine's language. Rasping calls of 'Kark kark kark' signified displeasure or anger, its intensity indicated by tempo. Wails of 'Eep eep eep', often prolonged, were a form of pleading which, if they elicited no response, might (especially in the case of the falcon) harshen to a cry better phoneticized as 'Airt airt airt', finally moving towards the 'Kark kark kark' of downright annoyance. The falcon peregrine is not the most long-suffering of God's creatures. The most interesting vocalization of all is that which is often described as the 'rusty hinge' call. I record it as 'Squi-*cluck* squi-*cluck* squi-*cluck*' out of regard for the variety of objectionable sounds an unlubricated hinge may emit. This, of all the peregrine's calls, is the most subject to variations of tone and emphasis each, I am perfectly certain, with a meaning of its own and of surprisingly sophisticated significance. It is the material of everyday conversation between the members of a family, and possibly of a local tribe. It serves as a simple greeting. Inflected appropriately, it is news, delivered to a perched bird by its mate high overhead, that a flight of pigeons approaches. Uttered by a falcon with yet another inflection and accompanied by strange bodily contortions, it says to a tiercel in the plainest language, 'Leave that hussy up there alone and return to your conjugal duty.' In another context, it is a command from a falcon to a chick or eyas which reads 'Eat this and eat it *now*. Mother knows best.' Obviously, I did not gain experience at that depth during a single month of long-duration peregrine wardening, but by the end of it my feet had been directed onto the right path. One day, I expect to see these theories proved by sonogram in relation to recorded incident, and scientific distinction awarded to whoever conducts the experiments.

During each of my April spells of duty I paid one cautious visit to the top and peeped over for a few seconds. The originally wool-lined cup of the ravens' nest had been reduced by the peregrines to a bare saucer in the centre of which four beautiful orange-brown eggs lay, disclosed to my eye one day by the falcon's hasty departure at the sight of my face suddenly projecting above her horizon. She, a somewhat less elegantly proportioned bird than her mate when viewed at such close quarters, reacted much more sharply to the intrusion than he had done when viewed from above while on duty. A last glimpse on 22 April, by which date a hatch was due or nearly so, established that it had not occurred. Standing up for a better eyeball-to-eyeball, the tiercel uncovered all four eggs.

Anxiety increased through the 23rd and 24th, by which dates the falcon was sitting for longer spells, refusing reliefs, and the tiercel visiting more often than usual, sometimes with a small kill which he himself ate when the falcon refused to take interest in it. He, too, quite clearly knew the date and its implications – as well as I did, probably, or even better.

Was all well? Had I been giving myself lumbago and risking pneumonia for a clutch of dud eggs? These peregrines had been suspected of infertility until a remarkable international law-enforcement operation involving the FBI, the Royal Canadian Mounted Police and the Warwickshire Constabulary, virtually as a postscript, finally ran to earth in the English Midlands clutches of peregrine eggs dated and marked with the map references of the only mid-Welsh sites still occupied during the darkest days of the population collapse. That discovery had led indirectly to the invitation to mount guard. The fine investigative work had established the theft of highly relevant eggs. It had not, however, thrown light on their fertility or otherwise. So 24 April was quite logically an anxious day.

My wife was there to share both the anxiety and the discomforts of that spell of duty. At 11 a.m. a motor cycle roared up, sputtered and halted. The well disguised figure which dismounted proved on unpackaging to be the son who had accompanied me on the opening reconnaissance and had shared duty whenever he could escape the demands of his employer and his own family responsibilities. He, too, on 24 April, was prey to anxiety.

At 6.25 the falcon at last resolved our misgivings by accepting a meadow pipit from her eager mate, carrying it to an adjacent crag for part pluming, then taking it back, otherwise intact, to the ravens' nest in the cleft to be dealt with to an accompanying melody of muted 'squi-clucks'. Chicks, it seemed, were hatched with a dictionary in their little heads. Or were they familiarized with the language by sound waves penetrating those handsome orange-brown eggshells? The tiercel's wild jubilation took him 2,000 feet into the sky, back to the lake in a wind-ripping stoop, then the length of it and back in less than a minute, his breast and wing-tips throwing spray from the bolder wave-crests. If I still harboured doubts of the peregrine's capacity for emotion, I lost them then. 'Funny' he might once have seemed. 'Small', as peregrines go, he certainly was. No celebrated warrior, either, but, if this display was anything to judge by, he promised to prove an assiduous father.

Would he, I wondered, make an adequate provider? That afternoon had produced his first observed attempts on homing pigeons. Neither attack need have worried the loft proprietor's insurance company.

Act 2 had begun. Eggs were no longer the object of protection, which I had assumed at first to be central to the whole operation; it was now chicks that had to be guarded. These, in fact, were the real heart of the matter, as I had learned during an interview at Newtown a few days earlier. Also that the risk was not confined to the threat offered by casual, ignorant and fundamentally innocent intrusion, or by some clone of myself differing only in the degree and nature of his interest in birds of prey in that it demanded possession of them. A man like that, forestalled or intercepted, could be expected to give up, smile, shrug, apologize and try to talk me out of calling the police. Such, indeed, might try for the young peregrines when they had feathered, but the long shadow of professional crime, violent at necessity, loomed over all. In the previous year a professional 'knee-capper' from the London underworld, a man with a list of convictions for serious crime as long as my arm, had been caught on the site by the local constabulary. If the dish needed seasoning, the interview provided it. With no attempted intrusion of any kind as yet, I was not altogether displeased by the news. A sentry-duty in which one is never required even to call 'Halt, who goes there?' can grow tedious.

THE 'FUNNY LITTLE TIERCEL'

Perhaps not in this case, though. Peregrines, supported by the rest of the cast – kite, raven, crow, jackdaw, kestrel, sparrowhawk, occasional hen harrier and merlin, goosander, wheatear, stonechat, and now cuckoo – provided adequate entertainment on the finer days, of which there were now more than there had been a month earlier. Matters progressed and fears that the tiercel might not be up to his work faded as an ample stream of pipit-size birds, ring ousels, small waders with neatly pointed wings and long legs hanging, as well as occasional collared or turtle doves with their characteristically black under-tail coverts (neither officially present in the county in that year), were brought to the eyrie by their proudly screaming captor.

By 29 April the falcon, too, had resumed hunting and among the larger kills she brought in was a big black and white bird I did not immediately identify. How many of the four eggs, I wondered, had hatched? There was only one way to find out there and then and I took it, with due caution, on 3 May.

A companionable display flight the pair made high over the cliffs on that beautiful day had encouraged me to conclude that a brief intrusion would not now present any hazard to the chicks. I went up, wriggled to the end of the pinnacle and craned forwards. There stood the falcon, feathers sleeked elegantly to her shapely torso, with a fragment of flesh in her bill and her foot spread over a snowy chick smaller than its siblings which, so the falcon's attitude implied, was not to be allowed to evade sustenance. The siblings, just three heads protruding from what looked like a large lump of dingy cottonwool, joined their mother in staring me out of countenance.

They reposed on a mat of pigeons' tail quills – woodpigeons', from their size, although I had identified none among the prey I had seen carried in – and on the narrow rock ledge the nest's rim pressed against there were the unmistakable wing of a hen kestrel and the big bright-pink leg of an oystercatcher. Originally, two pairs of kestrels had shared the cliffs with their seniors, and I had noticed a few days earlier a reduction, so it seemed, to one pair and an odd cock. The original possessor of the big pink leg had, as I mentioned earlier, puzzled me when seen in the falcon's grasp. Odd how the legs had been concealed, though, as if she did not wish to advertise the identity of her unusual victim.

On 4 May my son relieved me and dealt with the first attempt at an intrusion. Two men were involved. The police were unimpressed. They had their own catalogue of villains to refer to; the faces did not fit. On 7 May I returned, checked that we still guarded four chicks, all now appreciably larger and dingier, as the first suit of down was supplanted by the second.

8th May is a date underlined in my diary. Stage by stage, peregrine wardening brought me a whole new circle of friends. This was the day I made the first.

I had by then established an observation post on the lake shore, out of sight of the lay-by and the passing traffic, from which I could look directly up at the ravens' nest. There I could sit, snug and hidden from all but eyes searching deliberately. At 3 p.m. that afternoon, a pair of singularly innocent blue ones in a nicely tanned face crowned with a neat cloth cap met mine from over the fence on top of the concealing embankment, rather as mine had met the falcon's the previous day 350 feet above us. Neither man disliked what he saw. A straightforward question was asked in a pleasant voice made yet pleasanter by a faint Radnorshire accent. I stood up and declared myself, the purpose of my presence and the situation up in the cleft. It was a risk I had not previously taken. 'Making a census of stonechats' was the usual cover story. 'Mind if I come down and join you?' enquired the pleasant voice. The body of the man who climbed over was not a large one but, as I was to find out over the next seven years, it housed a good mind and a hero's spirit. D. A. Barnes ('Barney' to the world, as he lost no time in telling me) had been a post office official at Llandrindod Wells for many years. On entering his seventh decade, high blood-pressure and associated ailments had compelled an early retirement. Since then, the local flora and fauna had been the prime interest of the childless widower. He lived alone, shy and self-sufficient, holding too passionately opinions which were strong and often controversial for him to make friends easily. We had toured the same range of mid-Welsh wildlife haunts, I learned – a discovery which led promptly to an exchange of

Hen harriers gathering to roost in winter (see page 198)

Peregrines over the north Devon coast (see pages 205–214)

information concerning an oystercatcher, a vagrant in Radnorshire. He knew where its vagrancy had carried it, to a small lake half a mile from the site. I could impart news of the outcome when he added the comment that he hadn't seen it for a few days.

A past preoccupation with the game of golf was balanced by mine (not yet wholly spent) with fishing. Barney was a far better botanist than I; my travels had taken me more widely in search of birds, and I had been at it longer. Thus I had greater experience to balance against the warmth of his newer enthusiasm. Fate had obviously engineered the encounter. Within a week or so, other haunts were neglected for the peregrine site; by 21 May the peregrines were under permanent daylight protection, much of it by a two-man guard. That was good; but the *tenfold* improvement – as I measure it – which a second pair of keen eyes adds to observation, assisted further by the service of a second pencil and notebook, was of a value no smaller. There is much more, not in need of labouring. Family had helped splendidly with the task as they could, but, with a virtual resident for comrade-in-arms, loneliness and boredom on days of low activity were at an end. Loneliness and boredom? Yes. Even for me, hawks cannot entirely replace human companionship and even peregrines cannot enliven as a matter of course the entirety of a 15-hour working day. They have other things to do, such as hunting somewhere out of sight and brooding their chicks.

Not that they failed to do their best to entertain, assisted by the most welcome form of intrusion, the other peregrines roving those hills that I have already touched on. To the best of my knowledge, there were only two pairs breeding in that latitude of mid-Wales in 1975 but beautiful young falcons in the lovely golden garb of sub-adulthood visited the valley regularly, as did three mature falcons with features to identify them individually, such as a missing flight quill, an unusually rangy profile in flight, or exceptional size. All were either responded to flirtatiously by the tiercel or seen off summarily by his robust partner. Apart from one glorious youngster, accompanied at times as she passed over the valley by a mature tiercel as stout and powerful as the Galloway bird whose eyrie I had half-wardened (as

I now viewed the exercise), 'our' falcon was as fine as any I saw in the area. If there had been competition for the site, small wonder she had emerged victor. A peregrine territory, I am certain, is the possession of a falcon: her smaller consort, just another possession, even though he occasionally adopts attitudes of male chauvinism. For example, his kills are *his* property, until voluntarily surrendered, a fact or convention the larger falcon acknowledges with comparative docility. Hers, however, tend to be a very different matter and heaven help a tiercel if he touches one uninvited under Madame's eye.

With Barney to share the burden, all rolled happily along until 18 May. That afternoon, instead of the scrappy remnant usually carried out for jettisoning somewhere over the moor after a feed (a hygienic mother, this falcon) the burden borne was larger than the whole kill had been on delivery. In colour, it was a dingy off-white. Consideration of the implications inspired a walk up to the top on the 20th. As feared, only three chicks then remained. Provision, in conformity with the weather's influence on hunting prospects, had been erratic. Had it been fatally so? On the 23rd I went up again. Dark quills had begun to sprout about parson's noses and from the ends of long off-white wing-limbs, but there were now only two chicks left.

The 'funny little tiercel' became that 'bloody little tiercel'. Why, instead of getting off to work, must he now sit for hours, static as a museum specimen, in a tree growing from the rock, almost at the very foot of the cleft, from which little could be seen of the sky and the altitude of no passing pigeon reached until the quarry had passed beyond all hope of overtaking? Barney and I having conferred, I sped to the telephone and called Authority. Would it not be better to send a man down on a rope, retrieve the last two chicks before parental incapacity accounted for them, too, and have them hand-reared for subsequent release by some trustworthy expert? Surely such were available on tap, with the peregrine situation so worrying generally?

No, out of the question. There was no such expert and, if there were, no arrangements existed for the emergency issue of the licence which would be required to authorize the operation. Nature must be left to take its course.

I returned to my companion, fuming with rage. What slanders were

THE 'FUNNY LITTLE TIERCEL'

heaped on the head of Authority that afternoon were nobody's business. Then the tiercel flew out, killed quickly and came back. Making no attempt to offer his prey to the falcon, he flew low with it and vanished into dead ground near his new perch in the low tree, obscured from our view by a hump in the intervening hillside. With a string of obscenities regarding fathers who feed their own fat faces while their children starve, I stumbled along the road at a clumsy sprint to improve my view of his misbehaviour.

There he stood, blue-backed and handsome as ever, by a large boulder in the heather, solicitously feeding a fat white chick which had obviously survived a fall of about 80 feet, apparently undamaged. From then on, he made her the principal object of his attention, leaving her brother and sister to the falcon, who also contributed to the sustenance of the 'Drop-Out', as Barney promptly named her.

Good news, but an additional anxiety. Foxes and polecats had now been added to the hazards faced by our charges. But no fox or mustelid made the attempt. Prudently, perhaps. A five-week-old eyas is as big as its parents and its talons are beginning to curve and sharpen. By the month's end all three eyasses were handsomely in feather, two of them wing-exercising vigorously on the rim of the nest. (Was this how Drop-Out had dropped? It seems likely.) She, now dwarfing her loving father when he visited her, wing-exercising from the top of the boulder she had made her new home.

But could she contrive to fly from it? We – and she – suspected not, as she demonstrated by fluttering across the heather to a system of minor jagged crags at the foot of the cliffs and spending the morning of 5 June working her way systematically up them until she had 30 feet or more of empty air at her command, then making a competent first flight of 200 yards at 1.15 p.m. We had watched her closely as she plucked up courage in the gusting wind. There had been much ducking and craning, but when the psychological moment arrived she just spread her shapely wings, side-stepped into the moving air and flew. Lovely!

Her brother, promptly named 'Red Barron' by Barney, had been up since the 3rd and had already made an ambitious attempt at a displaying meadow pipit. His other sister, for all her advantages, gave the appearance of being a comparatively timid soul and did not risk flight until 8 June. Not all young peregrines realize that they are birds. Some seem imbued with the notion that the evolutionary step from lizard has still to be taken, and would much prefer some other individual to be first across that terrifying rubicon. Later on, I watched a fledge on a Galloway coastal site in which eyas No. 3, a falcon, lost her nerve after a fine confident flight over the little bay, alighted near the cliff-foot, then struggled up to join her brother and sister at the top using the technique of a green woodpecker climbing a tall forest tree, wailing with misery all the way.

Barney was there to witness the Red Baron's first flight. Bill Race, who had arrived from the United States for the climax of the drama, was watching when the meadow pipit had its near squeak. Margaret and I saw the first flights of Drop-Out and her unenterprising sister. Drop-Out, double-fed, had become a magnificent bird. A suspicion that a moron with a ·22 rifle put a premature end to her as an adult a few years later, on the next occupied territory to the west, saddens me deeply. She was ripe to challenge for the title of finest peregrine falcon in Britain. That site was attended by ill luck. No falcon seemed to last for more than three years and, finally, a whole brood of well grown chicks was blown or sucked from the ledge by an exercising RAF helicopter playing some dicing-with-death game.

Barney, week in week out, remained in close touch with 'our' brood until it dispersed in October. Margaret, Stephen and I joined him for some memorable – and untroubled – days. That is the tangible reward of successful peregrine wardening. The sky offers no other spectacle to equal the aerial play of wild, free, maturing eyasses. In terms of cost incurred and earning opportunities forgone, I valued the fledged eyasses at £600 each, not a negligible figure in 1975. Be that as it may, I considered the investment a sound one.

nine A SLANDER WITHDRAWN

When Barney, I and one or two new helpers assembled at the rock to begin the 1976 season, one thing struck us immediately with some force. In place of the 'funny little tiercel' we now found a broad-breasted fellow in residence who looked half-a-pound heavier, although still as blue-mantled as the bird there in the previous year.

Soon we had a visit from a friendly NCC officer, making his annual search for kites' nests. He had travelled from his home on a nature reserve some way to the south, where he too had one of the few surviving pairs of peregrines nesting. 'Do you think', he enquired casually, 'that tiercels continue to grow after they have begun to breed? If not,' he continued, 'I lose mine every winter. About this time, I always see the falcon with a bigger mate.'

As the tiercel we were watching resembled the 1975 incumbent in all respects except bulk, we provisionally allotted him a new name – Boy Blue – and reserved final judgement. The pair had moved 200 yards along the cliffs to a long narrow ledge unprotected by any worthwhile overhang to keep off vertically falling rain, sleet or snow, but which was nevertheless invisible to eyes looking down from the cliff-top above.

Again, incubation began early in the fourth week of March, to be followed by a pattern of events familiar from the previous year, but with one marked change. The spasmodic antagonism which had been shown towards the neighbouring ravens in 1975 had by March 1976 blossomed out into an evidently rabid detestation. One could not guess the reason for it. The behaviour of the ravens gave evidence of no significant change, although they had littered the top of the old nest the peregrines had used in 1975 with a jumble of broken branches, some of them thick enough to serve as a walking-stick for a man. Barney had watched them at the work a week or two earlier. The peregrines might have been inconvenienced, but as they had not interfered with the operation while Barney was watching it seemed hardly enough to justify a declaration of war. Yet on 19 April the falcon launched upon one of the ravens the most savage attack we had seen her make on anything. The first stoop knocked it to the ground; the next twenty kept it imprisoned under a projecting slab of rock beneath which it had sought refuge, offering its tormentor four inches of lifted dagger bill to eviscerate herself upon, but nothing vulnerable to strike at. 1976 was shaping up violently, but the participants in the conflict appeared well matched.

So they did on 5 May, when both peregrines made a set-piece attack on both ravens for no apparent reason, bursting away small puffs of black feathers several times to dance on the breeze, but doing no greater damage. Then came 8 May, when violence reached its peak, although not its conclusion. A 'Red Alert' first thing in the morning set the scene. Two parties of chick thieves were reported to have arrived in the county. The next twist was given to the screw by the fox, whose successful theft of a cached pigeon had started the trouble on 19 April, by exploding the falcon's short-fused temper.

Conversation with a shepherd had established that she was a vixen, widowed in a recent fox drive, with cubs in a deep earth at the foot of the cliffs. Desperate for food, she gave evidence of the fact that morning by clearing out an accessible kestrels' nest in minor rocks half-way up the bank, starting with a sitting hen too bold for her own good. That snack accommo-dated by her litter down under the cliff, she surfaced again to ring the bell for round two. Her target this time was the remains of a pigeon the falcon had cached on a high larder, but not high enough to be fox-proof. But it was a

A SLANDER WITHDRAWN

hundred yards from the mouth of the earth, and the way back was exposed. A battle royal developed. Falcon and tiercel, up on pitch at the first glimpse of the vixen, plummeted down in turn – falcon, tiercel; falcon, tiercel; falcon, tiercel – again and again, as the animal cast about for a safer route, turning at bay a very few yards to flatten herself in the heather and raise her mask to snap, snap, snap defiance at her tormentors' terrifying stoops, stoops which terrified the spectators down by the road from concern for the audacious peregrines as they clearly intimidated the victim, rightly fearful for her scalp, spine and eyes. As the falcon zoomed back to pitch after her final reckless stoop, the vixen, by now in the mouth of her earth, seized the opportunity to turn and dive in. The following tiercel clawed one fistful of fur from the disappearing brush; the falcon banked off pitch, stooped to the heather twenty yards from the earth and snatched up the bare girdle of pigeon bone, feather and gristle at the root of the contention, which the vixen had finally been forced to drop.

THE HAWKWATCHER

Its return to the larder did not assuage the falcon's fury. Dropping to a favourite pinnacle from which her scrape on the long ledge could be seen, she surveyed the valley. Rasping as she took off, the falcon sped to expedite the departure of two crows already hurrying out of trouble. As she returned one of the ravens, for reasons unknown, chose this unpropitious moment to fly along the face of the cliffs. With a bang which, down on the road in the unusually still air of that morning, sounded like hands smartly clapped, she struck it between the wing-roots to send it fluttering down into the heather like a broken mechanical toy. It did not rise and we did not see a pair of ravens on the site again until towards the end of the season.

The survivor continued to feed the raven brood in the concealed nest the pair had built newly that year in a big horizontal gash in the lower rocks near where the vixen had destroyed the kestrel site, but Madame had not yet finished with the ravens.

On 16 May she attempted to complete the orphaning operation begun eight days earlier. The incoming surviving parent was knocked out of the air base over apex three times in rapid succession, to end up on the road by the cars, blinking, dishevelled and limping painfully as it gathered its faculties to resume work. Nature being notoriously hard on losers, a posse of carrion crows tried to complete the falcon's self-imposed task when the poor raven reached the dead sheep on the hill across the lake to shear off another cropful of minced carrion mutton for its voracious brood. In the end, the falcon did not fulfil her ambition. The raven stuck to its guns, kept a warier look-out and finally attracted a new mate which, in the final stages, worked just as hard for the welfare of the brood as the slain natural parent had done. In some ways, the morality of birds can put ours to shame, except when we live up to the very highest of our aspirations.

The fox nuisance did not end there. May 19th developed into a day hot enough for July. As west-facing eyries are exposed to the afternoon sun and peregrine chicks in down are vulnerable to its burning rays (a fact of which their mothers seem perfectly well aware), the falcon stood that afternoon facing inwards, wings extended to form a spreading sunshade under whose shadow the chicks would find protection. There could not have been a worse time for an 'innocent' intrusion to take place.

Having suffered five of these since 11 April, when the first pair of trippers attempted a climb to the foot of the cliffs to improve their view of the valley, we were on the alert. This time, though, it was no tourist, willing to come down for a blast on a whistle and a shouted request. An elderly farmer from the head of the valley, accompanied by a younger man and five shaggy Welsh foxhounds, came into view from the left, already on the hill and pursuing a diagonal bee-line which must bring them to the foot of the cliffs if they persisted in it. Persist they did, plodding on impervious to whistle blasts, a chorus of shouts and a waving thumb-stick. Clad fittingly for November, they soon felt the heat, halted, laid down the spade and sack they had been carrying, collapsed onto a pile of boulders by the earth and fished out a packet of cigarettes. Soon they were smoking in contented relaxation oblivious to the fortissimo rasping of the falcon and tiercel as they circled anxiously overhead, or indifferent to it. By now the peregrine guard had become something of a social magnet for local people in sympathy with its aims, so there was quite a gathering assembled by the parked cars – hence the chorus of shouts. More of these having been ignored as studiously as the first, I decided that the time had come for someone to go up and see what might be achieved at shorter range before we troubled the police.

Younger men present having declined the invitation, the task fell to me. Fair enough – it was, after all, my idea. The bank is steep; I am no stripling. Eventually, though, I arrived at eye-level with my adversaries' belt-buckles. Explanatory appeal was met by dogmatic assertion of traditional rights (illusory in the circumstances) and a flat refusal to budge. How long might it take to dig down as far as they wished, to deposit the strychnined stillborn lamb I could see they had in the sack? Grunts. They had forgotten the crowbar, so it might take 'four hours, maybe'. I restated the legal position, forcefully. A murmur in Welsh brought the most hostile of the dogs, its larynx rumbling, its teeth bared, to where my throat was within easy reach. The younger man grinned vacuously.

THE HAWKWATCHER

What to do now? Seized by a sudden happy inspiration, I uttered a snarling roar, lunged at the dog's face with mouth agape and ginger moustache abristle. I have rarely seen two men more taken aback or a dog go into reverse more expeditiously. Turning round, I called down. 'OK, Barney,' I bellowed, 'go and phone for the police.' There are hill-men in Wales who do not welcome Authority poking a nose into their concerns. The senior intruder being of this persuasion, the incident was over.

With me and the intruders on the way down (now chatting amicably), the falcon was soon back on sunshading duty. While the altercation was in progress, cloud to veil the torrid sun had been sent by Jehovah, Horus or whatever other minor Divinity is deputed to keep a watchful eye on the welfare of genus *Falco*. The chicks remained unscorched and something else had been gained, too – heightened local suspicions that I was a man on the borders of dangerous lunacy, which stood me in excellent stead thereafter throughout all my eyrie-protection adventures in central Wales.

Otherwise, though, it had all been in vain. The following Sunday exhaustion at last overtook me, with fatal consequences. Days spent with eyes kept skinned for fifteen hours or more in the twenty-four, following and succeeded by even the minimum of domestic chores demanded by eating, sleeping and keeping a billet decent, take their toll. My alarm clock performed its duty at 5 a.m. on 23 May. Switching it off without taking the precaution of putting my feet on the cold floor first, I fell asleep again immediately to dream a vivid dream of rising, dressing quickly and driving swiftly to the site. When next I awoke it was an hour later. Knowing in my bones the scale of my offence, I took only ten minutes to drive the twelve miles to the lay-by.

But for the soft cooing of ring doves in the oak wood across the lake, all, on the face of it, was as peaceful as a sunny May morning in a remote Welsh valley ought to be. Searching the rocks, I found the falcon on a familiar crag. Fluffed out and relaxed, she was engaged in plucking small white contour feathers from her breast. Falcons begin the annual body-moult while they incubate. A big red Mercedes saloon approached, its crew of four turning to smirk at me as they drove by. So what? Fishermen often came early, and as often smiled, from friendliness or in derision. The falcon continued to preen. Little – if anything – comes higher on a peregrine's scale of priorities. Feathers are not only its heat-retention and ventilation system; the major ones are the tools of its trade.

Four hours went peacefully by. Then two characters I did not fancy the look of walked by along the embankment without a 'good morning'. Odd. I climbed the fence and followed at a discreet distance until satisfied that their plans did not include crossing the road out of my view where I sat by the car, to climb to the cliffs or behind them.

The peregrines had remained quiet and inactive. Again, no great cause for surprise. Saturday had been a big pigeon-racing day, with enough casualties inflicted on the passing flights to feed the family for a week. All known larders up on the rocks were well stored. When I returned from my surveillance stroll, though, the falcon was no longer on view, but a fresh pile of plucked pigeon feathers caught my eye. At 11.20, there came a deafening burst of 'squi-clucking' from the ledge. It was repeated. Ten minutes later, the falcon emerged bearing a white pigeon, apparently intact, showing not a trace of blood or torn flesh. Then the tiercel came in, calling. The eyasses, whose juvenile 'squeeps' we had been hearing for several days by then, made no response. Still asleep, I assumed, gorged into insensibility on yesterday's gargantuan provision.

People began to arrive – Barney, the usual weekend collection of RSPB members who had heard of the site, the guard. They had come to be innocently entertained. Pigeons began to fly through the valley again. The peregrines pursued and broke up formations, but did not press home their attacks. No pigeon died to swell the larder of cached kills spread among the minor crags and little grassy platforms among the rocks. The day wore pleasantly on to mid-afternoon, but still no kill had been carried to the ledge and consumed with the expected ceremonies. The earth's daily travel caused shadow to be cast on some previously well lit features up on the rocks, but brought others more positively into the sun's full light. Among these latter was an oak tree growing from the rock directly above the peregrines' ledge. From it there now hung a length of blue climbing rope never noticed before.

Had the ledge been visible from the crest of the cliffs, I should have gone up earlier, just to check that the long fast had no sinister implications. I went up now, accompanied by a young friend from over the Montgomeryshire border who had recently joined the guard force. We found the rope, faded and frayed, one end lying near an old staple hammered into the cliff-top by climbers of an earlier generation, but unattached. We pulled on the rope, to find the other end trapped somewhere out of sight below the oak. Hoping that it was connected to the broken-necked body of a peregrine-thief, we left matters at that, for the time being, and went down to report. All felt uneasy, but no one was convinced that the time had come to sound a formal alarm. Minds went back to earlier false alarms, the exaggerated fuss I made over the 1975 'Drop Out', and so on. Only one aspect of matters really disquieted us – the cessation of the usual feeding programme. Tomorrow should right that.

It did not. Again the falcon took in kills, called the command to feed at the top of her voice, brought the prey out intact. Next, falcon and tiercel visited various ledges together, with kills, calling and calling, as though no longer sure which of the ledges was the one where their young should be. It was obvious now that they had lost them. To pigeon fanciers, I at that stage presumed, who had found some way of dropping a poisoned bait to the ledge. The peregrines had not exactly refrained from offering provocation. Authority, sceptical of my conjectures, was consulted and in due course a trained rock climber arrived. His descent (which I did not envy him in a wind risen to gale force) established an empty ledge and no remaining trace of chicks, dead or alive. There had been chicks, we knew for certain. Small white wing-limbs raised in exercise had been seen several times and unmistakable voices heard.

Did we need to see and hear these things to be sure? Yes, we did, and later experience was to prove us correct in taking this view. While the carrying of kills to the eyrie ledge by the falcon at the right stage in the cycle spells chicks surely enough for the assumption to be safely made in 99 cases out of 100, one cannot rule out completely the possibility of a sterile or damaged falcon experiencing the avian equivalent of something known all too well to dog breeders – phantom pregnancy. In a later chapter, a tale will be told with a bearing on this.

The robbed tiercel demonstrated shock by moulting major quills several at a time, as I have heard that canaries sometimes do when shocked deeply by a determined attack on the cage by a cat. I returned home for a few days, sadder, wiser and shamed.

Educationally, there were compensations. I had now learned the appalling fact that the birds themselves could not be depended on to signal robbery, an assumption on which my tactics had placed great reliance. While they may rasp angrily for an hour or more when disturbed by the mere sight of a fox, it seemed that a falcon could relax calmly by a robbed ledge as soon as the biped robbers had gone from her view. In that and in other ways, major deficiencies had been exposed in the peregrine's capacity to relate cause and effect. Were they, after all, no more than feathered lizards with wings and warm blood, as some scientists were then asserting? My mind turned to bereaved human mothers I had heard of visiting missing cots in empty bedrooms weeks after a funeral; to the exultant aerobatics flown by the bird once known as the 'funny little tiercel' when first he set eyes on a brood of newly hatched chicks; to his unbelievably ragged silhouette 72 hours after their loss. If peregrines are no more than feathered lizards, are we more than apes in skirts or trousers?

I had learned two other salient facts. To demand too much of oneself physically is to invite disaster. Now I knew as never before why an army needs eight men or more behind the front line to keep one man in it. Following on from that, I had to recognize that the brunt of a dawn-to-dusk peregrine guard could not be borne by one man unless he literally lived by the rocks. His water and food must be supplied to him, or he must be relieved to fetch them himself; without a caravan, his bed must be a seat in his car. Future success was going to demand an acceptance of a higher level of discomfort and privation than had ever been foreseen. Like 1974 in Galloway, 1975 in Wales had been only a playing of romantic games.

While I sat in my garden in Worcestershire mulling over these conclusions, Fate was playing her own hand. In a little place called Aberedw I had a friend, a fine naturalist and expert wildlife photographer, who ran classes under the auspices of a county trust. On 26 May he phoned me. 'I think I know where your stolen peregrines are,' he announced. 'They have been heard calling in a house next door to the aunt of one of my ex-pupils. He's just called to tell me about it.' A quick call to the appropriate police station soon established that a big red Mercedes was parked outside that house. Before the 1981 Wildlife & Countryside Act came into force, the law which nominally protected birds was wrapped in red tape and creaked painfully when called into action. While a magistrate puzzled with knotted brow to discover how far his writ to issue a search warrant ran in such circumstances, the red Mercedes left for London. Rumour credited a police car with a capture missed by inches near Watford after more than 100 miles of pursuit, but that was the end of the 1976 story. Bill Race arrived from the United States just in time to receive the bad news, adding one more touch of irony to the unhappy situation. There was one compensation, though: the identity of our enemy was no longer a mystery. It was not, after all, the knee-capper, nor had it been anyone figuring in the Red Alert of 8 May, but it was a man – a much younger man – known well enough to the police in other connections.

Encouraged by his success, he came again in 1977, making another dawn raid and taking three chicks still in down from the eyrie the pair had established on the other face of the feature, much nearer to the old landmark. This time, I did not operate alone but in support of two paid full-time wardens. The 1976 robbery had stimulated interest and some anger throughout the county.

The 1977 raid failed. The delinquents were captured, the chicks, one male and two female, recovered after a long and stuffy ordeal concealed in an abandoned railway tunnel. One female had been left in the scrape 'for us', as the thief self-righteously protested when Fate gave me the opportunity for a few pointed words with him face to face. The little tiercel and one of his sisters fledged successfully ten days after their adventure; what became of eyasses three and four remained a mystery. After his conviction, the delinquent boasted of a return to the hillside after dark one night and failure turned into success. Lies being part and parcel of his kind's stock-in-trade, no one was impressed. We judged it likelier after noise was heard from the rocks after dark one night that foxes had taken advantage of a premature dispersal and halved the brood. The detestation foxes inspire in peregrines is not a matter of mere superstition and the character of the 1977 site – just a scrape behind a big rectangular boulder on the hillside – enabled the eyasses to stray from it by use of nothing but their feet.

The following year found the pair back on the big cliffs, where they reared two eyas tiercels again under full-time paid wardening with volunteer support. In 1979 they returned to 'Rowan Rock', as we named the hump on the hillside housing the scrape from which their young had been taken in 1977. Once more, paid and volunteer help collaborated to achieve success. Three eyasses flew without interference.

By 1980 the peregrine recovery had advanced too far for a case for further funding to be made out. But not for the volunteer group to stand down – by then, these peregrines had become part of our social circle, friends we could not desert without a sense of betrayal. Barney kept in weekly touch with them and as each season began the first preoccupation was anxious scrutiny of silhouettes in the sky, of patterns of thoracic decoration and the tints the sun drew from the mantles of birds in motion against backgrounds of rock and heather, to satisfy ourselves that our friends were still the peregrines in possession. Barney would always have an opinion after his winter watching, but was always anxious for confirmation.

Each season brought its own crop of excitements, novelties and titbits unreflected in the textbooks, extending and broadening our experience of the species, some more memorably than others. The tiercel, passing over at 1,000 feet one morning, dropped the connected wings of a consumed ring ouzel at my very feet, feathers most handy for use in the Greenwell's Glory trout fly and obtainable at that time by no other lawful means I can readily bring to mind. One fine afternoon we saw him clumsily knock the tail-end charlie of a starling flock into the lake, then descend like an osprey to retrieve it successfully without wetting a feather. On a cup-final day I recall a group of us clustered about a car with the radio switched on, but with our attention on the tiercel high in the sky, closing on a pigeon. Grab; lose; grab again; lose again – with our spectators' cries of 'Oh! Oh! Oh! Oh!' emitted in strict time with the wails and roars of the Wembley crowd as the ball struck the crossbar, rebounded, was shot in again and misfielded by the goalkeeper. Others in earshot, tuned in to other car radios, had no notion that our excitement had a separate origin.

On one day of ferocious wind, he, too, had his private adventure with ravens. A white pigeon forced its way desperately into the gale, Boy Blue struggling as hard to close the gap, both birds pinned to the grey sky like china ducks to a suburban wall. Finally, after what seemed to us below like an eternity, he made it and his talons closed on flesh. Labouring down with it (a domestic pigeon is no insignificant burden for a tiercel), he chose for his landfall a spot on the shoulder opposite where a pair of ravens had been busy for several minutes beetle hunting, out of sight in deep heather. Such was the mutual shock that the tiercel's toes spread involuntarily and the hard-won pigeon esaped with its life, whirled to safety before its captor could get back into the air. By the time he did, the ravens were ahead of him, fleeing in horror. Letting the wind carry him like a dead leaf to an attacking station, the tiercel furled all canvas, fell like a bullet behind the second raven, rocketed up in a looping hook and bound to its breast to be given a lift by it upside down with wings hanging for fifty yards or more. On breaking away, he obviously felt better, but I cannot speak for the raven. It survived the grip, but I should dearly like to study autopsy reports on all the peregrine's larger neighbours in some upland valley, irrespective of how they met their ultimate fates. The healed wounds I should be sure of reading about would hint at fascinating histories.

Textbooks tell of peregrines evolved for service in open skies above country equally open. True, I am sure, yet there came an evening when we watched this pair scrambling about like monkeys in the bare branches of a budding oak, attempting to grasp or flush a pigeon which had taken doubtful refuge there. The length of their wings seemed small handicap. And when one year we visited a scrape after the eyasses had flown, we retrieved the plumage of the woodland-haunting great spotted woodpecker for inspection with the rest.

I made one midwinter visit when by pure coincidence five voluntary wardens chose the same day to renew acquaintance with their charges. The falcon, perched on a favourite crag when the final arrival drove in, took a hard and knowing look at the assembled cars, flew down to her previous season's scrape and settled down on it. 'Ah well!' she seemed to say, 'if *they* are all here again, it *must* be the nesting season, whatever the negative messages I am getting from my biological clock.'

After her raven slaughter in 1976, the falcon grew no less formidable. On 28 March 1978 she relieved feelings after a long drenching so heavy that skin showed through her saturated body plumage by dragging a kite out of the sky by one wing to suffer more damage out of sight behind a skyline, resulting in a sadly disfigured flight profile when it was seen in the sky again on the following day. There were less dramatic incidents, no less memorable in their own way. I arrived to meet Barney on one midwinter's day in snow bad enough for a Radnorshire spring, dismounting from the car just as a flight of pochard passed over at about 500 feet. Boy Blue launched himself from his crag, clawed up towards them, vanished into the base of the snow cloud at the tail of the formation to provide as aesthetically pleasing a spectacle as any a peregrine has ever favoured me with anywhere in Britain. How I longed for a palette and brushes – and the skill to employ them! One of hawk watching's golden memories, to say the least of it.

The peak year for Boy Blue and his ferocious mate was 1980, with four eyasses elegantly on the wing on 14 June; their laying date, having since 1975 retreated from 21 March to 1 April in step with the climatic conditions of the early springs, had begun to advance again. There had been another attempt

THE HAWKWATCHER

at robbery – at dusk this time – thwarted with heroic panache and determination by a single-handed volunteer sentry living in a tent on the hill. It was the young Welsh friend who had been stationed with me above the colonel's eyrie on the night of 28 May 1977, morally armed to die – or kill, at need – for the right of peregrine falcons to breed in Wales without criminal interference. No hand was laid on an eyas; three guilty intruders faced charges and conviction, but whether fines were ever actually paid I cannot say. There we come to the Achilles' heel of the present wild bird protection measures. Pleading his way out of paying is a vital part of the skills package of the professional law-breaker. Until society nerves itself to confront that fact with brutal realism, the law will figure in our affairs chiefly as a lucrative profession for lawyers, and as little besides.

Broods of four peregrine eyasses are usually of mixed sex. This one in 1980 was not. All were tiercels, one of whom was sadly destined to cast light at last on where the young mid-Welsh peregrines might travel in the months between brood dispersal in the autumn and their return the following spring for aerial play with their father before the falcon's territorial imperatives drive her to break up the fun amid astonished wails from the children she had once loved and tended so solicitously.

In April 1981 we saw only three 'red hawks' (as falconers term the immatures) playing above the rocks. Later that year, news came from the British Trust for Ornithology that the leg-ring which had been fitted to the fourth eyas before he fledged had been retrieved from a lead-riddled cadaver found decaying on Bodmin Moor in Cornwall in January that year.

That was the last brood of eyasses this pair of peregrines fledged. Happily, Bill Race arrived from across the Atlantic to be among those who enjoyed their aerial antics. In 1980 I gave 340 hours of my time to the pair, by day and by night, fitted in between other duties on the sites to the north and to the south. I did not grudge those hours at the time; I rejoice in my recollection of them now. From the three sites, nine young peregrines flew.

In 1981 the falcon appeared to have laid in a deserted buzzard's nest on the wall of a gully between the landmark and the point of the spur. An

130

unseasonable blizzard on the night of 25 April immured her and closed the road to traffic for three days. By the time we could get through, the nest was abandoned and the peregrines behaving as though the breeding season lay six months ahead. At the assumed disturbance of eggs, as opposed to loss of chicks, the peregrines displayed no distress detectable by the human eye.

By 1982 Barney had become too sick a man to play a large part in a wardening operation. His heart was on the way out and the shock of witnessing a disturbance to his beloved birds could have been enough to arrest its beating irreversibly. Bewilderment and associated anxiety were in themselves almost enough to do that as the falcon gave ledge after ledge on the feature sufficient sampling to convince at least one of us that eggs had been laid on one rather than another. Matters were gravely complicated by the arrival of another falcon in 1981 – a bird of distinctively harsh voice and so distinctive an appearance that she fully justified the name of Dusky that Barney soon wished on her. She tried to establish a separate territory on the tall cliffs round the corner and alienate the affections of a tiercel whose blue mantle had always exerted a fatal fascination on the susceptibilities of the opposite sex.

In 1982 Barney saw a falcon fight in Buzzard Gully which ended with a wrestling match on the actual nest, which must have shattered any eggs then present. It upset him so thoroughly that he abandoned his watch there and then. Whatever happened at that nest, no eyasses flew from those rocks that year either.

On the morning of 13 July Barney phoned a friend to say that he felt very ill. She made all speed, but by the time she reached his flat he lay dead on his kitchen floor, a pot of tea half made. An admirable life had come to an end more merciful than some. The peregrines – and I – had lost an irreplaceable friend.

The pair we had watched so happily together for so many years were still in occupation of their territory in 1983, again giving indications of an intention to raise a family on Rowan Rock. A ewe and lamb strolling through the scrape while the falcon watched without protest from a rock above on a date when chicks should have been active there confirmed the suspicions we had already formed that the intention had not been fulfilled. These peregrines were no longer young. Not that too much could be made of that, because the spring weather of that year with its cold rain from the east caused many peregrines to fail, throughout Britain. Peregrines select ledges on the assumption that the wet winds will blow from the west.

On 24 March 1984 the falcon gave me my final view of her. I was across the lake, telescope trained on Rowan Rock. She sat preening on a small crag. Suddenly she turned her fine head, stared hard, took off and flew across the lake. She alighted on a jutting rock twenty feet above me, craned, uttered soft 'squi-clucks', the conversational tones used inside the family. Soon they hardened to a rasp and she flew away to climb and close with a longer-tailed young falcon which chose that moment to appear in the sky overhead. If a fight followed, I did not see it.

Boy Blue re-mated, probably with the young bird which had disturbed my tête-à-tête with his previous consort. They reared one fine eyas tiercel in a very old and well sheltered ravens' nest situated in full view of a water authority establishment manned twenty-four hours a day by men who were interested in the peregrines' welfare. He lost her in circumstances unknown in 1985, during which season I saw him several times, appearing quite contented with his unmated status, burning off energy by breaking up pigeon flights for sport.

I saw him for the last time in March 1986, flying like a champion, still bluer of mantle than some cock merlins. In March 1987 the rocks were occupied by a dingy little tiercel scarcely out of his rompers and an unfamiliar falcon showing a breast white enough to figure in soap powder advertisements. An era had ended: an era had begun. I had no great wish to be part of the new one. As many will remember, the winter of 1986–7 included some bitterly cold spells and the usual number of wintering thrushes was much reduced. They, I strongly suspect, are a vital source of winter sustenance for inland peregrines in Wales.

The date at which the old falcon vanished from the scene implied the mercy of a death in battle with pulses racing fiercely to the very end. For the tiercel, though, I see no such termination. The mind's eye pictures a figure stripped of its muscle by hunger, huddled on some familiar crag in frozen moonlight, feathers full-fluffed for insulation but now to no real purpose. Blood thickens; pulse rate drops and drops yet further. Soon after first light a raven examines with caution the iron-hard thing on the scree a starving fox has already nosed, attempted to bite, rejected in disgust with a whimper. A ray from the risen sun catches a reflection in an eye still luminous beneath its coating of ice. The raven croaks in alarm, backs away, decides on a policy of safety first, takes to its creaking wings.

All that remains on earth of a tiercel once called funny and little is allowed, for that morning at least, to lie in state, resting in peace.

ten # WATCHING THE
SUMMER MIGRANT

Fate ordained a poultice for the after-pain of that miserable 1976 failure in Wales. A pair of hobbies applied it in July of that year by hatching chicks in a highly visible tree on the Warwickshire shooting estate within half an hour's drive of home where so much of my local bird watching is done.

The hobby, like all other raptors except the kestrel, had first arrested my attention from the pages of a book, Kirkman and Jourdain's *British Birds*, which gave all the essential information then available, including the hobby's unique status as our only summer-visiting falcon, its reputation for hunting prey as remarkable as swallow, swift and martin, and the fact (or factoid) that no use had ever been made of the bird in falconry.

Enough, for sure, to mark the hobby for a special place in my affections when and if I should ever encounter one in the living flesh. That book was discovered in 1936, when the bird was widely believed to limit its presence in Britain not only to the summertime but also geographically to the counties which – by and large – lie south of the River Thames. The first rumour of hobbies nesting in my own county, Worcestershire, came my way in 1964. In 1965 I was shown the site, a straggling plantation of unspectacular birch and leggy oak, but the tree occupied in 1964 had been felled soon after the brood fledged.

No hobbies came to the wood in 1965. This I attributed (mistakenly I am now certain) to the loss of the tree. I was destined to learn that while hobbies in the Midlands may be faithful to an area they are not so to a particular wood, much less to a particular tree. In this they are governed by the nest-building habits of crows, whose structures they take over after the crows have finished with them, and by the survival prospects of corvine architecture through a wet and windy winter after a brood of hobby chicks has added to the dilapidations inflicted by the crow family as chicks hatched, grew fat and picked at the building materials to alleviate boredom.

Systematic visits paid to Salisbury Plain and the New Forest (the classical hobby country in Britain) while the local pair had nested unknown to me twenty miles away, and more made in the years which followed immediately afterwards, proved fruitless. In this there was a reflection of hopes and expectations disappointed twenty years and more earlier, when every 'hobby' glimpsed above the Plain from the turret of my tank during training exercises there had turned promptly into a kestrel as soon as binoculars were trained and focused on it.

The breakthrough came in 1970. First, on my North Devon cliffs, when the first hobby of my life did its species no credit by fleeing ignominiously before a kestrel enraged by trespass on its territory; second, over my lower Wye valley hill, when the hobby, coming presumably from the Forest of Dean nearby, gave a mixed flock of wheeling swifts and sand martins the shock of their lives by 'stooping' about a hundred feet *vertically upwards* into their midst with wings closed right in to its body, an aerobatic tactic only the hobby, in my experience, attempts or, perhaps, is capable of, starting from level flight.

After that, hobbies began to haunt me. At Draycote Reservoir in Warwickshire; on the Long Mynd in Shropshire; at Blenheim; on the Warwickshire estate where they eventually nested; even on Salisbury Plain, where I still went occasionally in deliberate search of them. A strong fancy for seeing a species in the surroundings I had been taught to regard as traditionally typical had long had an influence on where I preferred to take my binoculars for a day out.

One of those expeditions to the Plain was unforgettable. A well shaken grapevine had yielded fruit. The place to find hobbies there in that year, went the message, was the Army small-arms range at Bulford. Was one allowed in? Yes, there was limited public access – but keep a weather eye open for red flags at the hoist.

The range flagpoles were bare when I drove in, drove on and pulled off the track under a small stand of pines. The view was downhill to the bed of an almost dried-out watercourse, then north-west across gently rising heathland to the skyline a mile away. Rough grass, heather and bracken mingled to form a broken sward; pine and juniper grew up through it sparsely; the course of the empty river was lined with fine old deciduous trees. Linnets twittered from clumps of tall gorse; from somewhere at hand a quail called 'wet my lips', the first I had ever heard in England. With the June sun shining mildly through high thin cloud, the omens seemed propitious.

The first hobby of the afternoon appeared in the sky unheralded, towards the horizon, where it performed for ten minutes a display of ground-buzzing I have never seen equalled since for speed, dash, scope, or aerobatic virtuosity. That, I was told later, is often the way in which Salisbury Plain hobbies crop fox moths in early June as the insects flit about low over the heather from which they hatch. Lepidopterists' reference books make much of the speed of this moth's flight, which, perhaps, has some bearing on this dramatic style of hunting them.

I sat, as usual, under the raised tail-gate of my car, parked where it would command the best view in at least one direction. After a half-hour lull following the flying display, a long-winged dark-backed bird appeared suddenly at shoulder height (a sitting man's shoulder height) from behind the sheltering pines, made for a split second as though to squeeze past me and enter the car, thought better of it, turned to fly on for a further fifty yards, then swept up to perch on the top of a trackside juniper. Only a cuckoo, I thought, as I raised the glasses to take a look at the surprisingly erect bird topping the small tree, could be daft enough to fly into a car with a man sitting by it. The binoculars disclosed scarlet tibials and a handsomely aquiline masked face terminating in an unmistakably hooked bill. Not

Soaring goshawk over clear-felled forest (see page 220)

Merlins in a moorland valley (see page 229)

imbecility, after all – audacity. I was looking at my first perched hobby. A splendid sight.

Taking a walk towards the skyline a little later, I put up another from high in the crown of one of the elms by the empty river. This one flew away without haste, employing a relaxed beat of its long angled wings which recalled the style of a black-headed gull. I was living and learning. I returned to the car to resume my static watch.

The 'pop-pop-popping' of machine-guns from somewhere behind had recently become a part of the background to a peaceful day, to be ignored as far as possible. Suddenly, though, with a rattle, crash, patter and the 'smack-smack-smack' of bullets passing not far overhead, severed débris from the branches and twigs of a well-hit pine tree came showering down on both car and over-relaxed driver.

Someone, it seemed, had run up the red flag in ignorance of my hidden presence behind the pines and someone else had aimed his machine-gun at the wrong target, sending a burst of fire outside the limits imposed theoretically by the stout brick bunker standing behind the official targets to prevent such excitements. Time to depart, perhaps? Yes, but I did not get far. Within 600 yards, I ran almost axle-deep into unexpected mud. It was as well that I am competent at unbogging vehicles. More random bursts of fire cracking by a little farther away at intervals provided any extra incentive I needed to press me into getting on with the job. As I said before, the day was an unforgettable one.

Back to Warwickshire and more placid hobby watching in the year of that miserable failure in Wales. It was the third in which I had seen hobbies over the estate, as well as the third year, as I was to learn later, in which they were known to have nested somewhere in the vicinity.

On 13 July I saw one shift a gear above the ridge haunted by all the raptors there to race away from mobbing swifts at a speed which left the pursuers standing; on 3 August the nest was found in a dying hedgerow elm by licensed BTO ringers I had alerted. The elm was climbed and three fat chicks in smokey-blue down were decorated with permanent means of individual identification, valuable should they ever be so unfortunate as to come to hand later in life. One of them, in fact, did – on Portland Bill the following spring, almost fatally emaciated after its first journey (other than as genetic material) from Africa. Prompt veterinary help gave it a second chance to attempt survival. Its career, to say the least of it, had been chequered from the outset.

The elm of its hatching was a tall one and, as mentioned, fatally infected at the time. The nest, a crows', into the exposed bulk of which the keeper had emptied his gun unavailingly a number of times while its builders were in residence, had not gone unscathed. The young crows had suffered no proven damage, but the foundations of the structure had been loosened fatally. When I watched the robust second occupants moving repeatedly to the edge to exercise their wing-limbs on the afternoon of 8 August, I noted with apprehension that the platform of no more than barely adequate size had developed a marked tilt.

My visit of 10 August produced no view of young moving on the nest, or of a parent visiting with prey. The same on 12 August, by when a further complication had been added. Beyond the hedgerow in which the elm stood, wheat had been harvested, leaving an aftermath of short stubble and straw bales scattered about the field. Something down there was preoccupying the parent birds, both of which made repeated stoops at some point on the ground obscured by the hedgerow vegetation.

They had one preoccupation; I, another, which blinded me for several days to a fact which should have been obvious far sooner. The excitement of having nesting hobbies to watch had been heightened by the arrival on the scene of two new and unfamiliar raptors which hovered at times like kestrels, were not quite the colour of hen kestrels, had profiles in flight more strongly resembling those of the hobbies and a marked – and fully reciprocated – inclination to fight with the hobbies.

Time and closer views of these birds established them to be red-footed falcons, mature and immature females, presumed to be mother and daughter strayed unaccountably after the year's fledge from some home in the Balkans, as some do in most years. As no male was ever seen (and there is no bird of prey on the European list easier to identify with certainty), we did not suspect the local nesting which, had it taken place, would have been an ornithological event to put the affairs of the hobbies completely in the shade.

However, these attractive strangers and the identification task they presented to us took all eyes off the other ball until 13 August, and mine until 15 August, the day I was told of a visit by the BTO group on the 13th, when the nest was found to be tilted yet further and empty. Beneath it in the stubble lay the scattered remnants of one well-feathering young hobby, and one of the others, alive and apparently well, perched somewhat insecurely along a branch of a small crab-apple which stood as the elm's insignificant neighbour in the long hedgerow. Of the third nestling, no trace could be found.

Hobby nestlings not being a common target of bird thieves (the eggs are a different matter), the watch until then had been a relaxed affair, conducted for instruction and pleasure. Now the tensions of the failed peregrine operation entered the equation. The surviving hobby 'nestling' – or 'branchling'? – might not be under threat from human neighbours, but how about foxes, if it should happen to fall farther? And what of stoats, if it should not? Stoats, I knew, were perfectly capable of climbing a tree the size of the crab-apple. Something, most probably a fox, had killed and dismembered the youngster whose remnants had been found.

Something had to be done. The trunk of the crab-apple leaned for ease of climbing, but not so invitingly after I had done a morning's work with coiled scrap barbed wire and timber from a broken and discarded gate in the field. A ditch gave concealed access from two directions for any vulpine or mustelid prowler. It did so less attractively after I had established my 'cordon insanitaire'. The great-nephew of gamekeepers had learned early in life that a man's bladder provides something in fair abundance which can be made to form a line which Britain's small mammalian predators do not cross with easy minds and unalerted instincts. Additional to these precautions, a more formal watch was set up in case boys wandering on a nominally harmless trespass from the nearby village should spot the feathery lump with eyes in the crab-apple and overcome the obstructions rigged to obtain an unusual pet. The minutiae of the law protecting birds is neither universally known nor universally respected, even by the commonly law-abiding.

So my reference earlier to the chequered character of the young hobby's history should now be thoroughly appreciated. All, however, turned out well for it at that stage in its story and I had the great pleasure of watching its flight-quills lengthen for a week, and then be put to use on 22 August. Soon the bird was several hundred feet up in the sky, a third target for the ladies from the Balkans.

By the following summer the big elm had died completely, been felled and reduced to ash. The hobbies did not return to the estate. Perhaps discouragement kept them away, because the losses told of here had been their second misfortune in consecutive years, as I learned later. Their nest in the previous year had been in a rookery nearby after the rooks had vacated it. In that nest, though, the builders had woven a length of the twisted orange-coloured cord used these days as binder twine. That year's third nestling had trapped a toe in the frayed twine to remain imprisoned and die of starvation after its siblings had flown. Its withered remains, with a foot still entangled, had been recovered during a rook-ringing expedition. The adult hobby, it seems, is not programmed by instinct to feed nestlings indefinitely simply because they do not leave the nest.

Twenty-four months to the day after the first sighting of that Warwickshire pair, east Worcestershire offered an encore. This pair's site was also a disused crows' nest, one situated not in a hedgerow tree but in an old stag-headed oak, one of a clump among several other stands in fine, well cared for parkland. In France, the hobby bears the word 'hobereau' in its name – 'the country gentleman' – and not by accident, I am certain.

The oaks were bounded on one side by a fence. Within two yards of it stretched one bank of a shallow oblong pond about fifty yards long, densely weeded and highly productive of dragon- and damselflies. A branch project- ing horizontally from the trunk of one of the oaks provided the male hobby with a perfect vantage-point from which to stoop and snatch at the gaudy insects as they took their first (and at times, last) flights. On both Salisbury Plain and the Long Mynd I had wondered whether the distribution of *Odonata* might have a profound influence on the distribution of *Falco subbuteo*; what I was to see on this Worcestershire site strengthened those suspicions. There are a number of similar pools in that parkland, equally productive, taking one year with another. Hobbies bred on or adjacent to it to my certain knowledge in four out of the eight years which followed that first observed nesting.

To my even greater satisfaction, there was good cause to believe them to be the same birds each time. As I have written of peregrines, individuals show idiosyncrasies in plumage and these are usually sufficient (unless some remarkable coincidence intervenes) to identify them to the watcher. All hobbies I have seen at close range have had some degree of pale markings on the nape. Some have a white line, faint or bold, outlining the superciliary ridges above the eyes, usually connecting above the cere. The male of this particular pair had markings on his nape so pronounced that they resembled a mask duplicating his face – hence the name 'Janus' which we gave him – while his mate was so well endowed with superciliary decoration that she received the name 'Whitebrow'.

Textbooks bestow on all adult hobbies bright rusty-red tibial and belly feathers, but nature does not. Some show colour so faint as to be barely gold, which may reflect youth or a genetic factor – even diet, perhaps – but Janus, and Whitebrow even more so, were splendidly tinted in this respect. Why should the reappearances of these birds be so surprising? Could they not be taken for granted? No. Hobbies winter in Central Africa, where the First World's manufacturers of toxic pesticides sell the products the law often denies them the right to distribute at home, often for money provided by UN institutions. As if that was not hazard enough for a bird whose winter diet is almost bound to include locusts, the hobbies' migration routes take them over Mediterranean islands where shooting hawks as they fly in to rest is a traditional 'sport' and mounting the bodies of the smarter-plumaged species for inclusion in domestic décor a profitable business. Perhaps Janus and Whitebrow used a route which took them from Land's End to Mauretania without crossing any dangerous European land, and from there on without meeting half-poisoned locusts.

In the first year we knew them, they fledged two attractive progeny, sex undetermined because, although Whitebrow herself happened to be distinctly larger than her mate, sexual dimorphism in hobbies is not generally pronounced, and often merely marginal. Much of our pleasure in the family was enjoyed after the fledge, as magpies were put ruthlessly in their place, young kestrels of the same vintage happily squabbled with in and above the oaks of their mutual hatching, and the sole fledged offspring of a pair of nearby green woodpeckers sent in frantic haste to the hole in the solitary ash of his hatching from which he emerged under the juvenile hobby eye at his peril. So close was one shave that one of his pointed tail-feathers, designed to be pressed helpfully into the bark of any tree he climbed, came into my collection of avian bric-à-brac via the talon of the young hobby which had extracted it from the young woodpecker's rump with a foot extended just far enough as its victim vanished into sanctuary. The hobby turned and dropped the quill; I strolled over later on and retrieved it from beneath the tree.

I do not suggest that hobbies a week on the wing prey on woodpeckers young or old, but nothing as colourful as *Picus viridis* is likely to escape the mischievous attention of any lively young falcon across whose path it trails its coat.

These young hobbies, the first I had seen on the wing from the day of their fledging, taught me one new fact of interest immediately. On fledging, the hobby has almost the blunt wing profile of the sparrowhawk; about a week later, that of the kestrel; but not until it has been about a fortnight on the wing does it develop the profile it will display for the rest of its life. Ere that, though, it may be seen in the sky with its parents, riding the air currents at altitudes where 10-power binoculars are only just up to the task of identifying it with certainty.

On 24 August of that year, I enjoyed the memorable experience of having eight hobbies in view simultaneously – two perched in the staggy crowns of the old parkland oaks; six in the sky far above, racing in and out of the cloud-base as though jet-propelled. The pair from the other site in the county, the one discovered in 1964, abandoned and since reoccupied, had flown over with their brood for a tribal celebration. Hobbies, like other falcons I have watched, can at times be remarkably sociable towards each other.

Two months later news came of hobbies on the Warwickshire estate, too, in that year. The keeper, walking the rounds with a companion, had seen 'two of them ruddy hobby-hawks of yours' on the ground. 'Are you sure?' I enquired. He grinned. 'G—— put a shot into the ground between them,' he confided. 'They soon showed us what they were. Don't reckon they stopped till they got to Africa.' To that there could be no answer from a friend (who had turned a little pale, admittedly) but to confirm that Africa, in October, should be definitely where they were heading for.

They may not, of course, have been the product of the estate. Hobbies are not common birds anywhere in Britain and I have had enough autumn sightings of strangers on the territory after the resident family has left for the south to surmise that hobbies migrate via routes which take them systematically through the breeding territories of their kind, one outward-bound bird after the other.

The next year presented me with but one hobby sighting, but in quite memorable circumstances. On 13 July, a date which has an uncanny way of figuring repeatedly in my hobby adventures, I sat in dense white mist on the cliff-top above the North Devon peregrine site. Suddenly, without a trace of warning, two dark shapes loomed out of the mist, one to pass a yard from my left ear, one a yard from my right. With a whirr of wings, two hobbies were in transit, proving that radar was something needed by only inferior human aviators. I knew there was a site somewhere in that vicinity, in one of the inland combes, but June, July and August, the prime time for seeing hobbies, are months in which I do not eagerly visit the somewhat crowded counties of the south-west.

THE HAWKWATCHER

In both 1980 and 1982 Janus and Whitebrow came back to the Worcester-shire parkland or its neighbouring farmlands to nest in woodland cover and in each year they successfully reared three fine youngsters. In 1983, still the same birds, they chose a crows' nest surprisingly low in a hedgerow tree and fledged only two young from it. Whether there was a cause-and-effect relationship I do not know, because I did not discover the nest until the young were on the point of leaving it. One thing is certain: the nest was highly vulnerable to egg theft. One light and agile man standing on the shoulders of a sturdy companion could have inserted a hand without the least difficulty.

But my sightings post-fledge may not have been the first that I had of Janus and Whitebrow that year. On 28 April, which must have been very soon after their arrival from Africa, two hobbies visited a 40-acre lake just three miles away from the hedgerow tree which was to be occupied later. I happened to be afloat on the lake casting flies to rising trout when suddenly a hobby flashed past within six feet of the boat's bow. It then rose spectacularly to snatch a house martin which its companion had manoeuvred for it against a screen of bankside trees, too dense to escape through. The action was so fast that I could not even put down my rod before it was all over and the hobbies gone, much less lift the binoculars hanging at the ready about my neck and train them on the dashing targets. They were certainly hobbies but they offered me no chance to examine their brows or napes.

In 1981 my friend from the United States, Bill Race, had entered the year's hobby adventure for the first time, despite earlier attempts in years when I had none to show him, or had not learned of their whereabouts until he had returned defeated to Michigan, time being limited. July found Bill – now in his early seventies – convalescing from a heart bypass operation. Anxious though I was to see him again, I was concerned at the risk of overexertion if he had to walk too far.

By a stroke of great good fortune, the Warwickshire hobbies were found again, on a farm a few miles south of the estate, on land owned by one of the nicest farmers I have ever met (and that is saying something, because likeable farmers have been a marked feature of my bird-watching life) and a keen conservationist. He grew some cereals and reared cattle on land still as clean and congenial to wildlife as it had been fifty years earlier, before organochlorines had been even dreamed of in nightmares.

The hobbies were in the largest hedgerow oak on the farm, in a crows' nest on which the telescope could be trained from about two hundred yards away, a proper and lawful distance. Hearing of Bill's likely problems, Farmer Neil found a route through his fields by which a car could be driven in reasonable summer conditions to precisely the point from which the nest could be viewed at that range. Remarkably, the dry weather did not change to frustrate the planning.

Among the birds Bill had spent his Manchester boyhood dreaming of were hobbies. Hobbies in his diary would complete a foursome of rare raptors encountered under my stewardship, starting with kite and reaching this final day of triumph via merlin and peregrine. I itched for the day to be a memorable one. As I awaited his arrival in a nearby pub car-park, my own heart, sound to the point of embarrassment in those circumstances, had a tendency to flutter. The discovery that a once conspicuously active friend has become an invalid before one's eyes is a shocking experience. It had happened to me before, so I knew what I might be in for.

God be thanked, it was not like that at all. As chipper as ever, Bill could hardly wait to exchange greetings before he was transferring himself and his gear into my car. Fifteen minutes later his eye was glued to the 'scope, with two fat hobby chicks in smoky down, upright on the nest's rim, exchanging scrutiny. Mamma was on guard high in a taller tree behind, where hedgerows met to form the sharply acute angle which bounded the field in that quarter. It was 11 a.m. on a perfect summer morning. At 11.10, chick number three awoke and joined the appreciative audience. It is not every day that Warwickshire-hatched hobby chicks are offered the chance to watch a man who has travelled more than 4,000 miles to accord them the privilege. A knowledge of that fact and a grasp of its implications could not have intensified their apparent attention.

THE HAWKWATCHER

At 12.30 the hen took off, vanished briefly behind a screen of small wych-elms, reappeared, made an elegantly banked turn, flew to the sky directly above us and circled at about 200 feet to give Bill a view of hobby plumage a film cameraman might have had to wait days for. He murmured that she must have thought she was competing in a beauty competition. Back to her tree she flew for more guard duty, with the chicks perched on the nest immobile as, and resembling, three suet dumplings.

At 1.20 she left the tree at speed, her target the approaching cock, a kill in his talons. I saw the aerial transfer. Bill, having wandered off a short way to examine another length of horizon, did not. He saw the feed though, which took only three minutes, and did not miss the next air-drop from cock to hen, at 2.15. This time the cock, too, remained on the scene to complete Bill's study of the entire family.

All was not yet over, however. At 2.45, the cock repeated his mate's earlier soaring flight over our heads and set a final seal on the day by ascending to where even our 10-power binoculars would not have established his identity had we not already known him for what he was. My calculation of altitude? 7,000 feet. Bill, too, kept him in the glasses until a faint white speck in the blue was all that remained of a 13-inch bird whose spread wings spanned more than twice that measurement.

At 2.32 the hen had begun to feed the chicks. Feeds usually take about twenty minutes. When we lowered our glasses from their target high above, she was back in her tree. Small wonder our arms were aching. When other commitments obliged us to leave at 4.30, Bill had not witnessed a swallow hunt, nor had we succeeded in identifying either of the kills we had seen delivered. Otherwise, I thought, ten out of ten for 21 July. It had been the memorable day so much hoped for.

When I returned to the hobbies on 28 July , Bill was back beyond the Atlantic, a contented man. I visited the hobby family again on 1, 2, 5, 8, 10, 15, 16 and 20 August. The nest was vacant on 5 August; it took me until the 16th to make observations of hobbies moving about the area good enough to satisfy me that all three young birds had survived the challenge of the fledge.

WATCHING THE SUMMER MIGRANT

This was a major relief. As the reader will by now have discovered, one becomes emotionally involved with these young raptors, whatever one's intentions may have been.

I made my final visit that year on 22 September. On my arrival a rook proved that at least one of the young hobbies was still on the site by chasing it over my head at tree-top height, to receive a come-uppance from Mamma, still, it seemed, providing protection. Later that day I was treated to a cranefly hunt better than any I had previously watched. Three hobbies were involved, operating at a mean altitude of about 500 feet and clearing craneflies from about 5½ million cubic yards of airspace. Daddy-long-legs rise to a remarkable height above the ground in the right weather conditions, and in impressive densities, as anyone who has strolled observantly through old turf when a hatch has been in progress will know.

When hobbies are cropping them some hundreds of feet above the grasslands which produce them, one is aware immediately that something invisible to the naked eye is being caught and eaten. The birds dart about strangely in a particular part of the sky, pausing every few seconds with tail briefly depressed and spread, one foot extended. Foot and bill then connect adroitly for a split second and the spectacular flight continues. How the spindly-bodied fly is held for even a split second in the skeletally spare toes and talons of the falcon is a mystery which a close examination of either will do nothing to solve, but events are exactly as I describe them.

When first I saw this performance, over the Worcestershire site, the binoculars could detect the small quarry, but could not enlarge the image enough for identification. Then it occurred to me that my telescope, which zooms to ×60, might, if the legs of the tripod on which it was mounted were at full extension. Not the easiest of exercises, but the telescope did all I had hoped for, and on only ×30 magnification. The size of the small single-eye window of a zoom telescope reduces in proportion to the enlargement of the magnification. Having to follow a hobby moving swiftly and erratically about several million cubic yards of sky was a task which gave me cause for gratitude when I discovered that ×30 magnification was enough to pick out enough of the wing-blur and bunch of trailing legs which characterize the insect in flight, in at least the lower-flying specimens the hobbies were catching.

On this day in Warwickshire, the catch rate was so high that I began to time it. The resulting discovery was that each hobby caught and consumed something between six and twelve flies per minute, every minute they were engaged in the hunt. As the hunt lasted for an hour, broken into three spells of roughly twenty minutes each, the hobbies accounted for something between 1,000 and 2,000 craneflies that afternoon without farmer Neil having expended a penny on insecticides. The cranefly is the adult form of the leatherjacket, a soil pest high on the farmer's hit-list, whether he grows cereals or grass to feed stock. When I told him before going home of the work his hobbies had been doing for him, Neil smiled happily, a man bathed in a sense of virtue properly rewarded. The farm, alas, is no longer in his hands. His heart, too, has paid some of the price which a lifetime of hard work can exact. The old turf he gloried in went under the plough. Intensified cultivation – 'mountains' notwithstanding – has changed the face of the land. The hobbies have never returned.

The ability of these birds to catch craneflies on the wing is astonishing, but that is not the end of the marvel. Watching Janus and co. at work in the sky on a humid afternoon in August 1983, I noticed that there were no craneflies emerging from the grass about me. Mounting the telescope for a sky-scan, I began a search on ×30 magnification. Whitebrow was discovered as she checked in flight with her spread tail depressed, bent her head to her raised foot, spread her wings again and flew on. I had seen her clearly enough, but not the insect captured.

Could I find her again, with a better result, with magnification raised to ×50? By comparison with the usual speed of a hobby's, her movements on that heavy afternoon verged on the lethargic, so I found her again, but again I saw only the action, not the object of it. Try again. This time I picked up one of the youngsters, but again with the same result, or lack of it. Only one conclusion could be drawn. The hobby can seize with the foot and hold not only the cranefly, with a body like an inch of fine-gauge valve-bubber, but smaller insects, too, down to the size of a large gnat or smaller. There was no shortage of large gnats in the lower air that afternoon.

What else was I taught during the six seasons in which I had watched hobbies closely? First, that they are capable of astonishing speeds. When so high in the sky that 10-power binoculars only just make them out as hobbies, the specks nevertheless may move so fast that the watcher struggling to keep on target (once lost, lost for ever, in all probability) is spun so far round on the balls of the feet that there is a risk of being toppled over. When eyes are focused on a moving point half a mile overhead, balance is at hazard. *A speck in the sky* moving fast enough to have that effect is a bird travelling at immense speed.

One afternoon, I saw Janus come 150 yards (paced out later) from a tree-top perch to intercept a blue tit before it could complete the crossing between two oaks only twenty yards apart. When Janus picked it off, the victim had travelled no more than half the distance required for sanctuary. How fast did Janus fly – 120 m.p.h.?

In theory, a bird weighing about 8 ounces cannot possibly fly as fast as birds of similar shape but three or five times that weight – namely, male and female peregrine falcon which I have timed in level flight at speeds of that order. Yet I still believe the hobby to be the fastest flier in level flight to be met in Britain.

Hobbies are certainly fast enough to catch young swifts, as I learned from the unmistakable plumage of one found beneath a well-known plucking-post on a tree branch in 1976. When I watched another swift go bit by bit into the crop of one of the young hobbies watched in 1981, it was confirmed that the 1976 kill was no isolated piece of exceptional luck for the hunter. House martins, another species not prone to dawdle, are brought to the nest as a commonplace.

Moving on from questions of speed and agility in flight to that of prey in general, the majority of the birds seen delivered were passerines which could not usually be identified, although some could, usually the titmice, from their distinctive hues of blue-green and yellow. One passerine brought in by Janus was almost certainly one of our scarce Worcestershire corn buntings – so scarce that if I wish to see a member of that species it is quicker to drive to the Marlborough Downs for the purpose.

I saw a song thrush have a narrow squeak in 1976, after a twisting, dodging escape down two hundred yards of hedgerow which never allowed its pursuer to develop anything like full speed. The same hobby pair had one young partridge, possibly two, presumably from the ground. These the keeper reported, and at the same time declined to claim the indemnity I had offered for every gamebird the hobbies were thought to have killed on the estate. A tempting of Fate, if you like, with the invitation made in the knowledge of the late Colonel Meinertzhagen's loss when backing a pair of Hampshire honey buzzards ('honey'!) on the same terms attracted a bill for £5 17s. 6d., representing 47 pheasant poults at half a crown a head.

So hobbies rear their chicks on a variety of prey, not all of it necessarily taken from the sky, although I am sure that by far the greater part of it is. For all I could prove to the contrary, the hen might join in the hunting from quite soon after the hatch, but that was never my impression. Paternal delivery and maternal guard-duty was the pattern I picked up, even after the brood had fledged and were catching at least their own insects on the wing. The hen at that stage occupies vantage-points near the young's chosen loafing tree, as she did near the nest while they were still occupying it, to fly out fast for a food pass, aerial or on a tree-branch, when she sees her mate on the way in with a kill. There might or might not be an exchange of vocal greeting before the transfer (resonant 'tew-tew-tewing') and excited hoarse screaming while it takes place, which happens somewhere within two hundred yards or so of where the hen has been perched, even in the very tree if she herself has not forestalled that possibility.

The prey is stripped by the hen of all or most if its quills somewhere out of reach of the young before delivery. When it is presented or offered in fragments, competition for the kill between members of a brood is not usually intense. Manners tend to be exemplary. Not so, however, before presentation, especially when the young have grown strong on the wing and the cock has begun to deliver kills to his family directly by aerial transfer.

Then, I suspect, the hen may take a sabbatical for a few days (as I am certain falcon peregrines do), with the burden of education in addition to that of provision devolving on the brood's father. Induced competition for the kills he carries may well be an important part of that education, and the need for it among birds which must develop advanced aerobatic skills in order to survive, the prime reason for the length of time post-fledge falcon families remain together – at least two months in the case of hobbies.

While the feeding is Mamma's exclusive responsibility, she may carry remnants of kills unconsumed by her progeny into some private tree for a snack before discarding the final debris by dropping it at random in flight – more evidence to support a theory that she herself does not hunt at that stage in the proceedings. When her mate's kill rate exceeds immediate need, kills or some portion of them are cached in trees near the nest, poked in holes, wedged in crotches, or merely laid on some substantial branch.

I have yet to see crow or magpie attempt the piracy I always expect, but when one of Janus's offspring clumsily dropped a kill just presented by his father, jackdaws were down and after it eagerly. Eagerly, but not quickly enough to beat a duly alert Janus to the target! Perhaps hobbies do in fact lose the odd kill to corvids. Not, as yet, having camped on a hobby site from dawn to dusk, from hatch to fledge and beyond, I cannot give a certain answer.

Up-to-date reference works depict hobbies accurately, although it should be noted that adults do not in all cases display so rich a shade of red on the lower under-parts as artists delight in bestowing on them. Young birds, as seen through the binoculars, differ from adults principally in the smaller contrast between the dark upper and the paler lower parts. Like those of the young of other falcon species, the tails of young hobbies terminate with an extremely bold cream-coloured bar, which is often a critically useful aid to identification when the members of a family, young and old together, are on the wing in poor light.

The sexually dimorphic size difference between the birds of a pair is often so slight that some other feature by which they can be sexed in the field is needed. It is found in the wing-tips as shown in the usual gliding silhouette, always pointed sharply, but those of the hen a little less sharp than those of the cock. As it is rare for hobby territories not to be shared (reluctantly) with kestrels, a means of species identification at a distance when birds are perched high in trees, as both hobby and kestrel often are, is helpful. There is one: the shape of the head. Kestrels have rounded crowns; hobbies have rather flattened heads, the odd shape never forgotten once noted.

Are hobbies distributed more widely in Britain than once they were thought to be? I believe they are, but so sparsely north of their traditional haunts that they go unrecorded, mistaken for the kestrels people are accustomed to seeing. And, however often one reads of similarity between the profiles in flight of hobby and swift, there are flight postures in which a hobby can easily be mistaken for a kestrel, especially when the angle of view is unhelpful.

Clive Varty, a fine ornithologist whose home is in Yorkshire, came to Worcestershire in 1982 to watch Janus and Whitebrow in my company. Since he thus familiarized himself with the species, hobbies have been identified nesting somewhere in those broad acres. Farther north yet, I have seen a pair displaying over a Lake District peregrine site I was watching, and good evidence has come my way of hobbies in Galloway.

The Mynd hobbies in Shropshire – far more than a single pair – add a measure of extra mystery to the distribution conundrum by never having been seen by me with a family of identifiable young. Regarding this component of the population, I have a good story to tell. A mature acquaintance who has dwelt there since boyhood was told in his early youth by an old keeper that the merlins they were discussing nested freely in the extensive oak woods at and near the Mynd's foot. 'And do you know,' he concluded interrogatively, 'that when you pick up a little merlin you have shot and fold its wings along its body, their tips extend nearly an inch beyond the tip of its tail?' Verb. sap.

I failed in 1985 to find a hobby site locally, in either Warwickshire or

WATCHING THE SUMMER MIGRANT

Worcestershire. I don't think there was one on either territory. An unavoidable increase in workload in 1986 and 1987 denied me the opportunity even to go and look for hobbies during the summer. That phase is now behind me. I close this chapter in hopes that the years ahead will renew the contact and with it the birds' opportunity to teach me more of their fascinating way of summer life. The Midland hobby and the typical terrain occupied by it – an undramatic mosaic of field, hedgerow and small acreages of mixed woodland – offer special advantages to the spectator.

The inland peregrine on the wing often salutes recognition by vanishing promptly behind the lofty skyline bounding its upland valley; the ground-skimming merlin by the even swifter withdrawal from view that moorland undulations facilitate. For the judiciously positioned hobby watcher there can be a limitless ocean of sky for the high-flying birds to perform in, with the view of them interrupted by nothing more obstructive than the leafy crown of some inconveniently situated hedgerow tree.

Small wonder I seldom bring hobbies into sharp mental focus without drifting towards a conclusion that they, of all the falcons, are the birds for which I feel the warmest affection. The conclusion is a sound one, one which survives all contradiction – until I make my next successful visit to an occupied peregrine cliff, or to a high moor on a day of sun and brisk breeze, with its merlins put into the right mood for their inimitably lively displays of fun and games.

Bill Race's hobby watch in Warwickshire, followed by a tour of Wales to renew acquaintance nostalgically with the other birds he had come to know intimately in my company, marked his last hawkwatching visit to Britain – to date. Since then, I have kept him posted on successes and failures, on birds seen and birds once familiar, seen no longer. He will enjoy this chapter, bringing back as I hope it will clear recollection of past delights. And I hope I have made it possible for others to share them.

eleven   THE COLONEL'S ROCK

For the peregrine falcon in England and Wales, the 1960s had been the decade of collapse. The latter 1970s were the years of recovery. The cause of the collapse, the side-effects of organochlorine pesticides, is well known but exactly how Fate engineered the connection in Wales remains a mystery. Use of the pesticides, apart from inclusion in sheep-dip, was then confined to arable land. Wales was, and remains, largely pastoral and, while wool scraped from fleece by thorns and wire barbs might have affected birds collecting it for nest linings, peregrines do not line either scrapes on ledges or the old ravens' nests they at times take over – indeed, they commonly scratch and kick out any remnant of wool lining found in a nest.

Crops, early potatoes in particular, are grown intensively in Pembrokeshire, near the coastal peregrine territories, but the great thin-out extended from Liverpool Bay to the Severn Sea, from the coast to the most eastern sites looking down on the Marches. Was the population, perhaps, more mobile than supposed – wandering in winter from the uplands of the wild inland counties to where trouble might be found in England or wherever in lowland Wales arable farming might have been on a sufficient scale for pesticides to be used in volume? There is no evidence of it and what I have since observed in the uplands would cause me to be incredulous if ever told of an adult territoried peregrine travelling outside a circle ten miles in circumference centred on a Welsh eyrie rock from the day it took up possession to the day it lost its last battle with frost, raven or younger falcon.

Can we blame conifer afforestation, or at least put it in the dock to share the guilt with the pesticides? We cannot. The blanket had yet to develop when the peregrine began to decline; tree-cover has in fact increased year by year as the bird has recovered. Coniferization has cost us some sites, as hunting territories have been blotted out, and, I am painfully certain, is destined to cost us more, but it cannot be blamed for the losses between 1955 and 1975.

There was one suggestion that a massive winter passage of woodpigeons into Wales from the toxic Vale of Evesham (where most of the vegetables for the industrial Midlands came from!) might have lain at the root of the losses. A promising theory, if only there had been such a passage and peregrines had more enthusiasm for killing woodpigeons. My experience suggests that woodpigeons are at greater risk from hen sparrowhawks. Most peregrines will kill the smaller pigeons until further orders, but a big fat woodie does not commonly attract, nor does it suffer from suicidal impulses. Wood-pigeons share all the inland territories I have wardened, but show me one on the move while a peregrine is 'waiting on' overhead! So we are left with one of modern ornithology's great conundrums, one to which I can offer no solution.

That being as it may, the recovery was real and began to have a bearing on the strategy of protection soon after I became involved in the work. What should the priority be: to concentrate effort to guarantee peace at a few of the sites – the more vulnerable, defensible or productive ones, perhaps – or to spread protection thinner so that there was at least a token presence everywhere at some time, in the hope of deterrence? I did not arrive at a neat series of conclusions capable of satisfying myself as soon as the dilemmas surfaced, nor, I believe, did the ornithological establishment. I saw a variety of strategies tried between South Wales and Galloway, from thirty wardens serving one site, pair by pair, to one warden trying to service twelve.

My first distraction from the affairs of the original pair on the rocks by the reservoirs – Boy Blue and his formidable mate – came as early as the second year of the Welsh operation, when a valley not far to the north was reoccupied. The rock is the most magnificent in the county and its neglect by the birds in favour of those to which I had been anchored through the 1975 season and the first weeks of that which followed was a choice I have never fathomed. But then I have only a poor human mind, not a noble peregrine's. The rock reaches 1,200 yards from end to end and stands at its highest point 800 feet above its roots in the 800-foot contour to cut off a short valley which gives its name to one of the farms lying below in the rock's long shadow.

That farm is 'The Colonel's' and the crest of the rock is where I spent the night of 28 May 1977, after the taking and recovery of the neighbouring pair's three chicks. The colonel's pair had bred successfully in 1976, under a guard mounted so discreetly after the robbery in the other valley that neither he, nor his lady, nor the occupants of the two other neighbouring farms frowned on by the rock formed the least suspicion that it was in progress. The eyasses flew a fortnight later than their cousins over the hills would have done, had they been left in peace to have enjoyed that privilege. The colonel's peregrines had a more orthodox notion of the date on which peregrine eggs were supposed to be laid.

The crest of the rock was approachable by a long walk over ankle-deep grass. The song of larks overhead and the piping of golden plover as they ran from bilberry patch to bilberry patch was sweet to the ear. In July and August 1976 I made the journey several times to sit in the sun, gazing over the broad valley below as the colonel and his lady busied themselves with hay-making, drove their cattle from pasture to pasture and performed the score of other routine tasks inseparable from farming on the hills.

Perched on rocks about me would be one or more of the lovely young peregrines, chocolate-gold above, golden-cream below, reciprocating to the best of their ability the interest Barney and I were showing in them. Young peregrines are like that. No one who had become familiar with them in the wild could ever believe that our distant ancestors who first took the species into captivity were likely to have found the task of training them either burdensome or uncongenial.

THE COLONEL'S ROCK

The old year faded from the calendar and 1977 took its place. March arrived with the news that full-time paid wardens would in due course become central to the operations in the valley to the south. The door was open for an expansion of responsibilities, but not, I decided, on the same semi-clandestine basis as in 1976. Disclosing the location of a peregrine eyrie was – and is – no light matter, but glances and 'good mornings' had been exchanged in that year with both the colonel and his lady and tactful inquiries pursued with the 1975 circle of local acquaintance.

Every instinct urged me to lay aside the cloak. After all's said and done, how could we hope for these vulnerable birds to re-establish themselves generally if their presence was kept a dark secret from all human neighbours, irrespective of the welcome and good will which might be extended to such interesting creatures? Could the presence of birds whose raucous screams would be heard half a mile away be kept secret indefinitely? I doubted it.

On 20 April I nerved myself for the encounter, bumped up the long, rough drive to the farm, parked the car and got out. A tall figure, elegantly erect and bearded like a conquistador, strolled across the yard to confront me eye to level eye. I gave my name, address, occupation and business, succinctly stated. The bushy eyebrows rose, the face broke into a smile. After a few preliminaries came the first important question. Had I ever served in the Army? Yes, I had. Enjoyably, on the whole, in both tanks and armoured cars. The smile broadened into a beam. He, on the way up, had done a stint as a technical adjutant. I, eventually, had reached the eminence of technical quartermaster-sergeant in the same corps. It seemed likely that in many matters we should speak a common language. Yes, he had noticed the noisy birds up on the rock and had wondered about them. So, I shortly discovered, had his lady, who joined the conversation at that stage with a proposal that it should be continued over coffee in the greater comfort of indoors.

In her I found a second kindred spirit. By the time I left the farm that morning, a caravan had been put at my disposal, what is termed a 'Radnorshire second breakfast' put into my stomach and something like joy unconfined into my heart. Duty here would not entail rising and bed-making in advance of the sun's reveille, urgent journeyings with the risk of fatal delay. This site could be wardened at first light from a seat on a bed left in an untidy muddle until it was convenient to attend to it after as lavish a breakfast as I fancied, made and eaten in the dry when the first-light high-risk period was over and only casual intruders to be expected during the next few hours. I was, one might say, sitting pretty, and within fifteen minutes' drive of the professionally wardened site when my help was needed there.

From 1976 to 1983 the colonel's peregrines reared their families in a scrape beside the remains of a derelict ravens' nest on the floor of a big triangular alcove high in the rocks, gouged out by some spectacular rock-fall in prehistoric times. Fifty feet of vertical cliff formed its foundation; a great lintel-rock jutted from above, projecting several feet to provide shelter from all weather not blown on a north-east wind, and to enable a man making a descent by rope to see – but not to touch without the greatest danger and difficulty – what might lie in the scrape. This was established on 30 May 1977, when an official descent to mark and ring chicks still in down kept the falcon off them for forty minutes on a chilly evening. Another expert descent, arranged this time by me in the following August, after the brood had fledged, confirmed the difficulties to be met by robbers, but not the impossibility of an attempt. After a robbery, though, the thieves had either to come on down with the booty to run the gauntlet of men and dogs awaiting them below, or retreat across the moor beyond the rocks to reach a car parked where it would not be all that difficult to find. Assuming prompt detection of the attempt, police traps should be set on every line of retreat by the time the ledge could even be reached.

In 1976 I spent 60 hours wardening the site; in 1977, 170. In 1978, 440 hours would be given to the site, and more thereafter, until more vulnerable rocks elsewhere began to demand their share of the attention and priorities changed once more. In all, the colonel's rock had my binoculars or telescope focused on it for not less than 2,000 hours spread over twelve years while its handsome occupants moved steadily up the league table to become of all

THE COLONEL'S ROCK

peregrines I have watched in Britain the pair I came to know best. The falcon, who has often posed for the telescope in the bright early-morning light of a fine day in June which permits a ×60 magnification, differs from all others I have seen in having her breast and flanks barred in sepia, not the usual black or dark grey. Her mantle, too, has remained brown enough in adulthood for one to mistake her for one of her own daughters when a fledged family including a daughter has been on the wing.

She arrived at the colonel's rock mated to a cantankerous old tiercel who demonstrated a marked dislike for his three offspring, especially the two sons, and did not survive the following winter. The change was signalled, as they quite often are, by a pronounced shift in behaviour. By the time the 1976 nesting season was into its second month a particular grassy hump among the rocks was white with pigeon feathers, as though a feather mattress had been torn open and shaken over it. Use of a single plucking-post is common among merlins, but for a peregrine it is an idiosyncrasy. It was soon obvious that the 1977 tiercel took the orthodox view of this matter, lending confirmation to a suspicion already formed that we now watched a bird as small and slender as his neighbour had been two years earlier, and therefore a newcomer.

Certainty came when progress on the scrape eased pressure on the falcon. Freed from the need to brood the chicks or stand in close attendance, she would emerge on fine days to display overhead with her new mate, as though to say 'Look up here and see the nice young chap I have attracted'. She might have said more, because kills came in at a record rate and paternal attention, when the brood fledged, was assiduous. Where his grumpy old predecessor had shown, at best, indifference to his juniors, this tiercel seemed never to tire of a part in their sky games.

Was he, we began to wonder, Red Baron, son of Boy Blue from over the hills and heir to his father's lively personality? Research in the United States had established the tendency of peregrines to return to the area of their hatching at maturity, in the second or third year of their lives. This would certainly be the area and the time was right enough.

THE HAWKWATCHER

True, his mantle was not conspicuously blue, but the genetic inheritance derived through his mother must also have had a part to play. When the profile of his full-spread wings passed through the binocular window, with its suggestion of tips clipped by secateurs, we were tempted to a firm conclusion. One day, perhaps, the inheritance patterns of the peregrine will be as well documented as those of Friesian cattle or Landrace pigs. Until they are, though, we can but conjecture, with reservations. As well, maybe, for charm can fade as certainties increase.

Some certainties, though, are welcome. As the years ran on from 1976 to 1987 the falcon at the colonel's rock was a bird whose plumage never conventionally matured. She always favoured the same perches about the crags, as did her consort, whose torso broadened for a few years, but whose other features remained unchanged, including the most extensive bandit's mask the telescope has yet magnified for me on a peregrine's aristocratic visage.

Broods were fledged year after year, with never a robbery by human agency and few failures. Four eyasses flew in 1980 and 1981, three in 1976, 1977, 1978 and 1982. Two only flew in 1979, 1984 and 1985. In 1983, a year of national failure on a massive scale, this pair, too, hatched no chicks. In 1984 the sheltered alcove was used for the last time. An attempt was begun there, but when chicks were belatedly hatched it was on a grassy ledge, behind a screen of wood sage, above the apex of the alcove. Why the failure and move we never knew for certain, but one of the farmers dwelling in the shadow of the rock had occasion to blow a raven apart after it had ruined five of his lambs by blinding them and nipping out their tongues in full view of the house. That this rogue had such temerity (for rogue it was, in coexistent Radnorshire) implies a temperament which would not stick at taking peregrine eggs. If I was pressed for a guess at the cause of the initial failure in 1984, that raven would get the blame.

In 1985 the pair made a radical move half-way down the rock to fledge a son and daughter on a surprisingly open ledge. In neither 1986 or 1987 did the colonel or I discover any attempt to make a scrape or lay. The pair remained on the site, looking healthy enough, but they had reached the age which is the norm – although certainly not the record – at which peregrines reproduce for the last time. In 1987 they did not contest a successful attempt by the ravens to resume tenancy of the alcove. That struck me at the time as a significant development.

The pattern of 1987 and 1986 was maintained in 1988, but with one important difference. I could no longer be certain that both peregrines on the site were the familiar ones. The telescope established that the unusually brown-mantled falcon was still in occupation, but the colour schemes of the pair, seen as they flashed to and fro in flight against the background of the tree-clad rocks, appeared not to contrast as positively as before. If the light was not playing even more tricks than usual, that suggested a different tiercel, mature but only just so, with another moult to complete before perfection was accomplished.

It seemed that Red Baron (if our guess at his identity had been well-founded) had outlived his father by only the two years which separated their ages. But he and the mate which had survived him had together more than justified their occupancy of the colonel's rock. The debt of nature has to be discharged – by us all – but one could have wished that dutiful tiercel a more prolonged retirement.

A balanced output of male and female progeny would seem to be a useful biological economy. Thanks to Dr Newton's work on sparrowhawks, we know that this can be achieved collectively over extensive areas. Whether a single pair of peregrines commonly achieves a similar balance over the span of a breeding lifetime I do not know. Perhaps someone has investigations in hand. Whether or no, let the colonel's pair make their contribution, such as it is, to the statistics.

Their total output to 1985 had not been evenly sexed. Six broods out of the nine I recorded to my absolute satisfaction. The two broods of three and one of four with which I did not wholly succeed were definitely of mixed sex, but endeavours to determine the exact balance were frustrated. Fate, as ever, played a leading part, abetted by unhelpful weather, the chatelaine's disinclination ever to grow a plumage incontrovertibly adult in all visual circumstances, and the fact that the colonel's rock, untypically for the site of a peregrine's eyrie, gave anchorage to the roots of more than a thousand trees, large and small. Trees hide birds.

So of twenty-six eyasses fledged between 1976 and 1985 I can vouch for eight young falcons contributed to the population and fifteen little tiercels. In total, of course, the mix had to be either eight and eighteen, nine and seventeen, ten and sixteen, or eleven and fifteen. However many of each, I watched a total of more than twelve make their maiden flights – a privilege indeed!

Sexing a brood of fledged peregrines is a compulsive recreation, fascinating one by the combination of skill and luck it requires. It is, fundamentally, an exercise in the art of elimination as birds wheel up into the sky over a site in a variety of combinations, or perch there in view in happy companionability. One is helped by the fact that newly fledged young falcons look larger than their mothers (plumper and with longer tails), while the juvenile tiercels are appreciably smaller than well matured fathers. Sisters, therefore, look much bigger than brothers when at play in the sky together, while daughters usually look larger than their fathers by a bigger margin than their mothers do. Since the bottom line is a thorough knowledge of an adult pair as individuals, readers are not recommended to lay down the book, fill the car with petrol and set off for the north or west immediately on an eyas-sexing holiday. But for those who choose to ignore that advice let me assist further with an example. You know that a site has fledged four young from head-counts by telescope while the final feeds are in progress. (It is surprising how often peregrines, topography and telescope technology co-operate for this to be possible.) Your arrival is greeted by a grey-and-white peregrine flying in with a larger and browner specimen in noisily anguished pursuit. They disappear. Next, two even-sized eyasses shoot up into the sky to practise 'fighter tactics', as I usually term such evolutions, to be joined by a larger and probably clumsier one. Eyas tiercels develop faster than their sisters, and usually fledge a day or two faster, too. The larger eyas loses interest, falls to the cliffs, flies swiftly along them, goes to a perch screened, typically, by a clump of small rowans. A moment later, the adult falcon appears from somewhere in that vicinity, with a screaming eyas on her tail.

They twist and jink, changing the angle of view continually and therefore giving no certain indication of their relative sizes. As they drop below the skyline, your trusty companion announces that he can see the bird which dropped earlier from the game perched in a tree to which she has just moved. Then she too takes off and flies over the skyline – just when you have begun to congratulate yourself on having one, at least, nailed! The two eyas tiercels then tire of their sport and dive down to join her.

Six times in the next two hours, either two even-sized eyasses go up to play, or three, of which two, even-sized, are smaller than the third. While just two are up, no parent obliges by arriving in the right area of sky to be either distinctly larger, slightly larger, slightly smaller or much smaller. The conundrum remains just that. Finally, on a lucky day, three incontestable eyasses go up, tails full-spread to give final proof of their status by showing the broad cream-coloured terminal bars which, in virtually all lights and at all angles of the sun, are diagnostic. White bars terminate adult tails, too, but they are never so conspicuous in flight.

Glory be! Two of the eyasses are even-sized, *and the third much smaller*. Now we know at last: two of either sex.

But might not a youngster from a neighbouring site have flown over to join in the fun and complete the confusion? I cannot absolutely deny the possibility, but a lot of watching has pretty well convinced me that parents on territory do not tolerate intrusion by nieces, nephews and the children of more distant cousins or other kinfolk. Where a group of mixed-age peregrines familiar enough to their regular audience to be known as a family dwells amicably together until autumn or later, the odd youngster is seen occasionally to be chased off angrily by the adults as soon as it tries to join in sky play.

In that general connection, there was a strange difference in the behaviour of the birds on these two adjacent Welsh sites. On Boy Blue's, every breeding season following success was heralded by the arrival of a party of golden-plumaged eyasses in the same number and sex ratio as the previous year's brood. The only exception was 1981, the year in which the arrival of a party of *three* eyas tiercels followed the successful fledge of a brood of *four* – and that was the year in which the reported casualty occurred on Bodmin Moor.

On the colonel's site, I saw the occasional last season's eyas – or one assumed to be such – but never a group corresponding to the previous year's output. Did this mean that one pair of peregrines fledged young better adapted to long-term survival than the neighbouring pair, or that one pair was more welcoming than the other? Peregrines, if I judge rightly, can detect others of their kind in the distant sky at distances I could not equal with even 20-power binoculars. Many urgent bee-line journeys are undertaken by peregrines for reasons obscure to the human viewer. It has seemed to me at times that some of them might have been for the purpose of warding off intrusion before it occurred.

For all her ferocity when dealing with ravens, mine (and Boy Blue's) original light o' love was never hard on eyasses I judged to be her own. When the time arrived to clear the valley in the interest of renewed reproduction, her way was to fly up to them, pass them at enormous speed, then lead them racing after her until out of sight. Her commonest form of return from such flights was a vertical stoop to the cliffs, alone, from an altitude at which I had not even detected her presence.

Above the colonel's rock, though, I saw the brown-backed incumbent close one summer day with an intruding immature, grapple and fall with it through about two hundred feet of oaks and other deciduous trees growing from the rock, falling from one to another, breaking flight-quills in the eyas's plumage and losing half of one of her own tail feathers up there in the process. When they emerged tattered and dishevelled from the tree screen, the tiercel joined her in the assault, sending the poor eyas screaming from the valley, giving me my sole experience of a peregrine showing fear.

I never saw a raven struck in the colonel's valley, but a carrion crow provided drama on a late April morning in a year in which the alcove ledge fledged three eyasses. A few crows haunt the rock in most years and in this one a regular party of six spent much of their time there. Eventually, with both peregrines briefly away, one of the crows broke away as the flight passed the alcove and ventured in. It emerged immediately with an orange-brown object in its bill which might have been a scrap of pigeon or, more likely, one of the eggs, because it is not the habit of a falcon to take a kill to the eyrie while she is still incubating her eggs there.

The escaping crow travelled about fifty yards before the falcon came down from on high like a thunderbolt to hit it squarely, sending its mortal remains tumbling head over heels through the trees. As she hooked up with the impetus of her stoop, I saw that she was shaking herself to free one hind talon of a small jet-black burden. It, too, fell to the trees below – and was presumably the crow's severed head. Had it been merely a cluster of torn out feathers, it would have floated down rather than fallen. I had read a number

of times of such decapitations by peregrines and seen many a headless pigeon carried in to a site. Never before, though, had I witnessed the execution, and I have never seen it since.

The maximum speed a peregrine might reach in the stoop has provoked its share of discussion over the years, but less ink has been spilt over speeds achieved in level flight, interpreting the adjective broadly. The colonel's tiercel has twice shed light on the debate; the falcon, once. The times and dates were 7 p.m. on 16 April 1987, 3.58 p.m. on 1 October 1983 (the falcon's attempt on the record) and 4.02 p.m. on 10 February 1985. In each instance, familiarity with every feature in and about the valley, on map and ground alike, enabled me to measure the flights. An art I had acquired of counting seconds reliably to within a 10 per cent margin of error enabled me to time the flights reliably enough to make the assessments worth reporting. Timing by stop-watch would have been preferable to my second counting, but a stop-watch is an artefact I do not possess.

The first of these flights, in which Barney shared the witness, the counting and the arithmetic, as well as the conclusions, covered a distance of not less than 800 yards in 17 seconds. The points on the map between which flights two and three were made were so specific that the distances can be quoted without any margin of doubt. The distance in both cases was 600 yards. The falcon, the purpose of her journey undiscernible, covered the distance in 6 seconds. The tiercel, his sights on a kestrel rising to hover in the middle of a bitter February frost, took the same time to cover the same distance. In 1987 he gained height over the 800 yards plus; he lost some in the 1985 trial, as did the falcon in 1983. Wings were beaten all the way in all three flights. Loss of height in 1983 and 1985 was not such as to justify even the thought of the word 'stoop'. On all three occasions the breeze was light – so light that I did not trouble to note its direction. Two small and simple calculations yield round figures of 96 m.p.h. and 204 m.p.h. How I wish I had been sitting stop-watch in hand, with advance information as to what the birds were about to demonstrate! Obviously, the shorter the period counted in seconds, the greater the probable error, but an assumption of even a 50 per cent error in the calculation of 204 m.p.h. puts into interesting perspective references I have read of 60 m.p.h. *and 30 m.p.h.* as the likely maxima.

I would assume a peregrine to be capable of flying at 30 m.p.h. in still air without actually stalling, as I can walk at 1 m.p.h. without serious risk of falling over, and of cruising at 60 m.p.h. in circumstances which would stir me from a dawdle to an amble. In the absence of more acceptable data than those I quote, let the issue rest there.

Much more could be written concerning the colonel's rock and its peregrines. Only the North Devon cliffs can compare with that rock in terms of the pure pleasure I have derived from watching falcons. Elsewhere, greater drama has been paid for with greater anxiety and bitter-tasting failure. Drama is what one seeks principally in youth and the habit dies hard. But as maturity ripens in the evening sunshine one recognizes increasingly the force of Montesquieu's memorable dictum which translates roughly into the English phrase, 'Happy the nation which has no history'.

Compared with my adventures on three sites to the south of it, the benign shadow of the colonel's rock figures as something of a backwater into which I can float gently from time to time to pursue the study of peregrines free from sharp and often urgent anxiety over their welfare.

One day, the rock will again be the home of fertile adults and a succession of eyasses. When that day dawns I hope that my binoculars will be among those present, and that an era will follow as untroubled as the one on which the curtains are now being drawn. Before they can again be opened, though, it seems that Red Baron will have to be followed into the shadows by the falcon with the touch of dusty brown in her mantle which made her so difficult to distinguish at times from her new-fledged daughters in seven of their mutually productive years.

twelve   PANDION PAYS A CALL

I was fishing for eels at the time. As an eel gives more than a hint of its intentions when attacking a bait, this form of angling calls for less in the way of concentrated attention than most of the others. Fifty acres of shining reservoir rippled in front of me; binoculars hung round my neck, ready for immediate employment. Ducks dabbled in the shallows, grebes dived to search the deeper water off-shore for roach and small bream. Gulls soared and dipped, screaming raucously. The reservoir presented the personality it usually displays on a fine day in late September.

An impulse spun me round to inspect a short line of ancient oaks which stood in a field behind the shore from which I was fishing. An exceptionally large bird was climbing above them on wings beaten slowly but with powerful deliberation. Gulls were diving and veering towards it to mob. The big bird banked, turned a breast almost snow-white to the direct rays of the afternoon sun. It was undeniably an osprey, making a September day in Worcestershire typical no more.

Soon the mobbing gulls were joined by lapwings, crows and an indignant kestrel distracted from its hovering. Woodpigeons lurched frantically about the sky in panic, in preparation for urgent departure to some less alarming environment. Ospreys do not hunt pigeons, but how were they supposed to know that? As usual, the arrival of a big and unfamiliar hawk had precipitated pandemonium.

PANDION PAYS A CALL

The osprey sought for and found a thermal, rose effortlessly to shake off the labouring mobsters, then flew to patrol the broad shallows at the north end of the reservoir, indifferent to the few birds – all crows – which had not by then lost interest. It was the second osprey I had seen that month. The first, three weeks earlier, had been in Galloway, emerging as I spotted it from a big re-entrant which bites deeply into the western flank of the Cairnsmore of Fleet massif, which dominates all Galloway between Loch Ken and Wigtown Bay.

That osprey, too, had soon picked up an escort of resentful gulls, crows, lapwings and – in this case – quite a large flock of starlings. Unaccountably, the course it flew was one to take it towards the north, the exact opposite of what was reasonably to be expected at that season.

My Worcestershire osprey, in the right latitude at the right time, conveyed no suggestion of anything beyond an intention to take a break while working south by easy stages until the time came to cross the seas and oceans which lie between the British Isles and the osprey's winter quarters in Mauretania. If the pace was a relaxed one, that would be in keeping with tradition. With the nesting season in Scotland ahead of them, ospreys often hurry on their way north, but the return journey is usually made by easy stages.

The stage enjoyed by this bird in my parish was certainly that, lasting for twelve days. I spent six of them in its company, and with a ring-side seat from which to study a bird which was not merely rare in the days of my youth but positively extinct as a British breeding species, I learned much of value.

Calls to reinstate the values of the Victorian age do not attract an automatic 'Hear, hear!' from me. That was the era in which a set of decent recreations for countryfolk mushroomed into a cult in which the scale of the mayhem among gamebirds and salmonids was of only marginally greater interest than the annihilation of the vermin believed capable of competing in their slaughter.

The osprey was the most conspicuous of the victims, its demise ensured by two other Victorian obsessions. One was the systematic collection of eggs;

the other, birds stuffed and mounted in glass domes or cases to be part of the domestic décor. Oologists thirst for not just an egg, but for eggs by the clutch, demonstrating all the variations in colour and pattern a species produces. If a species is brought to the verge of extinction, up goes the value of its eggs – a vicious circle if ever there was one. No mounted specimen exceeded the splendour of the osprey, standing nearly two feet tall when posed to display its smartly contrasting plumage and usually in possession of a handsomely spotted fish duly mummified to complete the taxidermist's composition.

So from the first decade of this century to the sixth the only ospreys seen in Britain were birds in passage to and from Sweden. In 1956 I was told by a fishing-tackle dealer I visited in Elgin of a breeding attempt somewhere near and of his involvement in the protection of the nest. Memories still relatively fresh of Dannet wire crawled through painfully on army assault courses inspired a suggestion that the trunk of the nest-tree might thus be usefully obstructed. It was, but whether on my suggestion I know not. Coils of barbed wire extended to entangle had been a salient feature of many lives at intervals between 1914 and 1945, including that of the late George Waterston, the rightly renowned RSPB officer to whom the successful re-establishment of the osprey on Speyside is so largely owed. He, after capture on Crete, had spent the rest of the Second World War behind the stuff.

Not long afterwards, the return of the ospreys had become a front-page story for the national press and the protective measures adopted by the Royal Society for the Protection of Birds a symbol for all wild bird protection. Successful nest robberies occurred, despite barbed wire, dedicated wardens and electronic aids. One villain even concealed his success by substituting painted eggs taken from the poultry-house and making accomplices of the robbed ospreys for long enough for his escape to be completed. But, villainy notwithstanding, one nest at Loch Garten became two in the Spey valley, followed by others until by the time my local reservoir received its first visit twenty pairs or more were attempting to nest in Scotland every summer.

A view through the Loch Garten telescope at a crested head reared above that famous nest, the osprey seen so recently in Galloway and an earlier osprey at Blithfield in Staffordsnire – the first I saw in England – detracted nothing from the excitement felt at this more intimate opportunity.

My first local osprey was an adult, signalled by upper wing surfaces and mantle of unrelieved sepia. The dorsal contour-feathers on a bird from among the season's output of juveniles would have been cream-edged, giving at a distance a stippled effect. Experience could therefore be presumed. The bird would not remain unless the catering was up to standard.

There were two reservoirs in the same valley and a chain of three small trout ponds. The larger reservoir by which I first saw the osprey feeds the canal and is densely populated by a variety of 'coarse' fish – roach, bream, perch, pike and eels. The smaller, into which surplus water from the canal is fed at times to control the canal's level, although nominally a stocked trout fishery, receives many coarse fish with the influxes of canal water. In all, small trout ponds included, there is about 80 acres of water surface.

Where would the osprey choose to fish – and for what? Knowing that the Loch Garten ospreys travelled some distance to catch small pike found basking on the surface in a number of Spey valley lochans, I did not expect any determined assault on the trout ponds. Nor was there any. I was witness to the capture of three bream, two roach and two perch. Also, I saw the bird flying back to its base by the bigger reservoir from the smaller one, where it had caught one of the bream the committee was anxious to be rid of, a fish I judged to weigh about three-quarters of a pound.

I knew the theoretical length-weight ratios of the fish species the osprey might catch there: I knew the overall length of the bird to be something approaching 24 inches. As it conveniently shuffled all captures for carriage head or tail foremost – never turned at right angles to the axis of its own body – one could make a calculation of the prey's weight which should be accurate to within 25 per cent. Not more accurately than that, because eye judgement has its limitations and fish vary in condition, making theoretical ratios no more than that, useful though they are. There are fat fish and thin fish, as there are fat and thin human beings.

PANDION PAYS A CALL

Captures seen by other watchers when I was not there, the anxious bailiff included, persuaded me that this osprey, at least, preferred prey weighing between half a pound and a pound, experiencing difficulties if it tried to carry smaller fish. The smallest I saw it capture was a roach weighing about four ounces, a fish almost dropped several times as it continued its struggles to escape in the sky and so nearly succeeded that it hung from only one talon when its captor finally reached the tree which came to be known as 'the dining table'. No matter where caught, all captures were carried there for consumption. The view that a fish weighing a pound or not much more was near the osprey's upper limit was founded on the immense difficulty it had in rising from the water with a bream of that size on a calm day. Three times the bream dragged the osprey below the surface. Only by a tremendous thrashing of wings on water was the bird able to emerge and rise, shaking itself like a wet dog when it got into the air, to rid itself of a considerable burden of water. From records of osprey skeletons washed ashore on Scottish lochs, still locked by their sickle-shaped talons to the skeletons of pike, one assumes that like other raptors *Pandion haliaetus* is constructed to maintain and enforce its grasp rather than to relax it easily at will.

The osprey knew that a fish lost in flight is better dropped over dry land. This fact it demonstrated by turning with its prey as a matter of course towards the nearest point on the shore, to follow the shoreline overland all the way to the 'dining-table' tree, however much farther that tactic required it to fly. Only once was it seen to make a direct journey there over water, which led to interesting speculations.

Was the osprey intelligent enough to relate firmness of grip and prey behaviour in the talons to the risk of loss? It seemed as though it might be – a proposal to disconcert those experts who regard birds as no more than feathered lizards with wings instead of forelegs.

Water depth, light intensity, turbidity and the effects of wind on the surface are all matters of great importance to fish as they prospect for food cautiously enough to avoid becoming just that for some predator. Anglers learn to interpret the interplay and assess the significance of these factors, or to end up with little to show for their efforts except a fine repertoire of hard-luck stories. The visiting osprey taught me that they, too, acquire this awareness, or are hatched with it already planted in their small brains by instinct.

Sight, in this context, is the critical sense, for both hunter and quarry. What has not been seen will not be caught; what can be seen coming – the earlier the better – can be escaped. Before rain fell heavily and caused discoloration to spread throughout the reservoir, the osprey concentrated on the deeper reaches, where fish could be seen swimming some feet below the surface, provided the wind did no more than ripple it. Bream shoals are known to post sentries higher in the water when they are feeding: I believe it was the dark shadow below formed by the shoal that attracted the osprey and a sentry that provided it with a capture. The bream I saw it catch never involved the bird in a deep dive beneath the surface to grasp them; yet all were taken from water not less than ten feet deep, as I well knew from fishing it myself over the years.

As any experienced aviator will confirm, the higher the aeroplane, the deeper the view into the sea. This aviator knew this too, selecting both the altitude for its prospecting patrols and the part of the reservoir it would cover in terms of this fact and the others I have mentioned, especially that of surface disturbance, with its profound capacity to distort the images of submerged objects. When windstrength from the north was enough to build ripple into foaming waves racing the length of the reservoir, the osprey's catch-per-plunge rate – one in three or four in calmer conditions – would fall drastically. The bird would then circle up to expand its view of the valley and leave for the lower reservoir, a water less exposed to the force of the wind.

After the change in the weather, the upwind shallows were the first water to discolour. The osprey reacted appropriately, as though it, too, knew that fish would be emboldened to come inshore. It soon caught a roach of about a pound in weight (twice the size of those usually seen in the anglers' keep-nets) from a foot of water where no angler believed there was ever anything to be found except shoals of fry and the occasional pike or perch rushing recklessly in from the deeps beyond to raid them. We live and learn.

It was not the osprey's first visit to these shallows, though. Nothing it did during the fine weather of the first week surprised me so much as its alighting there every so often to stand belly-deep in the water, ducking and scooping with its sickle-shaped bill, even immersing head and neck completely, as though looking for fish in their own element. Fry shoaled there by the ten thousand, but whether the osprey was catching them to eat as a child eats sweets, drinking in sips, or washing its face and splashing its shoulders I could never be sure. At that time I lacked the telescope I acquired later, one of a calibre to settle the question beyond reasonable doubt. As such duckings and bobbings were often followed by a full-scale bathe in which the same techniques were used as those practised by starling or blackbird in a garden bird-bath, I suspect the latter. Perhaps the osprey fed or drank and bathed, in succession.

It demonstrated sound judgement in the matter of dead trees. One of these, standing on the shore in a position commanding the osprey's favourite shallows, was hovered over undecidedly several times but the bird never alighted. Crows and magpies used it often, kestrels occasionally. A week after the osprey left, a gale stripped the tree of all its higher branches. The osprey, it was assumed, knew enough about the stresses to which dead oak timber should be subjected not to exceed them by a couple of pounds or so. Instinct, or intelligence converting experience? And are we correct when we draw so sharp and positive a distinction between them? I doubt it. I suspect that the one evolved from the other by too gradual and untidy a progression for dogma to be appropriate.

The other birds did not in twelve days grow accustomed to the osprey's presence. A sudden appearance as it arrived from the lower reservoir panicked pigeons, plover and black-headed gulls as they had been panicked when first they saw it. Crows continued to mob it aggressively, as they mob all hawks except the peregrine; even the usually placid kestrels took their opportunities to molest it when it was burdened by a kill. Magpies, as they so often do, appointed themselves to form a committee of vigilance. Organized into small raiding parties, they allowed the osprey little tranquillity when perched. One magpie, while I watched, even nerved itself sufficiently to land briefly between the big hawk's shoulders for a hit-and-run peck. The osprey, well aware that its bill was for tearing dead flesh, not for striking at the living, defended against the more impudent aggressions with buffets aimed by its powerful wings, a crest erected to intimidate and the bill, opened wide, merely to reinforce the moral effect.

People strolling, often with dogs, were either ignored or inspected from little more than tree-top height as the bird circled briefly above them before losing interest and making off for a high branch in some tree in one of the fields less subject to trespass.

The only feature of life at the reservoir which the osprey found intolerable was the dinghy sailing at Saturday- and Sunday-afternoon density. Confronted by this, it would decamp to one of the quieter waters for a few hours, remaining there until the bar opened, the boats came in, and the starting-gun and the klaxon had fallen silent. After the bird had gone the reservoir seemed a strangely dull and lonely place.

Why do they go? That thought has intrigued me for years. Our summer migrants – swallows, swifts, warblers, and so on – come here to exploit a summer harvest of insects, still substantial despite modern pesticides. When these hatches are ended by the onset of chilly autumn temperatures, they leave us. We then receive a winter influx from the north of lapwings, woodpigeons, duck, geese, wild swans and winter thrushes, finding here an environment still sufficiently benign to provide them with a supply of food – aquatic plants in water still free from ice, worms in unfrozen soil, hedgerow berries, as the case might be. If the Arctic follows them, as it does at the heart of many winters, they retreat before it, to Southern Ireland, to Iberia, to North Africa.

A typical English winter would not deny life-support to an osprey on an inland water for more than four or six weeks. The sea freezes in only exceptional conditions and ospreys suffer no inhibition forbidding them coastal shallows as hunting grounds. That fact is well recorded; I have myself seen evidence.

Twice departing ospreys have added to the entertainment on my favourite coastal beat in North Devon. One of them interrupted its migratory flight to fish, quartering the cliff-foot shallows with systematic persistence for half an hour before heading again for Land's End. It was not success-ful on that occasion, but the sport is one which guarantees automatic success to no one, as both bird and man watching it must have relearned many times.

Nor is the problem one of fish deserting coastal waters in winter. Some species do, but others move in to take their places. So why does the osprey not remain until conditions are bad enough to drive the winter migrants farther south, and then go with them? One can only guess that modern osprey behaviour is a continuing response to glaciation, and an endorsement of the classical view that evolution governs all, with Mother Nature operating her selective processes to her own uniquely unhurried time-scale. What is a period of 10,000 years to her, but a brief thaw in the northern temperate zone before the ice-sheet again comes between ospreys and their prey for nine months of the year?

Perhaps the ospreys are well advised not to change their habits too readily. None of us knows when the next glaciation might overwhelm us. Only the unthinking can bask calmly in the assumption that such phenomena belong irrevocably to the past.

Almost two years passed by at our local reservoir, more or less uneventful-ly, before another osprey visited. This one, a distinctly smaller specimen and therefore presumed to be a male, arrived on 11 August and remained until 20 August. Having a commitment in the middle of that period to visit North Devon for a look at the eyasses fledged successfully by a pair of peregrines I had watched there earlier in the year, I had less time to spend with the second osprey than with the first – 19¾ hours, to be exact, spread over five visits. It proved to be time well spent.

Naturally, I looked chiefly for differences in behaviour, making any allowance which seemed necessary for the difference in the dates – mid-August as compared with late September – and the fact that the level of the water in the reservoir was lower by three feet or so at the time of the second visit than it had been during the first.

The first difference to strike me was that, whereas the first visitor had often plunged spectacularly from a cruising altitude of 200 feet to take her prey from deep water, the second bird's technique was to patrol the deeps flying very much lower, surprising fish on or near the surface and taking some of them without wetting a feather. The female of the species a bolder hunter than the male? It seemed likely.

Indeed, dry feathers were the prime objective I assigned to the second bird in my assessments of motive, until I saw him splash down one afternoon into the shallows, to stand there with only his head in view until he emerged laboriously (and extremely wet) burdened by a bream of not less than 12 ounces in weight. That, though, was the largest fish I saw that osprey catch. His speciality was the capture of perch weighing from 4 to 8 ounces. That might imply that perch were more plentiful that year (their numbers fluctuate quite sharply) or that his sojourn in Scotland had influenced him in that direction. Perch are common in Spey valley lochans, roach and bream non-existent.

That line of thought assumes the possibility of highly selective fishing, by no means a fanciful suggestion. There is a school of well informed thought which holds that all raptors show a lifelong preference for the particular prey on which they were chiefly reared. Accepting that, one is faced by the catholicity of the other osprey's taste in fish. Can an attempt be made to account for that? It can. In the first place, birds are individuals, not automata. That means, among other things, that individual A could habitually hunt more, or less, opportunistically than individual B. In the second place, it is no more than assumption that the first (or indeed the second) osprey came from Scotland. Either could have been a member of the Swedish population (a hundred times the size of ours) and, if the original bird was, the fact that the carp family is infinitely better represented there than in Highland

PANDION PAYS A CALL

Scotland becomes extremely relevant. Cyprinids are likely to have been prominent among her first gastronomic experiences, and dominant thereafter while she was in Europe.

There were two other particulars in which these two ospreys, as observed during their Worcestershire sojourns, differed. The first, as I have already said, made a principle of heading straight for the shore with each capture, thus minimizing carriage over water. The second bird did not, going so far from the principle on one occasion as to change his mind after starting for the shore, reversing course to go back out over the deepest water to circle up to 500 feet and soar for several minutes with the small perch he had caught. Perhaps he knew that he had improved his grip; perhaps the perch had ceased its struggles. Perhaps he was an osprey which had dropped fewer fish back into the water to escape than his predecessor had. One can guess, but that is all.

The second difference was still more intriguing. The conduct of the first visitor conveyed no hint that anything but fish could hold the slightest interest for her. The second, after a particularly long spell of unproductive fishing one morning, flew purposefully to a nearby pasture, buzzed the solitary oaks standing in it one by one and flushed a number of wood-pigeons. Perhaps those which signalled the arrival of the first osprey with such displays of panic were behaving less hysterically than it seemed at the time.

Anecdotal evidence from the Spey valley and documented fact derived from studies of a Continental population both quote the pike as the fish most frequently taken by the osprey. Pike abound in our local reservoir, with plenty of young fish weighing less than 3 pounds, the limit of the osprey's theoretical lifting capacity. In late summer many of them haunt the shallows. Yet neither of our visitors was ever seen to catch a pike.

Far more important, neither bird was seen with a trout, or making a plunge into one of the trout pools – only into the lower reservoir, where the quarry was always a bream. The committee managing the fishing respected the law and were aware of the basics of wild bird protection, but I would not have cared to see their patience tried too sorely. It is, after all, a fishing, not a wildlife protection, committee.

A sample of two is not statistically significant, nor is Worcestershire in Scotland. Nonetheless, having watched the behaviour of these two ospreys with trout at their ready disposal, one is bound to look back a hundred years and ask whether the Victorian river keepers and gillies had a shred of justification for their exterminatory assault on these magnificent birds. When sea trout were running the rivers in their thousands, as they ran them in those palmy days, the ospreys, I am sure, took their share of them. They had done so since before mankind first set foot in these islands. And there were still plenty of both ospreys and sea trout when that benighted inventor found a way of loading a sporting gun at the breech with a composite cartridge.

The osprey which crossed my path most recently did so on 3 May 1987. The location was surprising; the course flown much more so. The place was Radnorshire, as it was once named; the course, although wavering a little, was basically east-south-east. After watching a peregrine cliff where nothing of interest had happened for an hour or more, I turned to scan those reaches of the sky which had been out of view behind me. What I discovered in an otherwise empty blue infinity was a raptor-shaped speck approaching in the far distance from the direction of Plynlimon, following the winding course of the upper River Wye.

It kept on coming, soon to become a silhouette with a strong hint of wings sharply angled at the carpal joints in the manner of a kite's. Why not? This was Radnorshire.

There was not much evident in the way of tail, though, and there were surprising glints of white flashing in the sun from some substantial feature in the plumage as the bird deflected or veered under control to correct its course in the gusty wind. May in Radnorshire is not like May in Eastbourne.

As three or four miles were reduced by the bird's steady progress to one or less, it became clear that this was no kite. The tail was not only without the diagnostic fork, it was even shorter than a typical buzzard's would have been. But, for all that, was the bird in truth an unusually pallid buzzard (such specimens are not all that uncommon) with a shorter than average tail and a wing profile distorted by some feather loss or injury, or even by an optical illusion? Bird watchers need to keep such possibilities in mind. The bird came closer still, still following the course of the river, keeping about a hundred feet higher than the high skyline to the north. Then and not before could I be sure that the bird I was watching with such concentration combined starkly contrasting sepia and white in its plumage – sepia above, white below – and that the gull-like crook in the broad wings was preserved as they were fully beaten. A buzzard often crooks its wings sharply while gliding, to spill air and reduce lift when it wishes to lose height, but it does not often hold them that way while beating them. Nor does one meet buzzards in two-tone finish. Dark buzzards, yes. Pale buzzards, too, but not sepia-backed, white-breasted buzzards.

The penny at last dropped. At long last. In the Spey valley, where eagle, buzzard and osprey would have been the logical probabilities, the bird would have been identified correctly at the first flash of the white breast in the distance. Here, there was some excuse for the extreme delay in recognition. One tends everywhere to see what one expects to see. Illusionists and confidence tricksters make careers out of the fact. One abandons with reluctance one's perceptions of the probable. In terms of bird watching, it is better so, for 249 times out of 250 the bird which has baffled one turns out in the end to be something quite commonplace, of the likely species, seen in the right place at the right time. It is only novices who fill their notebooks with hoopoes, saker falcons and sarus cranes seen in the valleys of mid-Wales.

Ospreys on passage there are not material for a phone call to the editor of *The Times*, but one flying an east-south-east course in early May was legitimately food for thought with a vengeance. Could it be, I speculated, that migrating birds might make errors, become aware of the fact and backtrack to correct them, seeking the point on the map spread out beneath them at which direction had been lost? Or did sub-adults, perhaps, leave the wintering grounds with the older birds flying north to nest, to spend that season in prospecting for new territories into which the species might expand its range? There could certainly be less economic ways for a species to achieve that end, and nature is not always as prodigally wasteful as it so often seems. A pity, I thought, that this osprey had not flown lower and nearer to give a better chance of making out the minor details of its plumage, and thereby estimating its age. If it was in fact a young bird, there would be grounds for speculating deeply on hypothesis number two.

The area being one in which several pairs of suitably interested eyes were often directed at the sky, I fed the news of the sighting into the local grapevine. No one, however, knowingly saw the osprey after it had passed from my view, which suggests that it did not linger. Twenty-four hours after I had seen it, it was probably back on course for the Spey valley and north of the border.

Luck often plays an important part in the recording of unusual bird sightings. Sometimes, a very big part.

thirteen   # THE SMALL VALLEY

My old route to the hills I searched so often for kites in the late 1960s led at one stage through a small steep-sided valley as romantically picturesque as a steel engraving in a nineteenth-century travel book. A small river threads its busy way through the boulders in the valley bottom; stern crags break through the turf to frown from its beetling skylines. Pipits there were in plenty in those days; wheatears bobbing and curtseying to the spring sunshine. Buzzard, raven and kestrel kept regular station overhead, joined occasionally by a wandering kite. Only the star was missing from the cast.

That was corrected in 1980, when, after an absence of at least fifteeen years, peregrines chose to resume occupation. But, forbidding though the valley's rocks could appear, especially when denser cloud veiled the sun, none was big enough to deter the thief in search of the rare egg or the saleable eyas. The return of peregrines there, of all places, demanded an expansion of responsibilities.

With one site of proven vulnerability already in care, and the colonel's to keep an eye on and cover at necessity, were we in shape to take on a third commitment? Histories and logistic and topographical factors had to be taken into account; high-risk and low-risk dates, times and periods. Related intimately to these was the overriding consideration of manpower, most of it not available on each of the seven days in any or every week of the season. Detailed calculations were made. Provided we did not end up by erecting three stools only to fall between them by attempting too comprehensive a cover for the small valley, the answer was yes: we could risk taking on the extra commitment.

Across the river from the road there stands a modest formation of rocks which just about merited being described as cliffs. Eric Hosking photographed peregrines there before the Second World War; it was there that these new peregrines gave the first indication of their intent to establish an eyrie. That was on 8 April. They were still there on 13 April, when the tiercel expanded my education by feeding his mate as though she were a chick as she sat crouched down in view, presumably covering or laying eggs. Neither such connubial feeding nor any hint of it had I ever witnessed before, but I was to see this tiercel do it again several times, both before *and after* the hatch, as she sat incubating the clutch or brooding the result of those labours.

By 26 April, though, that ledge, laid on or not, had been abandoned. If it had been robbed of eggs before abandonment, a large hole had been shot

through our strategic assumptions. On 4 May the falcon was on another disused ravens' nest, this one wedged almost invisibly (and so previously unobserved) in a small crevice high on the only rock in the valley not to be completely climbable without the aid of a rope. This lofty pyramid of rocks rose from roadside foundations on the side of the valley from which we proposed to guard. Whether it would therefore offer a tiresomely irresistible challenge to bank holiday and weekend scramblers – as well it might, thus located – only time would show.

From 4 May the site was attended more closely than before and we began to know these peregrines, too, as individuals – to discover a novel problem. Both seemed so large and each so closely resembled the other in terms of colour and markings that sexing was a matter of perpetual difficulty and much initial doubt. So, therefore, was record keeping as to nest reliefs and which bird should be credited with doing what. One, for example, had an unusually short tail, but it was not until 1982 that I finally satisfied myself beyond all uncertainty that I knew for certain which one it was.

Although both were exceptionally large specimens (unless the smaller scale of everything else in the small valley produced an optical illusion to that effect), the falcon was unquestionably the larger bird. Thus, if action began with helpful juxtaposition, we had a chance of recording confidently who did, in fact, do what. With such assistance I learned for certain that he, not she, was the particularly gifted hunter who watched from low perches, allowed woodpigeons to pass (there is no shortage of them in that valley) and then tracked them at their own pace along their own flight path, but six feet lower, to accelerate like a rocket when handy cover thinned out, and shoot up and attempt a snatch from directly below the victim. It seemed that he was lucky in his instincts or had been taught something by long experience concerning a woodpigeon's blind spot.

On 25 May I saw him score a near miss at a swallow, scatter a pack of crows like chaff in the wind, and go in to brood his chicks within twenty-four hours of our proving a hatch by observing the first feed. Not only a good provider, this one, but another tiercel with a generally well developed paternal instinct which his mate was willing to indulge. Not all are. The next day a cuckoo crossed the guard-post, calling with a still unbroken note. He came for it like a shot from a gun; the cuckooing ceased a moment after the birds had passed from view over the skyline above us. Twenty minutes later, the tiercel laboured back with his crop hanging as though containing a cricket ball. Years ago, a correspondent at the British Museum (Natural History) told me that all hawks detest cuckoos and kill far more of them than is generally supposed. This tiercel, at least, appeared to be privy to the secret.

On 27 May we had our first view of a little white head reared above the rim of the ravens' nest, watching mother perform an imitation of Hollywood's vision of a spaghetti-eating Italian as she dealt solicitously with some feet of viscera tugged from a middle-sized kill I had not identified in carriage. Thus are small chicks protected from the risk of choking or asphyxiation.

The weather in May of that year was kind, making the wardening of that site more of a pleasure than a chore. When the eyas flew on 25 June we had been troubled by only three intrusions, all made by sensible and courteous visitors to the valley who came down at our request and accepted the reasons given without complaint. One party (there is usually at least one) spent the rest of the day with the guard, learning how to enjoy bird watching from the inside.

This eyas (a tiercel, as it happened) made eight already flown from our patch – four each from the original site and from the colonel's – into a record of nine, which we have never again equalled from the three sites. It is possible that of the nine only one was a female. At most, only two; and, if two, both from the colonel's cliff.

A fledge in the small valley on 25 June implied a laying date at some time between 7 and 14 April. Peregrine eggs take between 28 and 32 days to hatch; chicks from six to seven weeks to fledge. So what of the falcon's sittings on the ledge across the valley on 8 and 13 April? We judged her to be a young bird laying for the first time; the story we laced up in retrospect strengthened that impression. Young falcons (and not only young ones, perhaps) have been known before to betray uncertainty as to where they really wish to set up home.

There was a comforting aspect to these calculations. Robbery of the ledge across the river later than 13 April would not have allowed time for a second clutch egg to have been laid early enough for its occupant to have hatched and fledged by 25 June. Splendid! Then another thought darkened the picture. What if all but the final egg of an original clutch had been stolen soon after 13 April and the clutch completed very prudently on the less accessible ravens' nest where success was achieved? Sadly, wardening does not necessarily supply answers to all the questions that events on a site might pose. That fact we were to have impressed upon us elsewhere in Wales, rather painfully, in 1985.

But that lay well ahead when, on 2 April 1981, Barney concluded with slight reservations that either laying or incubation was in progress again in the high ravens' nest on the tall rocks by the road. On 7 April I joined him, concurring in his opinion after a day's watching. On the 9th we saw the tiercel knock feathers, including a large scapulary, out of a kite trying to pass inoffensively over the rock, and, with the falcon's help, attempt the murder of one of the valley's buzzards right over our lay-by. Yet both peregrines permitted themselves at some time on that same day to be charged summarily off skyline anthills on which they were trying to relax in the sunshine by a ewe with a lamb at foot unwilling to tolerate the unfamiliar. One can rarely predict accurately the patterns of animal aggression and response. Peregrines, except during odd flashes of frantic displacement activity – as, for example, after otherwise uncompensated infuriation by the activities of a fox – certainly offer no threat to sheep and then only minimally. A scratch from a talon is the worst to be feared. Not, of course, that one may count on the ovine brain being up to appreciating that fact.

On 11 April the falcon returned from a trip out of the valley followed by a screaming eyas tiercel demonstrating belief that he had some claim on her by rolling beneath her in flight and begging noisily for the kill she was carrying to be dropped to him. The product of 1980, it appeared, had survived the winter. That visit was followed by others, culminating on 17 May in a pursuit of the tiercel to the very nest, where it stood for a few moments beside its 1981 siblings, imploring a share in the goodies delivered. Mamma ignored him; Papa took off and led him patiently away.

Every peregrine wardening inspires new theories. Now I had evidence to support one that it is sexual jealousy between mature and sub-adult females which finally breaks up peregrine families, not a generation gap as such.

A fortnight earlier, on 3 May, with the help of a tenacious red chequer racing pigeon, the tiercel had done something else to expand my comprehension of his kind and the limitations they may labour under. Rain had driven me into the car, where I remained in touch only by courtesy of the windscreen wipers. Switching them on for a check, I found two birds in the sky up-valley, sparring very close to a tall, sheer rock beyond the site. One was the pigeon, fluttering in search of cover; the other, the tiercel, trying to snatch it before it succeeded. The pigeon, though, could flutter. The tiercel, in the still moist air of that afternoon, could not. Every failure to connect gave him three options. One, crash into the tall rock; two, stall and fall to the ground; three, haul off into what faint breeze there was, describe a half-circle taking him a hundred yards away across the valley, and come in again, rather faster than was desirable in the circumstances. Having tried and failed by employing the third option twice, he attempted a compromise solution by hauling off about thirty yards and hovering like some great bulky kestrel in the mouth of the little gully closed by the rock.

After ten minutes of this wing-work (exhausting for a bird three times the weight of a kestrel) he did what I had expected him to do sooner – fly away as though he had lost interest and position himself on the skyline above the guard-post to cut off the pigeon's retreat when it plucked up courage to make the attempt. It did not, before dark, so my view of prudent tactics proved no more productive than the tiercel's had been at the outset. Not having seen the whole of the action I may have done him less than justice, though. He may have known that a fatal blow had already been struck, and that if the pigeon was not flushed from cover promptly he would be attempting the eviction of a corpse. To comprehend a peregrine's range of choices fully, one needs to be one.

And so matters progressed. On 10 May two white heads were visible at feeding time; on 15 May, possibly a third, seen for certain on 22 May. The following day produced a spectacular moment of truth. At 2.45 p.m. I spotted the tiercel dashing down-valley, pacing a flight of five racing pigeons from his preferred station thirty yards astern and six feet below. Homers, though, can be even sharper-witted than woodpigeons. This flight was alert, caught a glimpse of the tiercel as he began to rocket up, and scattered as though a shell had exploded in their midst. Alert they were, but not blessed with quite enough luck. Quickly choosing a single target, the tiercel deflected, closed, grabbed, sent wing feathers flying but, missing flesh, only knocked the pigeon lurching. Its staggerings took it right into the talons of the big falcon, positioned perfectly like a good slip fielder to take the catch without changing station by as much as an inch. I have watched hunts by peregrine pairs which seem to employ collaboration only to get in each other's way, to the benefit of most of the targets. This pair in the small valley, though, was different, as I was to see proved a number of times in that and the next nesting season.

Nothing more of note took place that May, except a bizarre attempt by a strange brace of trippers to propel a push-chair, complete with infant occupant, up the bank towards the eyrie after a careful explanation had been given as to where and where not in the valley they could explore without offence. It is not the birds that surprise one when on peregrine guard; it is some of the people. The fact that these two had binoculars about their necks, disclosed after the ascent had begun, did nothing to sweeten my tongue when I followed to bring them down.

And so we come to 1 June, when I returned after a week off duty to begin the 24-hours-a-day stage of the watch, moving the car at night to a lay-by directly under the eyrie and dozing there until the alarm clock proclaimed dawn to be only an hour away. By now my equipment included a powerful spotlight connected to the car battery and mounted for hand-holding. Not that I seriously expected a nocturnal attempt in that dangerously rugged terrain, but I wished to be prepared for one if I had guessed wrong.

The evening had been horribly humid, the sky at sunset frightening. A few minutes into 2 June there came a peal of thunder accompanied by an almost equally loud crash of rain on the roof of the car. Pandemonium then broke loose. Lightning forked before, behind, and below the car, the thunder-cloud reaching within minutes to the valley bottom. The roar of thunder was continuous for three hours, all but the loudest peals drowned out in the end by the combined voices of rain and river, the stream risen ten feet by dawn to boom over its boulders in a mad torrent. Giving myself up for lost at about 2 a.m., I philosophically consumed some of the choicest of my week's rations. The condemned man, after all, is entitled by tradition to such small considerations.

The first loom of light hinted at 3.45 a.m. that there would be a dawn. At 6.20 the fitful doze of a nervously exhausted man was interrupted by a clamour of sounds unmistakable in origin but not altogether familiar in tone or timbre. The rain having at last eased, I got out of the car with the binoculars and focused them. Both birds, wing and tail feathers saturated and stuck together to show gaps suggesting an attempt during the night to pluck them like poultry, tore through the grey sky overhead, making hysterical passes at each other and the ravens' nest, as they screamed brokenly and cried 'pep pep pep' in that tone never heard before.

There was no intruder, human or otherwise, in sight. What in God's name had happened? Had I invited disgrace again – this time by sleeping the sleep of the exhausted through an entire first-light raid, despite having been within arrowshot of the eyrie?

I decided that I must assume the worst and call the police. After the loss of another ten minutes while I struggled to dry out a short-circuiting ignition system, the engine fired and began to turn, and I raced down the road to the nearest telephone. The message delivered, I returned to carry out the remainder of the emergency drill. As I pulled into my daylight guard-post, the police car arrived, manned by two officers I had come to know well. After a few questions, they drove on, to find open ground from which the radio could be operated. Coming back a few minutes later, they halted at the foot of the eyrie rocks, dismounted and looked up.

With my binoculars also levelled at the site from the guard-post down-valley, the falcon chose that moment to alight on the rim of the nest, reach down into it, lift the dead body of a big but still downy chick by the scruff of its neck and dump it to lie limply on the edge, half in, half out of the nest. So there had been no raid with theft in mind. The disaster began to look more like the work of Nature in her guise as blind destroyer, aided, perhaps, by the falcon's reported decision on the night of 30 May that the time had arrived to start roosting away from the chicks. Exposure seemed the likeliest cause of their deaths, and her sheltering presence might have been just enough to avert them. Do Sod and his Law ever fail us? Whatever the answer, there were reasons enough to attempt recovery of the cadavers for autopsy.

After another trip out of the gorge to radio again, ordering a police stand-down to curtail waste of more time and petrol by other cars and crews, by then heading for cut-off points on escape roads, one of the officers made the greasy climb up the steep bank to see from above what might be accomplished. Nothing, he reported; without a rope. Arrangements were put in hand.

On 4 June a rope-man arrived, made the descent and recovered casualties. Taken straight to a handy field study centre, they were examined and weighed. There were only two, both of them weighing at between three and four weeks of age a dram above or below 2 pounds, only half a pound short of adult weight. The texture of their outgrown down reminded one of the flue on a pipe-cleaner; it no longer served any conceivable purpose, unless to evoke some aspect of parental response. Talons were well developed and sharp, but bills were no more formidable than a Rhode Island Red's.

Of the third chick there had been no trace, leading to an assumption that the site was not fox-proof. Had the delay in making the descent been longer, there might well have been nothing left to recover. The ravens' nest, however, was all too waterproof. A MAFF laboratory which performed the autopsies found thoracic haemorrhaging to have been the cause of death. That, I was told by a friend in the medical profession (another peregrine enthusiast by way of recreation), spelt death by asphyxiation, not exposure. So they drowned. A strange death for unfledged peregrine falcons, but there was a crumb of comfort. Analysis yielded no trace of organochlorine residues or of toxic heavy metals, another threat to the species since discovered. Whatever else, the hawks in the small valley had been proved free of chemical contamination. Consequently, we entered the 1982 season more certain than ever that the job we proposed to do was worth while.

Discouraged, perhaps, by the 1981 failure, the birds moved back across the river to Eric Hosking's cliff. I found them there on 9 April, and proved incubation by observing a relief on 11 April. On 10 April a car had driven up and halted for a middle-aged man of athletic build to disembark and introduce himself as Ken Whitehead, a Shropshire farmer with whom I had corresponded about articles written for *The Field*, and whose daughter I had taken bird watching at his telephoned request in August 1981 on Plynlimon, near where she then resided.

He was now a recruit for the guard and as our connection developed became another close and valued friend gained through wardening the peregrine falcon. Not all farmers, whatever the newspapers allege to the contrary, regard the environment solely as a source of profit. By the end of the 1982 nesting season, Ken and his daughter had given ample proof of that fact. She, indeed, had saved the situation one night during a period of high risk by wardening single-handed from dusk to dawn to fill a gap which yawned suddenly without warning in the guard roster.

In describing the events of 1982 I shall confine myself to what the year produced by way of novelty. The first observed feed, proving the hatch, took place on 11 May. On the same day we discovered that a pair of carrion crows had three sooty nestlings in a nest in a tree only a hundred yards from the eyrie. That, one could predict confidently, must in due course result in drama. On 12 May the tiercel distinguished himself by delivering no fewer than five substantial kills. On 13 May the falcon made a surprising hunting

THE SMALL VALLEY

trip; so soon after the hatch she might have been expected still to be preoccupied with brooding the new chicks. What she brought in with her, unobserved until she swept up to the ledge with it, raised eyebrows and set tongues wagging. A stout yellow leg, as thick and sturdy as her own, projected from a glimpse of snowy plumage figured in black which was all of it her mantling wings disclosed during the feed. Were we the witnesses of murder followed by cannibalism, or had she snatched a Light Sussex pullet from somewhere on the farmlands beyond the valley's mouth? Either was a disturbing prospect.

By then I knew the local farmers, one of whom I visited to ask questions. No. No Light Sussex or other basically white-plumaged poultry were kept in the area. We did not need to fear an outraged farmer with a twelve-bore shotgun. There being no other obvious candidate for identification, thoughts turned again to murder and cannibalism. Other peregrines had visited the valley and had been chased angrily away. I supposed it was only a matter of time before we witnessed a fatal encounter, or its aftermath.

I had seen through the telescope a fair quantity of débris knocked over the edge to fall to the turf and bracken below. When the brood fledged, the scavenging trip then lawful should reveal much of the true status of Madame – murderess or otherwise included. It was not to be. At 3.45 in the small hours of 15 June there was an outbreak of pandemonium recalling the clamour of the disastrous dawn of the previous June. Now, though, there was light from neither moon nor stars, nor any of significance from the yet unrisen sun. The big spotlight picked out first the glassy green eyes of a vixen and her cub, then their silver-gold bodies as they beat me to the scavenging at the foot of the low cliffs. Far more important, it illuminated in brighter silver the bullet-shaped bodies of the airborne peregrines as they stooped screaming in virtually total darkness at the impertinent intruders. Who says owls and hawks differ in that the latter are – and must be – completely diurnal by habit? Not Dick Orton, after 15 June 1982. Peregrines are at hazard from foxes, foxes from peregrines, both from *Homo* so-called *sapiens*. A feature of the 1982 watch were visits from scruffy little men from South Wales in beaten-up old vans laden with terriers and digging equipment. In search of fox skins or victims for illegal badger baiting, they were anxious to be told whether we had seen signs of either animal. The police were glad to be given the descriptions and registration numbers of the vehicles. Control being one thing and exploitation another, I was always more than happy to oblige the law enforcers.

As expected, war to the knife broke out between peregrines and crows, with ravens suffering some of the backwash from it. On 16 June one of the adult crows forgot itself so far as to stoop peregrine-fashion at the falcon as she stood on the ground enjoying a well earned pigeon. Abandoning it on the instant, she rose screaming with rage to tower, plunge, and send the crow, a confusion of broken flight-quills, crashing through the canopy of a clump of oaks beneath. The hint was taken, for the crows removed themselves four hundred yards down-valley.

By then we knew the brood to comprise one eyas tiercel and two eyas falcons – one of the latter a smart specimen, the other a late-developing oddity with so much unplucked down adhering to her head at six weeks of age that she seemed to be wearing a lawyer's wig. As usual, the little tiercel outreached his sisters in enterprise. So much so that he fell from the ledge before he could fly – drop-out number two in my experience of the species. He worried me much and Barney, now a man sickening towards death and fully aware of the fact, considerably more.

But this tiercel was a total survivor. Before night fell and the foxes began to prowl, he had contrived to clamber up out of danger. Eighteen hours later, a sudden and unexpected sighting of him over the road, gliding fifty feet above the car to bank, turn and beat competently back to the cliffs, established that he was safely on the wing.

While his sisters dawdled, his parents took to hunting the hillside behind me for I knew not what. Startled pipits and wheatears sped in panic before them as they quartered the slope like harriers, but no attack ever developed. Something else preoccupied them. Finally, when the falcon presented a capture to the eyas tiercel, almost on the road, when I already had the telescope trained on him, I discovered what had been hunted – *lizards*, one of which she was killing by holding it in her bill and by banging it against the rock. Her son played with it for a while, but abandoned it uneaten.

Time dragged on as the eyas falcons rested too comfortably in their nursery. My time ran out; Ken and Susie Whitehead took over. They ran out of time at 11 a.m. on 23 June, the eyas falcons, now unaccountably rejoined by their fledged brother, still ledge-bound. When Barney arrived at 1.30 p.m. all three eyasses were on the wing. What an irony! After the most time-consuming and totally committed operation we had ever engaged in, not one of us witnessed a first flight. It was the first time a successful operation had not included that consummating pleasure.

In 1983, a year of widespread failure throughout Britain, eggs were laid in the small valley, but not hatched. In 1984 egg theft had to be assumed before we could assemble a guard. In 1985 the peregrines left the valley at the beginning of the nesting season, after haunting it throughout the winter. In 1986 I found peregrines nearby on a hillside beyond a locked gate at the end of June. Whether they were the pair from 1980–2, I could not get near enough to determine. Someone, I learned, had kept an eye on them, however, leading to a happy outcome. In 1987 I again lost touch, and did not regain it in 1988.

In April 1989 I learned that the eyas tiercel which left the ledge prematurely in 1982 had come back into recorded history. On 26 May 1982 he had been fitted with a stamped leg-ring by which his identity could be determined if ever he should afterwards come to hand. On 8 November 1987 he did: lying with one wing broken by the roadside just outside a village fifteen miles from the valley where he had been hatched. Under veterinary care, his wing mended. As so often happens though, when injured raptors receive treatment in captivity, he died inexplicably during convalescence. Oddly enough, the village near which he was picked up is only one and a half miles from the little churchyard where Barney's ashes lie buried. At times, the ornithologist's world can seem a very small one.

fourteen
THE MOST PERSECUTED HAWK

Harriers, comparatively large hawks which hunt by quartering terrain systematically at low altitude, have been rare or scarce in Britain throughout and beyond living memory. The first one I ever saw – a marsh harrier – stared with the somewhat owl-like face common to all harrier species from the glossy surface of a cigarette card issued fifty-seven years ago by Messrs Players, one of a set entitled 'British Birds'. The handsome male chosen for the study stood characteristically by a nest amid reeds containing two well grown chicks in white down.

Thanks were due to the great George Lodge for the next encounter – a splendid male hen harrier posed on a moorland boulder gazing out from a colour-plate in Kirkman and Jourdain's book also entitled *British Birds*. That was four or five years later.

Manhood had overtaken me before a harrier in the feather came my way, which happened in circumstances almost terminal for the bird. I was driving an army truck along the coast road which bounds the Libyan desert when we met, near a place then named Misurata. Sweeping up from scrub on the left, the bird took just enough time to bank and declare itself *Circus macrourus* (pallid harrier, not found in Britain) before escaping contact with the windscreen by inches, to waft away in the light breeze over the scrub which thinned out to the right, towards the authentic desert inland.

I had a particular reason for recognizing it with certainty. There had been a

THE MOST PERSECUTED HAWK

fine specimen in Tripoli's little natural history museum, where I had recently occupied leisure hours in helping the Italian curator provide his collection with English-language name cards.

Then came a remarkable hiatus, broken at last in 1968 on what is now the A939, between Tomintoul and Cock Bridge in the wilder Scottish Highlands. The bird was a 'ringtail' hen harrier (female or immature male) following a covey of five red grouse a few feet above the heather. I was more than pleasantly surprised because when I had pored over George Lodge's picture more than thirty years earlier the species was thought to be extinct in Britain, apart from Orkney and the southern Outer Hebrides, where a few pairs were said to cling tenuously to survival.

Other raptor species 'threatened with extinction' had begun to receive publicity by 1968, but not those which had used the 1940s and 1950s first to escape from that threat, then to recolonize historical habitat outside the heartland. European wars which exchanged the gamekeeper's twelve-bore for a sniper's rifle were good news for upland wildlife; so, initially, were socialist taxation policies which left major landowners pressed too hard to meet the high labour costs of effective grouse-moor management. Not until the grouse moors began to vanish under a conifer blanket did most of us awake to the fact that there might be worse threats to raptors than a sport-crazy laird and keepers' overenthusiasm for the 'vermin-control' side of their duties.

My companions in the car that day, assured that they had been witnesses to an ornithological event earning a red star in the notebook, moved house shortly afterwards from Worcestershire to Comrie in Perthshire. Two years later still, I went to stay with them, breaking my journey an hour before tea-time arrival at the house to take the binoculars up Glen Artney for a look at what might be there.

There were black grouse galore, bending branches precariously as they disbudded willow trees, and, before long, a fine male hen harrier quartering the snowy March moorland across the Ruchel to catch the reflected light on plumage which might have been designed specially to make the best of it.

THE HAWKWATCHER

Apart from the yellow of the eyes, cere and legs, there are no true colours in a male hen harrier – just black, white and a lovely hue of pale pearly-grey. My disclosure of the news a little later over the teacups was met with smiles which, but for muscular restraint, would have been patronizing. There were, I was told, no fewer than fifteen pairs of hen harriers nesting by then on a restricted area of moorland within ten miles of the village.

It seemed that my ornithology was badly out of date, but here was a chance to amend it. I soon discovered a promising stretch of moorland easy to watch from beside the road to Braco and decided that early mornings and evenings should be spent there. The moor proved to be well populated by grouse, black and red; by curlew, snipe, redshank and oystercatcher; and by mountain hares still in white or mottled pelleage. Ringtail hen harriers came to hunt there two and three at a time and to battle for hunting rights with short-eared owls visiting in similar numbers at the same times of day. The hares, I noted with interest, ignored the harriers, but grouse fled in haste at their arrival.

The welcome news of the abundance had been accompanied by some less comforting. Keepers were already growing worried and illegal destruction had begun. Judging by the reaction of the grouse I had seen in hasty retreat, it was not altogether surprising. The recovery, however, continued for several more years, despite growing pressure to curb it. Between 1972 and 1977 a hen harrier had ceased to be a notable event in my bird-watching life. I could watch them almost to order each winter on the marshlands towards the mouth of the Dovey, on the heather slopes of the Long Mynd in Shropshire, and occasionally even nearer home.

A low-flying target pestered by a kestrel one February morning on my Warwickshire bird-watching territory proved, when finally tormented into visible response, to be a fine male harrier. It remained there hunting voles and starlings in and over an old rearing-field then becoming overgrown with scrub, before ringing up in my presence to about 5,000 feet at eleven o'clock one morning to continue its migration to the north. Harriers are usually noticed as they fly a few feet above the ground, but all species soar beautifully when the spirit moves them. Quite often it does. In a recent survey of hawks soaring over the Camargue the total time spent by marsh harriers in this exercise exceeded that of all other hawks recorded.

In September 1976 I took a holiday cottage on the Sound of Mull and could scarcely step outside it, so it seemed, without a ringtail passing by in view. There is a theory that single sex migration routes are used by the species to leave the nesting territories, and Morvern gave me no reason to question it. Ynyshir on the Dovey was another matter, but that was a destination, not a staging-post.

Where those birds came from was of particular interest. It was assumed to be the Berwyns, between the valleys of the Tanat and the Dee, where the RSPB found evidence of nesting soon after their Welsh Office was opened. What was yet more interesting was the discovery of an ancient shepherd who claimed to have known the harrier as a summering species since boyhood, when, according to the ornithological wisdom of the day, none bred in Britain outside Orkney and the Hebrides.

I found hen harriers of both sexes in the heart of the Cambrians in the late 1960s and should not be at all surprised if they never ceased to breed there either, in what was during the first half of this century one of the thinnest-populated and least trodden areas in the whole of Britain.

Cold linear dimensions cursorily referred to present the hen harrier as a hawk approaching buzzard size, ranging in overall length between parity and a shortfall of only two or three inches in twenty. Seen on the wing, though, the impression of size is more that of an expanded hen sparrowhawk. Comparison of weights clinches the point. A male hen harrier weighs, on average, only 20 per cent more than a hen sparrowhawk, while even the male buzzard may double or treble the weight of the harrier. Comparison of wing-spans – from 46 to 54 inches in the buzzard, from 40 to 43 in the harrier – also brings one nearer the reality the eye perceives.

By the end of the 1970s I had ceased to stumble on hen harriers in unexpected places. Murmurings from game-rearing interests in protest at the maximum class of protection accorded to the species by the law indicated why. Closer investigation confirmed the point. Some upland keepers detest all the larger raptors and destroy them whenever they can do so without risk of prosecution. Some draw distinctions, often sparing the golden eagle and the peregrine for the splendour of their size or flight. I have yet to consult one, though, who willingly spares the harrier.

This is not because they destroy more grouse than the other two; it is because the mere appearance of a harrier on a shooting day can fatally disrupt the management of the drives. The guns are in the butts, the beaters in position, the signal due. Along wafts a harrier from one flank; off go the packs of grouse to the other. Tweed-clad men sweating in the late August heat face more miles of rough walking through tall heather; guns who have invested heavily in expectation of hectic sport resent their deprivation. Wrong though it emphatically is, one cannot be surprised that the departing harrier is at times sped on its way with lead. Matters are not helped by the tendency of the harriers to form breeding colonies where food supply is generous and game preservation not rigorous enough to deny them the opportunity.

The fox is the chief natural enemy, as of all other large ground-nesting birds, and, especially when a decline in the supply of prey keeps the adults away from the nest hunting for longer than usual, the fox collaborates with the shortage to cut the harrier population back to what the terrain can support. If left to get on with it by their human neighbours, the harriers respond to the next explosion of prey by increasing the size of the clutches laid.

If only harriers did not interfere so unacceptably with the *mechanics* of the grouse shoot, such reasoning might fall less often on deaf ears within the community of the gun. With the canopy now closed by growth in the plantations the birds exploited at the beginning of the forestry boom, the situation is a most unhappy one. The grouse moor is again the preferred habitat of the hen harrier and numbers have declined so sharply in the last few years, after the post-war population increase which brought me my widespread sightings between 1968 and 1980, that the species, as I write this

THE MOST PERSECUTED HAWK

chapter, now occupies top slot on the RSPB's list of raptors in Britain needing priority protection.

Hartham's famous account of the birds of Worcestershire includes a report of a late-nineteenth-century shooting of a marsh harrier in a streamside field over which I can look from an upstairs window in my home in the village of Alvechurch. I doubt if one has flown there since. This hawk, whose prey includes ducklings, had been exterminated in Britain by the turn of the century, and made only slow progress towards recovery, virtually confined to a heartland in the reed forests of Norfolk and Suffolk, after recolonization in the 1920s. Like other raptors, the marsh harrier benefited from diversion of human energies during the Second World War and began to look set to establish itself securely in East Anglia at least. We did not, however, enjoy even a reflection of the quite dramatic expansion which occurred among marsh harriers in some other parts of north-western Europe.

That may have been because the British Isles are by geographical necessity on the margin of this harrier's zone of occupation, or because its heartland here was subjected so early after the war to the blast of expanded aquatic recreation which has since spread everywhere else in Britain where water lies in a lake bed or trickles over gravel. Had the marsh harrier been distributed more generously here at the onset of the drainage mania of the last three decades, that programme would no doubt have put the bird's progress into reverse once again, as it has curtailed expansion in similarly affected parts of continental Europe. Draining to create polders in Holland has helped the species increase there, but draining riverine marshes for cultivation elsewhere, as we have done here, has obviously had the opposite effect. Yet, in spite of these factors there are signs that marsh harriers are again returning to some of their traditional sites outside East Anglia.

However, I doubt if any of the debts due from bird watchers to the RSPB are as great as that owed for the chance to see marsh harriers virtually on demand in present day Britain. Their reserve at Minsmere in Suffolk is the one sure find, and its small but stable population of the birds an invaluable nucleus from which a few of the quieter places in the general area could be recolonized. Due, no doubt, to boat traffic, Hickling Broad and Horsey Mere, the sites benefiting first from the natural recolonization of the 1920s, were as busy as a Birmingham park pool and understandably devoid of harriers when I last paid a summer visit.

The Minsmere harriers can be watched from inside the reserve, but also from favoured vantage-points outside it – and anywhere 20 feet above sea level in that extraordinarily flat terrain qualifies for that description. From a public footpath just to the south of the reserve, I have watched two pairs plus an intruder engaged simultaneously in the spectacular mating flights which are possibly the marsh harrier's principal claim to ornithological attraction. It is the largest of the harriers seen in Europe and the only one to be mistaken excusably for a buzzard when detail is not discernible. When it is visible, a typical male is seen to be a handsomely decorated and unmistakable bird, with grey, black and sienna-brown patterning the plumage in a not entirely predictable formula. Females are much darker than all but exceptional males, with diagnostic help offered by their creamy crowns and similarly coloured leading edges to the inner wings. One of my most aesthetically satisfying hawkwatching recollections is of the spectacle made by a superbly coloured male as he soared up into a cloudless Minsmere sunset in the track of a starling flight swirling up ahead of him.

Outside East Anglia, I have seen marsh harriers only twice. One was a male grounded in a reedbed in the Nile Delta; the other, a female soaring in contentious company with a buzzard over my peregrine cliffs in North Devon of all improbable places on a sunny morning in May 1979. Had the upper surfaces of both birds not been below eye-level at the time and perfectly illuminated by sunlight streaming brightly from behind my right shoulder, I should not have believed what the binoculars were showing me. If before that occasion I had been asked where in Britain one would *not* see a marsh harrier, the North Devon coast would have sprung to mind second only to Piccadilly Circus.

Hartham's *Birds of Worcestershire* told not only of a marsh harrier shot in the parish where I now reside, but also of Montagu's harrier nesting successfully in a cornfield on an estate only six miles from the village.

Although rare enough for concern during the years of my boyhood, this was nevertheless Britain's commonest harrier at that time. I have lived to see it die out altogether in 1974 and to begin a recovery in 1976 when two pairs are recorded as having bred, and I, astonished, watched a female Montagu's soar in company and apparent amity for ten minutes one May evening with the peregrine falcon I was then guarding in Radnorshire. Had the peregrine not been there for size-reference I should have assumed the harrier to be *Circus cyaneus*, despite its evidently small size and slight build – slight even by the modest pretensions of all species of harrier. Identification was aided by my having seen a chestnut-breasted juvenile before 1974, fleeing before a crow pack over the sheep pastures behind the cliffs of the North Devon peregrine site. The chestnut breast was diagnostic; other features associated with it stuck firmly in my memory. A sighting of that bird there was not so surprising, because in that year they had bred just over the Cornish border, in new forestry.

I have since been favoured twice: on the western edge of Salisbury Plain, and in mid-Dorset. On 29 September 1984 I was parked on the Plain just short of an area closed to the public in the interests of safety and military training, there to share with companions a view with certain nostalgic connotations. The kestrel I had expected to see there had come to hover briefly, and had then flown from view into one of the Plain's characteristic 'bottoms'. Thus had it ensured (bless its ashy pate) that the binoculars were already in my hand when another hawk emerged from the bottom as though warned by the kestrel that it was due to go on bird-watching duty. It was a fine female Montagu's and she quartered the down between the car and the bottom for long enough for me to impress my friends – one of whom I had not seen in forty years – with the remarkable erudition since acquired.

The second sighting mentioned was over a newly harvested cornfield somewhere between Blandford and Puddletown. The harrier hovered like a big broad-winged kestrel, attracted no doubt by displaced mice or voles. The only place where I could have pulled off the road for a better look at the bird was already occupied by two dented cars and two irate drivers squaring up to discuss responsibility. Perhaps the harrier had been on view for some minutes and one or both of them hawk enthusiasts, too. Thinking it wiser not to inquire, I re-engaged gear and drove on. That was 30 September 1987.

I doubt if I should have seen Montagu's harriers twice in four years during my comparatively infrequent visits to Wiltshire and Dorset unless their numbers had made a quite remarkable recovery in southern England since 1974. Not that they are totally confined to the south. One pair, I know for a fact, bred successfully in a recent year in a field on the outskirts of a northern industrial town, within a few yards of a footpath.

That, of course, is not untypical of the species. Farmers in parts of France, when the species was common there and welcome as a rodent killer, used to erect platforms on the edges of cornfields so that the harriers might rear their young in greater security.

If my guess at a greater number visiting England to breed in recent years is not adrift, I might yet have the pleasure of training the binoculars on an adult male. It is nice to have a novel experience still to look forward to in one's seventh decade.

fifteen   PEREGRINES
MYSTIFY THE WATCHERS

In 1980 the peregrine recovery in Wales extended its southerly reach to include the Black Mountains and the Brecon Beacons. One of the traditional sites then reoccupied was one studied in the 1930s by Dr Charles Walker of Hereford, a natural historian of high local standing whose enthusiasm for the falcons had not been noticeably diminished by the arrival of his eighty-fifth birthday. Many and pleasant were the hours we spent together in 1980 and again in 1981, watching the year's family of eyasses on the wing, three in each case, soaring and playing over their lofty sandstone cliff.

On 17 April 1982 we construed a five-hour stint on the scrape performed by the tiercel as a message transmitted loud and clear that incubation was emphatically in progress again and that we could look forward in confidence to mid-June and eyasses again at play in the sky. At the conclusion of a visit on 20 May we left in good heart, satisfied that the falcon had been observed in the act of feeding chicks, although no chick had indisputably been seen.

On 2 June Dr Walker, visiting alone, had been rained off before either adult had visited the ledge. On the 11th, we were greeted with the news that a licensed ringing team had made a roped descent on the 6th to discover nothing but a single addled egg awaiting their inspection. The chicks which had hatched from fertile eggs in the clutch had vanished without trace.

With only two failures from natural causes in the sixteen peregrine nestings I had by then wardened – and both of them in conditions fairly to be described as freakish – I had no hesitation in ascribing this one to theft.

Early in the following March a meeting was held at the site to plan a guarding operation in which I should participate at some stage, as my other wardening commitments permitted. The watch began, but suspicions formed before April was out led to a roped descent on 6 May. It discovered only two eggs – a cracked one lying in the scrape, another undamaged but stone-cold lying outside it. By that year we knew that peregrine eggs were being taken by another class of thief for artificial incubation, covered by a pretence of captive breeding. Might this be at the root of our troubles? The leaving of two obviously unhatchable eggs on the ledge gave a strong hint that it might be.

For 1984, therefore, it was decided to plan a more elaborate operation, supported by the provision of tents for better protection from the weather, required by volunteers if they were to engage themselves again. The site could be watched from cars parked in the yard of the farm down the hill, but volunteers who had served in 1983 were anxious to be nearer their charges.

Better experienced than most in the full horror of what the Welsh uplands could inflict on those venturing into them, even as late in the year as June, I had my misgivings but did not press them. Others, perhaps, had equal experience on which to rest this trust in canvas, and Jeremiahs – especially know-all Jeremiahs – antagonize rather than influence their fellows.

A visit paid early on the morning of 23 May, following a report of a hatch on the 18th, found the guard-post saturated and abandoned. The absent sentries arrived soon afterwards, their faces masks of despair. With tents and 'waterproof' clothing reduced to sopping wet ruin by a violent storm, they had abandoned the post at dusk on the 22nd to go home and dry out. Returning dry-clad at first light, they had already sensed trouble. Failure was in the air.

As the day wore on, the behaviour of the birds confirmed it, pointing in the circumstances to an uglier possibility than we had imagined. Did robbery which followed the desertion of the post so promptly not imply a traitor in our midst? 'Traitor' was not too dramatic a term. All the local people, the gamekeeper included, had professed regret at the earlier failures and moral support for the wardening. Another descent for inspection again brought to light nothing but unhatched eggs, two of them, on the scrape.

The year passed into history and 1985 arrived. The time had come, thought Dr Walker, for a rolling up of sleeves. Money was raised, the commitment of the County Trust expanded, arrangements made to erect a properly equipped and fully waterproof wooden guard-hut large enough to sleep two. Troops were recruited sufficient to mount a 24-hour-a-day watch from the laying of the eggs to the date on which the young birds flew well enough to be safe from any attempt which might be made on them.

Not only had we the hut. Thanks to help from the local military, we were wired for virtually unbroken telephone communication all the way to the handiest police station. Never had I been involved in a peregrine-guarding operation with so much promise and back-up.

On 8 April I 'opened the batting' with an old comrade from earlier wardenings elsewhere in Wales, Jack Smith from Leominster, another fine local naturalist, but one, like me, who first saw the light of day in Birmingham, where, oddly enough, we had attended the same primary school, a fact we did not discover until more than forty years after we had moved on from it. Talk of skylarks had led to the discovery. 'I knew a square mile of commonland inside a city boundary where they sang by the dozen in 1930,' said I. 'I attended a school within five minutes' walk of a common like that,' replied Jack.

And so we began to watch, supplied with cooking equipment, even tea, coffee, powdered milk and sugar. The only chore, assuming we had arrived with all the food we should need, was to toil up the hill with water in two 4½-gallon plastic jerrycans every morning. The extent of my past experience made me a particularly welcome member of this guard, and had led to a request for written notes to guide the newcomers. I subscribed them gladly, confident that I could base them on four certainties.

THE HAWKWATCHER

1   Although tiercels share incubation dutifully, they do not visit the scrape for more than a few moments at a time until laying has truly begun. Hence: reliefs = eggs truly laid.

2   Apart from swallowing the odd morsel while feeding the chicks, the adult does not feed at the scrape between the laying of the first egg and the fledging of the last eyas. Hence: prey carried to the ledge (and not brought out intact soon afterwards) = chicks or eyasses there to be fed.

3   That an infertile clutch will not be incubated for more than a week or so after the latest feasible hatch date of the egg which was laid last.

4   That a peregrine knows by reliable instinct the difference between eggs and chicks, and exactly what is due to both.

Neither on 8 April nor the next day was there evidence of incubation having begun. Each time the birds seemed on the point of furnishing it on the 10th, they were disturbed by either RAF jets or helicopters, or some fusillade of rifle shots from below, as the keeper and his trigger-happy amateur help bombarded corvids in the trees by the brook, rabbits among the bushes, or whatever else took their fancy as targets. Other peregrines I had known were not gun-shy, nor were they visibly nervous when low-flying aircraft passed over. With hill-hopping so much practised by RAF pilots and fox control so essential a part of hill farming, Welsh peregrines are given plenty of opportunity to become familiar with the noise generated by both. These birds, though, were extremely nervous – a fact never disclosed during earlier visits. I began to wonder whether we really needed theft to account for the three-year run of failure.

By the time the first stint concluded on the evening of 12 April, though, several unquestionable reliefs had been witnessed and noted. I and many others did duty; the RAF obligingly consented to reduce low flying in the valley until the eyasses had fledged. The guard-book grew fat with records of reliefs, notes of kills brought in by the tiercel, of intruding peregrines – more than I had expected so far south – confronted and seen off by both tiercel and falcon. Weather was on the whole bad, sometimes awful.

Contact by telephone before my next turn of duty was due established that there had been no criminal attempt on the site. On 11 May, by which time a hatch was possible, I paid a visit to take a look at developments. There had been none, apart from continuing incubation. Although I had planned to travel on north to see how the colonel's peregrines were getting on, I decided instead to remain where I was and reinforce the watch. When I left for home late on the 13th there was still no evidence of progress. Incubation having been recorded continuously from 12 April, the first egg of the clutch, if fertile, should by now have produced its chick.

I returned on the 17th for my longest stint to be greeted with the news that a kill had been carried to the ledge and consumed at 5.30 the previous evening, followed by another at 9.30 that morning. At 1.30 p.m. I decided that there had been another feed. By the evening of the 18th, I had begun to have misgivings. Where experience affirmed that kills should be taken in by the falcon four, five and six a day and fed to the brood with just a few murmurs of encouragement for periods lasting about twenty minutes at a time, noise here was clamorous and continuous, timings erratic. The ledge, chosen for the first time that year, was high, overhung by both rock and a screen of ivy hanging from it. How I wished otherwise. There was scarcely anything I would not have given for a view through the telescope of what was really going on behind that ivy.

What I got instead was the first of a series of banks of mist which rolled in one after another for three days to close off all view of the eyrie and, for much of the time, of the rock itself. All my eyes were able to detect during those dreary seventy-two hours was thanks to a brief thinning of mist as the tiercel arrived on the afternoon of the 22nd, calling and carrying. Hobbies, it seemed, were not alone among falcons in being equipped with radar. Ears, however, were kept busy by every sound in the peregrine repertoire, all being heard at some stage during the 'white-out'.

By dawn on the 23rd the weather had changed. Calling began at 4.25 a.m.

Prey was carried from larder to the ledge at 6.50, to be followed by intermittent spells of 'squi-clucking' until 8.0 a.m. At 9.40, 9.50, 10, 10.45 and 1.10 p.m. the tiercel visited the ledge with kills, each to be rejected by the falcon, continuously at the scrape during this 3½-hour period. After a two-hour break to pick up a visitor, I came back at 3.30 p.m. to the news that the next feed was still awaited. During the eleven hours in question, the tiercel himself fed heartily on various ledges about the rock from several of the rejected kills. At 7.05 in the evening, the falcon at last carried a kill to the ledge, to remain with it silently at first, but the usual volume of noise developed eventually.

The 24th was spent by both birds in flying wildly about the valley – joyfully, so far as could be judged by the watchers. Visits to the scrape were few, so few that helpers began to question the deployment of their time. On leaving the site at noon on 26 May, I had little doubt that we were guarding no more than a single chick, but I was not yet ready to give up. On 3 June I returned to pay a social visit. A chick hatched on 16 May should now be showing at least a hint of its snowy presence during at least some of the parental visits made to the scrape. Ken Whitehead, then the duty warden, reported the falcon seen by telescope dipping her head and bill towards something in the scrape. The something, if a chick, should have lifted its head in response. Some believed they might have observed this. Others, Ken and his companion warden from the Hawk Trust included, did not. By the evening of that day I had become certain that what we now had under observation was a resumption of incubating behaviour, not the rearing of hatched chicks. Falcons brood chicks, but not continuously in hot weather (as the weather now was) when they are a fortnight old or more.

Arrangements were made for a rapid descent by a licensed investigator on 6 June. He found a falcon sitting on two fresh-looking eggs in a bone-dry scrape on a wet and windy morning. It was almost clinically clean, without the faintest trace of débris from the consumption of prey. When disturbed, the falcon came off the eggs without the slightest murmur of protest.

With the colonel's and a new site in the vicinity occupied by peregrines feeding chicks in accordance with convention at that date, I wished the birds on the Darren a not entirely fond farewell and redirected my efforts elsewhere. Some of the guard kept in touch with them and a second descent was made on 27 June. It disclosed a single cold egg on the scrape, now completely overhung with ivy.

The birds to which I had transferred my attention fledged between them five fine eyasses. The colonel watched his cliff at first light from an upstairs window, clad in a dressing-gown. I, helped by a kindly topography, watched both the other brood and the likeliest line of retreat by which villains would try to escape from his site, from a car in which I slept between dusk and dawn stand-tos.

To the south, we had begun our guard with one confident assertion to which all had subscribed. 'With a 24-hour guard maintained for twelve weeks or more, *whatever* happens, we shall at least be certain what it was.'

When the dust of incomprehension had finally settled, only one fact was clear. I knew less of what could be predicted of the behaviour of a pair of peregrine falcons than I had fancied four months earlier. So much for conclusions based on 'four certainties'.

In 1986 a pair of peregrines whose personal identities I should not like to swear to reared a single eyas behind the ivy screen, under renewed wardening in which I was not involved. In 1987 they reared three on the long open ledge where success was achieved in 1980 and 1981, and in many years before the population collapse, when Dr Charles Walker had been in continual contact with the site. In 1985, the year of his ninetieth birthday, he himself came up the hill several times to join us in the watch and share our bewilderment. In 1986 and 1987 his ascents were to witness the successes.

Sadly, Jack Smith was not there to join him. He spent the eve of his seventieth birthday sleeping in his tent rather than the hut, which I suspect him to have regarded privately as too great a concession to comfort. He did not see his seventy-first birthday. Within two months of that week we spent together in mist, wind and rain, he died of heart failure in his cottage near Leominster, quite probably in his sleep. He is much missed.

THE HAWKWATCHER

Neither Dr Walker nor anyone else climbed the hill to witness success in 1988. A pair of peregrines appeared to have laid in mid-April, but on an exposed ledge higher up the cliff than in 1987. The night of 30 April was wild and stormy. The scrape was abandoned and the birds spent the next fortnight paying spasmodic visits to the concealed ledge behind the ivy. If hopes were nourished for a repeat laying, nothing came of them. I began to wonder whether another name should be added to the short list of sites known to me as notorious for the confusion they contribute to debate rather than recruitment to the population.

In these chapters on the peregrine falcon I have tried to avoid repetition of a mass of well-known data. No other raptor in Britain having attracted so much literature at so many levels, this has not always been easy. I nourish hopes that I have neither failed in that aim nor left the less instructed reader groping for meanings and implications. If I have been guilty of the latter, redress is available by reference to Dr Derek Radcliffe's standard work, *The Peregrine Falcon*, and Dick Treleaven's *Peregrine*, an authoritative and highly readable personal statement.

Among the peregrine watching adventures space has not been sufficient for me even to touch on here have been some in Cornwall with Dick. My tally of kills by wild peregrines witnessed stands at forty-five. His century was passed several years ago. That statistic puts our relative status in the art of peregrine watching into fair perspective.

Henry Williamson wrote rather romantically of the peregrine in 1923 in *The Peregrine's Saga*; J. A. Baker, beautifully in 1967 in *The Peregrine*. What I have added now will not greatly expand what is known academically of the species but may, as Williamson's writing did for me when a boy of sixteen in 1940, open for someone else a window on possibilities previously unimagined. If so, I have ample grounds for satisfaction. There is more for me in the fact that there is now a secure and expanded population of peregrines for them to go and look at.

I shall offer no specific advice to readers in the north of Britain. To those in the southern half, though, I would mention the RSPB facility at Symonds Yat, near Ross-on-Wye in Herefordshire. Here a peregrine eyrie may be watched in the nesting season by all comers, with or without their own optical instruments. A telescope is permanently mounted, a collection box maintained. Last time I was there it was so full of £1 coins that the warden could scarcely lift it. Splendid!

Since the reoccupation of those rocks in 1982, I have kept in touch with the situation there. Two eyasses were fledged in that year, one of them flying soon afterwards into power-lines in the vicinity, to go into veterinary care with a broken wing, from which it recovered.

As usual in those days, the villains were soon on the scene. In 1983 the site was robbed twice – first of four eggs, then of three chicks after a repeat clutch had been laid and hatched. After further robbery in 1984, the site was placed under regular breeding-season surveillance by the RSPB and the Forestry Commission working in collaboration, and the public observation facilities already mentioned were set up.

In July 1987 I had the pleasure of watching four eyasses on the wing there as they played together for most of an afternoon at eye-level, above it, or even below, down between the steeply wooded shoulders of the Wye Gorge. The site was again successful in 1988, but I found neither time nor opportunity to pay my usual visits. A failure there would have been a disappointment to those hoping for a repetition of an aerial spectacle, but that is all. For the time being, at least, the British peregrine population is secure, the few areas not yet reoccupied well counterbalanced by others where the records suggest numbers to be higher than ever before this century.

Some of the peregrine's admirers, indeed, have begun to wonder whether quite so many of these formidable predators in such confined sections of the ecosystem should be viewed as a development entirely to be welcomed. As yet, one can only speculate on the full range of the implications, but the percentage of territories which hatch and rear chicks may already be falling to a figure lower than we became accustomed to in the years at the beginning of the recovery, when substantially fewer of them had been reoccupied.

THE HAWKWATCHER

Does one detect the mechanics of natural selection re-entering the situation more forcefully than of late? It seems likely; and, if so, by far a more desirable corrective to excess than anything we ourselves might attempt to contrive.

sixteen   GOSHAWKS REOCCUPY
BRITAIN

Notes contributed by one Murdoch Mathieson (presumed to have been a gamekeeper) to a book compiled in 1930 by Mr Edward Ellice, MP, refer to Mathieson's slaughter of a goshawk in Glengarry with the second barrel of his gun after he had emptied the first with equal success at a blackcap warbler, to prove the species really did occur in Glengarry.

The title of the book is *Place-names of Glengarry and Glenquoich*. It was published privately, but I am fortunate enough to possess a copy, not least because the famous (or infamous) 'Glengarry vermin book' is reproduced in the text. Mathieson was proud of his unusual left-and-right and one may guess that pursuit of the unusual was the reason for at least the first shot reported. Unfortunately, he did not date the event. Failing to do so may have cost him more in sporting status than he could have imagined.

For a man still alive in 1930 one assumes a birth-date not much before 1850 and the death of the goshawk an event not occurring earlier than 1870. If much later (as well it may have been, for Mathieson could still have been young enough for keepering in 1900), his may have been the shot which extinguished the species from the British list for about fifty years. Mathieson certainly described that gos as the only one he had ever seen.

Tracing the early history of the species in Britain is not easy and is further complicated by confusion in the old records between goshawk and peregrine. It is likely that both were at times recorded under the modern name of the other. Parish registers of bounty money paid out for 'hawks' killed as a threat to poultry in Commonwealth times and thereafter are our chief source of early information on raptors in Britain. They show that parish clerks, whatever else they may have been, were not commonly informed ornithologists.

News first came my way of goshawks in Britain during the present era when through Army circles I learned of attempts by the late Lord Alanbrooke to photograph them at the nest in Sussex in the early 1950s. The news which followed was of a fade-out; the next, utterly dramatic. Goshawks, I was told in strict confidence on 26 January 1975, were present in extensive woodland in our own county, and had bred there successfully for several years.

Parts of the area were open to the public and people had watched birds in general there for many years. There was no reason whatsoever why goshawks should not be looked for discreetly and watched with pleasure outside the nesting season from any vantage-point approachable without committing the offence of trespass.

Theorizing was one thing, finding the vantage-points another. They were not abundant, which may explain the success with which the secret had been kept for so long. My first visit found neither a good observation post, nor a goshawk; my second discovered both. I sat, binoculars hanging at the ready, on a hump of ground clear-felled of mature Douglas firs some years since, replanted promptly with Canadian red cedar in clumps, now grown into trees six feet tall and a little more, with seedling pines and spruces dropped in among them since. There was an extensive view over conifer and broadleaf reaching some miles to the north. Only to the east was the view cut off by tall firs, survivors of a thinning. To the west, there were only plantations of European larch of no great age. Unless the goshawks insisted on progressing with their bellies brushing the canopy, there ought to be sightings.

By 5 p.m. there had been plenty of sightings, but chiefly of couples walking dogs or of half-grown girls astride fat ponies. The nearest thing to a hawk had been a large but shadowy presence glimpsed passing quickly through distant tree-tops at 12.50 and 2.35.

Then, suddenly, there was something unbelievably majestic in the sky, soaring on wings almost full-spread and a well opened tail. The bird was the size of a buzzard, plus extra inches of tail. It was at least 400 yards away and 200 feet into the sky, but the face shown by the binoculars was a keen and ferocious one, with a glint of yellow in the eye. I was looking at my first wild goshawk. Why not 'goseagle', I thought – there was too much dignity here for a mere hawk. This was anything but the oversized sparrowhawk I had expected. How captivity diminishes a raptor! I had seen goshawks on their bow perches in the falconry exhibits at several game fairs, but they could have been a different species. I had seen a goshawk take a rabbit on film, but that whole flight lifted the bird not more than six feet above the ground. One needs the width of the open sky to do justice to the personality of a hawk.

The hen gos, for such it was, then performed, as though to settle matters beyond all possibility of dispute, the territorial display I had read of. Under-tail coverts were not only fluffed out; they were curled up almost to form a white patch on the goshawk's rump like that of a hen harrier. Stooping and zooming steeply, wings beating in a strangely slow syncopation, she made her way through the sky above her territory. Then all was over, the great bird having plunged vertically to a plantation of leggy oaks past which yet another girl was riding a pony, all unaware to the spectacle overhead. I was surprised that the pony did not shy. That was on 23 February.

I visited the site again for watches lasting at least six hours on 8, 15, 18 and 27 March, seeing on the 8th simultaneous but apparently unconnected displays by male and female. On the 18th a cock as grey-backed as a peregrine tiercel was seen twice, briefly, leading to speculation. The mantle of the big hen seen in February had a distinct touch of brown to it, although she wore the barred under-plumage of the adult. So, too, had the birds seen in the sky on 8 March looked brownish. Having now seen this truly grey-backed cock, I came to the conclusion that either adult cocks were greyer than hens, as sparrowhawks are, or that acquisition of full adult plumage by goshawks is by stages which take several moults to complete. Other sightings elsewhere have since moved me nearer that second conclusion. The two other watches that month were wholly unsuccessful, but two hens were seen fighting directly above the glade from which the goshawks usually came 'on stage' by a friend on 27 April.

Three more visits which I paid that year, in late summer and winter, were again unproductive. One thing in particular had been learned. 'Watching' goshawks was more a matter of glimpsing goshawks, an occupation calling for exceptional patience, rather like salmon fishing – long empty hours punctuated by brief spells of spectacular excitement.

There was, of course, a certain clash of interests. I could not be in Wales guarding peregrines through spring and summer and in Worcestershire woodland awaiting a goshawk sighting at one and the same time. Nor, as 1976 was to demonstrate, should I be able to reconcile the demands of watching for Worcestershire goshawks in late summer, when newly flying young birds would be about the site to add extra action, with making the best of opportunities to watch hobbies elsewhere in that or the adjacent county, where I by then knew them to nest. In the circumstances, February and March were the months I could spare best for concentration on goshawks. As well that these are also the months in which the species flies most conspicuously, in declaration of claims to territory and in response to challenges.

February 26th of that year produced a memorable display by the big hen; the 28th, another, and one by a young cock, brown-mantled and streaky-breasted. During these displays, of longer duration than those watched in 1975, I was able to form conclusions regarding goshawk identification. Because they are buzzard-sized, hens present no problem in Britain, notably short of buzzard-sized raptors; but males are a different matter. They and female sparrowhawks are so nearly of a common size that confusion is possible, especially when the bird in the binocular window is a hen spar broad-breasted with high condition as so many of them are after good hunting in clement winter.

One conclusion I reached was that the goshawk wing looks proportionally longer than the spar's and is often beaten with a more leisurely stroke, as well as being flexed so as to present a profile nearer to a symmetrical ellipse. Nor does the gos interrupt the beat with glides so obsessively as its smaller cousin, lacking, perhaps, the same physiological imperative to avoid building up the waste products of combustion. More conspicuously, the head of the gos protrudes relatively further and the tail, relatively shorter, spreads to end with a more pronounced curvature, calling to mind a kestrel's. Not all textbooks confirm these points, but that is what *my* eye recorded.

On 2 March 1976 my goshawk watching reached its first dramatic climax. Already aware that there were two males on the site, one a grey-mantled veteran, the other a brown-backed streaky-breasted sub-adult, I identified a goshawk passing calmly over a stand of oaks at the far end of the clearing as the former. Early-morning frost had been followed by bright sunshine and clear blue sky in which wispy white cloud had begun to form at midday. The light was perfect. Suddenly, without a hint of advertised intention, the hawk stood on his tail and began to climb on flailing wings at the steepest angle I had ever seen a hawk – or falcon – attempt.

Where a peregrine would have ascended by beating hard for half a circle and climbing the reciprocal with a banked glide, in a succession of spirals, the sturdy gos used his great wing area and an incalculable input of energy to reach his objective in a quarter of the time or less. Risking the loss of my target by ranging ahead of him with the binoculars, I got there first – to find a white homing pigeon passing over at an altitude of not less than a thousand feet.

In what seemed to be only a second or two the gos had overtaken the swing of the binoculars and was closing on the pigeon as though it were nailed to the sky. As unexpectedly as he had attacked, the gos swung suddenly away from the now accelerating pigeon, circled twice, then concluded the performance with a display proclaiming possession of that volume of sky above the clearing. Why should a goshawk treat a white pigeon as a territorial competitor? I can offer no explanation, but remain no less grateful for the spectacle and for the demonstration of the goshawk's enormous muscular power and stamina.

Two more visits in March yielded sightings of the young male but nothing of real note. With the year's peregrine operation over, I returned to the goshawks briefly in July. My son, also in the secret, found the nest by accident during an early morning walk with his dog on 18 July. It was high in a massive Douglas fir only 150 yards from our February-March watch-point.

Knowing the brood must be fledged or on the point of it, I arrived at 5.30 a.m. on the 21st. Following directions, I walked down a path never before trodden, half blocked by fallen trees. As I entered a glade overgrown with waist-high bracken, with a wall of larch on one side and plantation oaks on the other, shrill screaming on a broken note rang out from among the tall Douglas firs beyond. I walked in among them, looking up into their interlaced branches, but seeing nothing. Screaming came now from all about me. Selecting one of the larger firs, I lay down at the foot of it to await events. Immediately, the hen flew from somewhere unseen to alight in its neighbour in perfect view, the branch springing and bouncing under her great weight. A hoarser screaming broke out and a male gos in moult crossed to the tree, followed by a male juvenile.

Wriggling to a fresh position to end the growing intimacy between a fir-cone and one of my kidneys, I brought into view the bulky nest of woven sticks, wedged between the trunk and a major limb about two-thirds of the way up the tree. For the next half-hour I lay there, enjoying the noisy crash-landings of bird after bird in one conifer crown or another. Shrill screaming continued, interspersed with silvery calls of 'kik-kik-kik-kik', unexpected from such a throat, until the sun climbed and the air grew warm.

I had been told that sunrise was the time to visit goshawks; now I knew it to be a fact. That was the second dramatic climax experienced while watching the species. The young birds having left the nest, my close watching then constituted no offence against the law. It would be different now, under the stricter provisions of the 1981 Act. Not that the goshawk family registered any objection to my presence in 1976. Nor did a fox, which would have stepped on me had it tried to stroll by any nearer. Much woodpigeon plumage decorated the trunk of a tree fallen nearby. One could make a good guess as to the goshawks' principal prey in that territory.

Fitting visits round peregrine and other commitments, I kept in touch with the goshawks from 1977 on, but by 1984 the Douglas firs had been felled and trees on the mound which had been so useful an observation post had grown thick enough to obstruct access and tall enough to close the view down-valley. The goshawks still nest somewhere in the vicinity, but trying to watch them has ceased to be even a marginally profitable investment of time. They have spread out, too, but in doing so have attracted casualties. The area is one of intensive pheasant rearing in which keepers do not welcome the presence of so big and powerful a hawk. I have sought goshawks elsewhere, but terrain has always been a major problem, throwing into sharp relief the advantages to the viewer of a hawk which selects a ledge on a high and usually barren cliff for the establishment of its observation post and nursery.

I have visited goshawk territories in Carmarthenshire, Herefordshire, Shropshire, Derbyshire, Yorkshire and Galloway, but never found what I sought – a site on a wooded slope in otherwise open country which can be watched from across an unobstructed valley at a distance of less than half a mile. It is the comings and goings of hawks which chiefly fascinate me, not close-up views of proceedings at a nest.

In Galloway I had a memorable if all too brief view of a pair assaulting a golden eagle, and another of a fine big grey-mantled hen hunting a heather moor below a peregrine site with the tactics of a harrier. That 'moor' is now a blanket of 10-foot sitka spruces; the peregrine cliff, abandoned.

A day-long bird watch by a Yorkshire reservoir in December 1984 culminated in an attack by a young male goshawk which a cloud of common gulls chose to regard as personal. I judged peewits on the mud to be the true target. Confused by the gulls, the gos alighted on an exposed tree-stump on the shore for a sit and a think. His departure was not spectacular. That, apart from a hen crossing the road in front of the car between Leigh Sinton in Worcestershire and Hereford one April day in 1985, was my most recent sighting, but I hear news of the birds quite frequently. Usually, I suspect a misidentified hen sparrowhawk, because the word 'goshawk' has only to be whispered in a vicinity for people to report sightings. I, better than most, know how many hours of intensive watching a sighting usually demands. No other raptor in Britain, not even the merlin, resists the watcher so effectively,

albeit unintentionally. Goshawks are not shy birds, as evidenced by those –
not a few – which nest in a hedgerow tree within a field's distance from
some Continental farmhouse, and by a hen from heaven knows where which
paid several visits to a garden in a village between mine and Birmingham in
February 1988.

Until recently, though, they were treated as vermin in most Continental
countries, as they still are in parts of Britain. One of my colleagues on the
peregrine guard – incognito at the time – heard a Herefordshire keeper boast
openly to cronies in the local pub of having himself destroyed thirteen of the
birds since falconers established a colony on the border of that county and
Shropshire a decade or so earlier.

Whether some of the goshawks now resident in Britain stem from natural
immigration or not is a matter of conjecture. That most do not is a matter of
well-known fact, most occupied areas having been seeded with imported
birds to provide a domestic supply for falconry. Has this, perhaps, led those
who liberated the original stock to view the goshawk as unfitted thereby for
protection by British law and act as though it received none? The scale of nest
robbery in the Derbyshire–South Yorkshire sector of Britain's goshawk
country justifies the question, if not any snap answers.

Some might ask why wardening has not been more effective. Protecting
goshawks is an exacting task, meeting all too often with failure for the same
reason which makes such hard work of watching the species – the closeness of
the country they prefer. That which hides a goshawk's nest also hides men as
they approach to rob it and depart with the booty.

The goshawk is a fine robust bird which seems, like the peregrine, to be cut
out for survival, and no less fecund. Yet pressure has extinguished it once in
Britain during the past hundred years. We shall be lucky if it does not do so
again within the next twenty.

seventeen THE MAGICIAN'S FALCON

It was 5 a.m. on 28 June 1986. The car was parked in a roadside lay-by well up a remote valley in mid-Wales. Seated in it, I wrestled with a concertina of computer print-out paper, my mind but half occupied with the prosaic information which I was engaged on extracting from it. The good news was that the day's first cup of coffee was soaking comfortably into the lining of a grateful stomach.

Across the narrow road and twenty feet below, a river rushed through its gorge. Beyond the river and four hundred yards away, five merlin chicks were completing their feathering in a second-hand crows' nest high in the tallest of the hawthorns on the steep hillside. It was to them that at least half of my attention persistently wandered, and much more than half of my interest was directed – for all that fourteen months had passed since I bade an unregretful farewell to the enigmatic peregrines on the sandstone cliff, with my final duty to threatened raptors in Wales then complete, or so I insisted on telling myself.

Fate, however, had taken a different view. News of these merlins had reached me only a few days previously. A visit had shown that the road had been made too attractive for tourism for the site to be left to its own devices – at weekends especially, when most of the visitors came, parked, and ate their picnics. Stepping-stones afforded easy passage across the little river; the hillside and its trees would be bound to

223

attract younger people with digestion to assist and the energy to attempt it.

Adult merlins exercise caution when there are young to be protected, but the young themselves can be highly indiscreet, standing on or about the nest and attracting attention by flailing their growing wings for minutes on end. The tree would not be difficult to climb; nestling hawks have often been taken to be made into pets purely because they are pleasing to the eye and often do not make particularly vigorous efforts to escape capture. The law now forbids the taking of them, but would all who might cross the river and climb the hill be aware of that fact? I thought not.

These were the first merlins known to breed in this part of Wales for several years, because another unexplained decline had soon followed that from which the species began to recover in the 1970s. With no one else available to take on the duty of watching this fine big brood through to a safe fledge, there seemed no way I could decently avoid the responsibility. Those locally in authority at the time were glad enough to share that view, so, having reviewed my other commitments, I decided that what should be done at a desk could, at a pinch, be done in a car. Here I was then, and not sorry for the fact. My hawk-protection career had begun with merlins in mid-Wales – not unfitting if it should also end with them. Merlins, after all, had a special place in my affections, as they richly deserved. No other bird of prey can equal them for sheer charm.

It began, in Radnorshire, in 1972 – one year after finding my first Welsh merlins, in that same valley. That 1972 nest was also one abandoned by crows, which had built it with marked architectural skill in the biggest hawthorn of a clump of three standing centrally in an almost incredibly secluded horsehoe-shaped valley bitten from a steep hillside overlooking wide farmlands. Rock lined half its perimeter, a feature I found in later years to be highly important. I have yet to see a merlins' nest far removed from rock, the 1986 nest included.

That 1972 pair hatched three chicks, to rear two of them. The third, just coming nicely into feather, spoilt the morning of 1 July for itself and for us by lying dead at the foot of the tree when we arrived, still supple and warm, with no evidence of damage beyond a bead of congealing blood on a carpal joint. The body was retrieved and sent for autopsy, but however soon we had arrived at the scene of the little tragedy bluebottles had got there sooner. By the time the cadaver reached the laboratory bench, their damaged had been done, so the cause of death remained a mystery.

The two surviving chicks soon taught us why merlins enjoy a reputation for confiding natures. For a fortnight after flying they shared perches on the valley's rocky walls with us, even carrying kills presented in cautious haste by their parents nearer to us for consumption when crows attempted piracy. One could have supposed them to be comparing their standing with that of crows, and to know that crows, too, would be aware of the difference.

On 22 July the young merlins had quitted the amphitheatre. Never had a moorland valley seemed so empty. Empty of small birds, too. Pipits, redstarts, ring ouzels, wheatears, wood warblers and chaffinches had been there and free from interference until the young merlins had left the nest. Now, all were gone. It was the first hint I received, since confirmed by both merlin and peregrine, that an instinct in breeding falcons which inhibits the killing of small resident neighbours might have the useful effect of providing a supply of prey too relaxed for its own good for the newly fledged youngsters to practise on.

The following year brought me another merlin duty, this time in Shropshire. Two more additions to the population were again the outcome.

In 1974 I was back in Radnorshire, coming near to paying my life as the price of wardening merlins. The high ground in that county draws thunderstorms as a magnet draws iron filings. When on 16 June we arrived at the foot of the long slope leading up to the ridge overlooking the site – some miles across the hills from the horseshoe valley – a real brute was brewing up to the west, darkening the sky to a fearsome tint of deep orange where it was not the colour of a peregrine's mantle. It gave us an hour of watching as it gathered strength, then broke like the day of judgement. We lay on one waterproof, cowering beneath another, lashed by hailstones the size of overripe peas, dazzled through closed eyelids by incessant lightning, deafened by an almost unbroken roar of thunder punctuated twice by the explosions of newly riven hawthorns on the opposite slope, already littered with the wreckage from tempests of earlier years. Had I not had my wife with me to be calmed and encouraged, I, too, might have been trembling with terror before it was all over.

When a break at last came, our route, over moorland whitened as though by a snowstorm, was made circuitous as we sought to cross gullies dry on the approach but now rushing with storm water barely fordable in wellingtons. All hope for the three young merlins, just in feather in a nest high in the usual tall hawthorn and sheltered by only a few sprays of leaves, had been abandoned. Yet despair was premature. The next visit, made on the 18th, found all three in good order, well washed but otherwise unaffected by our shared experience. Hailstones which stung the hide of a sixteen-stone man through several layers of clothing had not battered to death five-ounce birds equally exposed to them. There must be more to feathers, I concluded, than met the eye.

These and kindred recollections passed in review as I sat in the car combining dull clerical work with more pleasurable duty. Thoughts then ran deeper. Why, I wondered for the hundredth time or more, had merlins come so near to dying out in the 1960s? The period, of course, was that of maximum organochlorine contamination nationally, and of massive conversion of open moorland to conifer blanket locally, in Wales. As with the Welsh peregrine, though, there was no solid evidence to link the fate of the merlin positively to the poisons. As much to the point, there was at that date still plenty of unplanted heather moor to provide nest sites, and meadow pipits for the summer hunting. But the merlins which should have been there to exploit the opportunities were no longer coming.

Had they picked up the toxins in winter, perhaps, while away from the uncontaminated uplands? If so, their winter journeyings must have taken them farther afield than was thought likely at the time, because the farmlands at the foot of the hill features, where merlins were sometimes seen in winter, were among the most traditionally farmed in Britain, with little arable cultivation and less of pesticides, except in sheep-dip. Should one consider the possible influence of wool used to line crows' nests? Perhaps – but merlins in this part of Britain were traditionally ground nesters. When their eggs were first found in crows' nests, the old keepers still on the moors did not believe they could be merlins'.

Intensive afforestation had attracted complaints from sheep farmers, who found the plantations to be impenetrable sanctuaries for the foxes they had always laboured to control. Had increased numbers of foxes, ranging abroad from them, imposed an intolerable pressure on ground-nesting merlins – explaining, perhaps, the transfer of interest from the heather to the hawthorns in the dingles? Other explanations equally tenuous had been offered, even a theory to account for the renewed decline of the early 1980s based on a fear that the peregrine recovery of the 1970s had been at the expense of the merlin. The remains of merlins, usually the brighter-coloured males, had been found bearing the hallmarks of peregrine violence – characteristic nicks in the breastbone made by the peregrine's stout, extra strong hooked bill as it feeds. But no one could show why coexistence, no longer possible in the 1980s, had been possible fifty years earlier.

Causes of both primary and secondary declines were speculated upon and theories advanced. What was clearly not in evidence was any kind of remedial action to check the ills that were suspected of causing the decline. In some ways, indeed, the situation seemed to be deteriorating from year to year. Yet some of us with a particular interest in the birds now had a feeling in our bones that modest recovery was again in progress. If it was – and still is – that, too, will be another mystery. Mystery surrounds the species. In February 1914 one of either sex was shot on the then semirural outskirts of Birmingham to be sold to a local taxidermist and resold by him after mounting for five shillings each to the city's natural history museum – hence the survival of the record.

Were they a pair? Had they an intention to nest in that improbable area? I know a nest site in a marshy meadow on Anglesey, and there were marshy meadows where those merlins were shot (no doubt for the shilling each the taxidermist would pay for the bodies) in the valley of the little River Cole. That I know, because there were marshy meadows still when I lived there as a boy between 1928 and 1935. Not only marshy meadows but also districts adjacent to them which included the word 'heath' in their names. Modern Birmingham has nineteen suburbs so styled. Did ancestral memory (something I strongly suspect that birds possess) lead the 1914 merlins to where they met their sad end? One thing about Birmingham is made abundantly clear by the Domesday Book. Whatever else it lacked (almost everything of economic value), the manor and its environs were well endowed with terrain of a type to attract merlins – 'Bleak and barren stony heath'.

If the two birds shot in 1914 were merely wintering, does their presence on the land of one small farm suggest that pair formation takes place on the wintering grounds, not in the uplands after the return there? Our lack of information on that point bears added witness to the elusive nature of the species. One day the moor is devoid of merlins; the next, a pair is in residence. And that is almost all we usually know of the matter.

Intriguing though the history of merlins in 1914 may be within 3½ miles of what was shortly to become Britain's principal small arms factory, one does not need to go back so far in time to find merlins amid bricks and mortar. In 1985 it was confided to me that Blaenau Ffestiniog was the surest place in Wales to see them. 'Visit the town in midwinter,' I was told. 'The merlins come in and hunt sparrows up and down the main street.'

Semi-urban merlins are one thing; plantation merlins another. The former strain my credulity not at all, in the numbers quoted; the latter strain it painfully, despite all the claims I have heard in recent years. That the claims emanate from sources in or near commercial forestry interests does not help credibility; nor the fact that such merlins as I have been taken to see at nests in plantation conifers or other improbable trees have been missing on the date of my visit, eminently debunkable, or, as more than half expected, very obvious kestrels.

Moorland hawthorns are used commonly by Welsh merlins, rowans twice to my certain knowledge. On both occasions the rowan was marginally the tallest tree bearing a crows' nest in a mixed clump dominated by the usual hawthorns. To adapt effectively to coniferization, though, the merlin needs not merely to take a collective fancy to discarded crows' nests deep in the forestry, but to replace a deeply ingrained instinct to hunt pipits and larks in open country with both the instinct and aptitude to pursue titmice and goldcrests through close canopy. That is all the merlins will find there, and not in any great abundance. I should therefore expect sub-average results from any merlins which did attempt the transition. My advice to them would be to come back to Yardley Wood, Birmingham, instead, and try a suburban garden near the River Cole. They would run smaller risk than their 1914 forebears of being shot for taxidermization, and the sparrows would be at least as plentiful as those in Blaenau Ffestiniog.

With reflections as inconsequential, my three long weekends of merlin watching passed pleasantly away without undue strain. But not without interest. I was given cause to suspect that a second hen merlin was on the territory, acting as 'auntie' to the brood by assisting with provision. If not, the frequency of some of Mamma's deliveries suggested that she had found pipits on sale at a hillside supermarket. I have long viewed merlins as the deadliest of all the raptors, combining the speed and agility of the sparrowhawk with the stamina of the peregrine, but there are still limits.

They began to leave the nest early on 5 July. Three fledgelings made it confidently to find perches high in the branches of the hawthorn from which promising take-offs could be made. Number four climbed a little way up from the nest monkey-style. Number five fell clumsily to a low branch, lost so much confidence in the process that it would not risk a further leap, and in consequence spent 8¾ hungry hours squeaking with misery while its siblings were fed again and again. The parents took a Thatcherite view but I found I had lost nothing of my capacity to identify emotionally with a young hawk in trouble.

Nothing to be done about the matter, though, either lawfully or with any prospect of not making the matter worse by exercising good intentions. Finally, the lizard took its life in its hands and embarked on life as a pterodactyl. Mamma, wise in her generation, then rewarded it. A head still downy when all others had been plucked clean established its status as the baby of the family. A fortnight later, he was indistinguishable from his brother.

That was an anxious day, but 30 June, when my heart was kept in my mouth for thirty-five endless minutes, had it beaten.

The curtain rose at 7.20 a.m. when a hitherto somnolent hen merlin ran forward unexpectedly on the rock uphill from the nest tree on which she had been relaxing for half an hour, took off and stooped. Her target was a small party of grounded jackdaws probing the turf near the foot of the tree, members of a flock of fifty or so which had quietly left their home in the high crags which rose behind the lay-by to invade the merlins' territory across the river.

A squawk implying a successful strike sounded the tocsin. As the merlin climbed back to pitch a cloud of angry jackdaws accompanied her, joined quickly by every member of the flock, well aware of the strength which resides in united will and collective action. Stabbed at from all sides, the merlin employed her agility to avoid damage and her exacerbated fury to turn defence into savage counter-attack on each daw whose temerity brought it within talon-reach.

Up swirled the cloud, elongating, truncating, fragmenting, coalescing, with the fiercely elegant brown bird ever in the centre, striking left, striking right, whikkering in angry excitement. Suddenly the cock too was on the scene, calling the hen from her sport to accept the first kill of the morning. Imperatives being just that, she tried to break away and obey the summons, but her voluntary grounding gave the enemy their chance to transfer the action to where the advantage was all theirs. The turf was instantly black with birds, most of them excited spectators of a noisy six-bird wrestling match which called to mind the swift ferocity of fighting tomcats. As suddenly, that round was over; the hen merlin escaped and dropped into the tree, still incredibly in possession of the pipit, while the cock was now fighting single-handed the battle the hen had fought before his arrival.

In the tree the hen fed a brood preoccupied with breakfast and completely unaware of their sire's problems. Or those of the jackdaws, as twice he fell earthwards dragging a foe with him in a cloud of small dusky feathers. After the second grapple on the ground, though, he decided that enough was enough (after all, he hadn't started the fight) and escaped to the peace of his hunting range up the valley. The feed over, Mamma sought hers in a bush a hundred yards away. Predictably, it was denied her. The jackdaws, out for blood, hounded her from branch to branch, from bush to bush, confronting her, outflanking her, the most dangerous of her enemies always the one trying to work round behind to take a snatch at a tail quill while another distracted her. Agility is the merlin's prime asset; the tail its rudder. Maim and deform that and the hawk is at the mercy of its airborne enemy. She was equal to every attempt, spinning round on the branch, like the lightweight champion she was, to confront every would-be plucker with hooked bill agape and hissing, daring the assailant to close.

Then – God help us all, I gasped – six broke away from the flock, flew swiftly to the nest tree and dropped into it, surrounding the nest. Now, I thought, I am destined to sit here impotent while the young merlins are stabbed to death and pulled to pieces. Even if I tried to intervene, I should not get up the hill in time. The young merlins turned to face the arrivals, but more, it seemed, in expectation of another pipit than in fear. (I ought not to have been surprised. I had seen one in Shropshire importune a passing Boeing 707.) Unaccountably, the jackdaws began to look away as though in embarrassment, and to preen. Having thus comforted their egos, they left the tree one by one and flew back to their rocks. Perhaps infanticide had never been seriously in mind, just a determination to extend their claim to freedom of navigation to its ultimate boundary.

Along the hillside the conflict swept back into the sky, the merlin obviously nearing exhaustion. Suddenly she stooped from the fray, flattened out at ground level, flew off in the wake of her mate and left the nest to its fate.

Perhaps she understood the inner truths of the situation better than I had. All but four of the jackdaws accepted this as a signal for return to the rocks; the four resumed probing the turf for grubs and worms as though nothing had occurred to disrupt the tranquillity of the morning. The hands of my watch recorded 7.55 a.m.

What had it all been about? Just a demonstration of the bird's instinct which transcends all others to defend territory simply because a claim to it has been laid and previously enforced, and for no more immediately rational a reason? That was my conclusion. Another was that the hen merlin had probably affirmed the unromantic fact of life that while a mother can always hope to produce more children a child cannot as easily acquire a new mother. Progeny in the wild, however vigorously they may be defended up to a point, are, in the final analysis, expendable.

If merlins had caused my confidence in their intrepidity to falter on 30 June, the hen acted to restore it on 7 July. My attention was distracted from the brood, perched decoratively about the hillside, by air expelled from corvine lungs in a painful grunting squeak up behind me. A raven sprawled spread-eagled on the turf at the foot of the jackdaw rocks. The hen merlin rocketed above it into the raptorial equivalent of the Spitfire's victory-roll. When the 3-pound raven recovered, its departure was with a limping wing-beat. The 7-ounce merlin betrayed not a feather out of place.

If it really was my final bow as a guardian of falcons, I was ending with a chord in a major key. But was it? Who but a fool attempts to foretell with certainty what the future might have waiting for him somewhere around the corner?